THE CONFEDERATE
—APPROACH ON—
HARRISBURG

THE CONFEDERATE
——APPROACH ON——
HARRISBURG

THE GETTYSBURG CAMPAIGN'S
NORTHERNMOST REACHES

[signature]

COOPER H. WINGERT

Charleston · London

THE
History
PRESS

Published by The History Press
Charleston, SC 29403
www.historypress.net

Front cover: Passing Through, by Don Stivers.
Back cover: A Sketch Showing the Earthworks for the Defense of Harrisburg, Pennsylvania, in
The Pictorial Battles of the Civil War (1885), colorized version courtesy of the author.

First published 2012

Manufactured in the United States

ISBN 978.1.60949.858.0

Library of Congress CIP data applied for.

Contents

Foreword

"If Harrisburg comes within your means, capture it." With those words, famed Confederate General Robert E. Lee set in motion a march toward the riverfront capital of Pennsylvania, the second most populous state in the Union. While his primary goals were to resupply his army from Northern bounties and to draw the Federal army out of Virginia for a potentially decisive battle, the chance to seize Harrisburg offered an important political prize. The Civil War had dragged on for more than two years, and Lee recognized that the Union, with its superior resources and manpower, eventually would win any protracted conflict. Invading the North, and possibly whipping the Yankees on their home turf, might bring the United States to the negotiating table.

Lee had invaded Maryland in September 1862 before being turned back in bitter fighting at Sharpsburg. Over the winter, he planned another attempt, commissioning maps of the Cumberland Valley and other key points in Pennsylvania. Following the battle of Chancellorsville in May 1863, Lee met with President Jefferson Davis and other key Confederate leaders to discuss his plans. On June 3, he began his aggressive movement toward the Shenandoah and Cumberland Valleys.

With the Union Army of the Potomac several days behind Lee's advance forces, the defense of Pennsylvania fell to an eclectic mix of untrained home guards, hastily recruited state militia and troops lent by neighboring states. Their officers and leaders also brought mixed talents, skills and experience to the daunting task of protecting the Keystone State.

In this book, Cooper H. Wingert aptly tells the story of the Confederate movement toward Harrisburg and the feverish efforts of Pennsylvania's governor and U.S. military officials to prepare for a Rebel assault. The author has pored through scores of primary sources such as soldiers' remembrances, old newspaper accounts, civilian postwar damage claims and other accounts to connect the story of the invaders, defenders and civilians caught in the path of two armies at war.

Scott L. Mingus Sr.
Civil War writer and lecturer, author of *Flames Beyond Gettysburg: The Confederate Expedition to the Susquehanna River, June 1863*
York, Pennsylvania

Acknowledgements

There are many who have made invaluable contributions to the completion of this volume, which has been three years in the works. Scott Mingus of York, Pennsylvania, has most generously spent countless hours editing and advising me on this manuscript, giving suggestions down to every trifle. Jim Schmick of Enola, Pennsylvania, has provided valued assistance throughout the entire process. John Heiser of Gettysburg made the wonderful maps that accompany this volume on short notice and, additionally, suggested many new leads that were most appreciatively used. Dr. Richard J. Sommers of the USAMHI in Carlisle provided his knowledgeable insight, along with many suggestions and sources.

Hannah Cassilly and all the good folks at The History Press have been especially kind and receptive, answering without complaint my mind-numbing and voluminous questions. Many others have done similar: Gregg Clemmer, North Potomac, Maryland; Ken Frew, Dauphin County Historical Society; Lawrence E. Keener-Farley, Camp Hill, Pennsylvania; Brian Stuart Kesterson, Lubeck, West Virginia; Carl Klase, assistant administrator, Pennypacker Mills, Schwenksville, Pennsylvania; Robin Lighty, Camp Hill, Pennsylvania; Jack Thomas, Hershey, Pennsylvania; Richard Tritt, photo curator, Cumberland County Historical Society. Additionally, the staffs of all the libraries listed in the bibliography were extremely helpful.

Chapter 1

Harrisburg in Distress

It was pitch dark as many of the senior commanders of the Federal Army of the Potomac huddled in council past midnight on May 4, 1863. Their topic of discussion would have been inconceivable to anyone in the group—or for that matter any soldier in the large Northern army—a mere week ago. Then, in the last days of April, the Army of the Potomac boasted over 130,000 men, an imposing size compared to the meager Southern forces opposing them. Nearly all were extremely confident in their ability to deal with Robert E. Lee's Army of Northern Virginia. However, the sheer thickness of the so-called Wilderness—the dense, overgrown woods that enveloped the area west of Fredericksburg, Virginia, and south of the Rappahannock and Rapidan Rivers—seemed to clog the thought process of army commander Major General Joseph O. Hooker as much as it did the pace of his army's march.

Hooker, who had frequently boasted of his upcoming offensive, soon stalled his progress around the Chancellor house when a bold counteroffensive by Lee and legendary corps commander Thomas Jonathan "Stonewall" Jackson stunned him. The battle took a turn for the worse for "Fighting Joe" when Lee dispatched Jackson as a flanking column. Stonewall's veterans reaped havoc on Hooker's bewildered army, whose right flank soon collapsed. Hooker's confidence and grand plans of a marvelous victory faded away before him.

So brought Hooker and five of the army's seven corps commanders to this unwelcome meeting. The befuddled Hooker thought of retreat and only that. "It was seen by the most casual observer that he had made up his mind to retreat," later opined Second Corps commander Major General Darius

N. Couch. "We were left by ourselves to consult," recollected Couch. A vote was taken, resulting three to two in favor of offensive operations. Hooker sauntered back to the tent and, after being informed of the vote, announced that "he should take upon himself the responsibility of retiring the army to the other side of the river." That was only another step in the beginning of the end for Fighting Joe's tenure at the helm of the Army of the Potomac. With that move, he did little to soothe his subordinates' anger.[1] As Fighting Joe lost the tenacity garnered him by his sobriquet, Robert E. Lee basked in it.

HARRISBURG

Laid out in 1785 and incorporated as a borough in 1791, Harrisburg became Pennsylvania's capital in 1812. The town's founder, John Harris Jr., boasted to one traveler in 1788 that "three years ago there was but one house built," and soon it had become a rapidly growing town on the eastern banks of the Susquehanna River. "Harrisburg is most picturesquely situated," raved one observer.[2] "There are few cities which in proportion have such a large number of merchants keeping retail stores," described eighteenth-century traveler Theophile Cazenove.

> *The lands watered by the Susquehanna are so excellent, that settlements are made hourly, and the farmers are generally supplied from here; also from here comes…products, that go down the river in boats…There is here a printing-plant, where an English newspaper is…published every Monday and costs 2 dollars a year for subscription; a school, where I saw about 60 children learning from only one teacher, reading writing, arithmetic, grammar, etc…A German church, where Lutherans and German Presbyterians have alternate services…The county-jail had one prisoner, a thief, condemned to 2 years imprisonment, and 3 noisy negroes…They are making the [new courthouse] building so large with the idea that the Pennsylvania legislature will hold its meetings here.*[3]

In 1794, during the Whiskey Rebellion, President George Washington visited the then-nine-year-old, rather insignificant town. "The Susquehanna at this place abounds in the Rockfish of 12 or 15 inches in length, and a fish which they call Salmon," Washington penned in his diary. After spending the night in Harrisburg, on October 4 he forded the Susquehanna, passing over Forster's Island, now known as City Island, in the middle of the river.[4]

"The river from the [capitol] dome is the most beautiful I think I ever saw," noted another spectator. "The river studded with Islands covered with rich foliage stretches away as far as the eye can reach above and below the town while the two splendid, bridges, almost, or quite a mile long, add very much to the picturesqueness of the scene."[5]

One of these two "splendid" bridges spanning the Susquehanna was the Camelback Bridge, a roughly mile-long covered bridge. In the early months of 1812, the Harrisburg Bridge Company, composed of many of the city's most prominent and wealthy persons, formed with the ingenious idea of establishing a toll bridge for pedestrians and wagons to cross the Susquehanna. The company contacted bridge builder Theodore Burr, who responded, "I am…more than willing to undertake your Bridge, and can build you one, on the most improved plan which combines in itself conveniences, strength, Durability and eligance [sic]; for $175,000 every way complete and properly secured from the weather[.]"[6]

Burr soon started work. On May 27, 1814, a sad reminder occurred of the dangers of bridging the mile-wide Susquehanna. Four men fell—one injured "pretty bad," breaking his leg—while three others suffered minor injuries, though Burr felt confident that they "will be able to work again in a short time[.]"[7] In 1817, workers completed the bridge, which opened up a new line of traffic across the Susquehanna. The idea that had begun five years earlier had proved an extremely profitable venture.

It was not long before the Harrisburg Bridge Company had to compete with the neighboring Cumberland Valley Railroad (CVRR) Bridge, which initially allowed foot and horse traffic as well as locomotives. In September 1847, the Harrisburg Bridge Company accustomed its tolls to those of the CVRR Bridge:

Pheaton Pleasure Carriage or Sleigh drawn by;
One horse or mule, 25 cents.
Two horses or mules, 50 cents.
Four horses or mules, 75 cents.

Loaded wagon or Sled Carriage or Sleigh drawn by;
One horse or mule, 20 cents
Two horses, mules or oxen, 60 cents
Every additional horse mule or ox, 5 cents
Each cord of firewood, 62½ cents

Single Horse and Rider, 15 cents
Horse, mule, or donkey without a rider, 8 cents
Foot passenger, 3 cents.[8]

However, in 1850, word came that Robert Wilson, toll collector for the CVRR Bridge, allowed cattle and other stock to pass for a lesser toll than the rates the two companies had agreed upon in 1847. Naturally, the Camelback lost substantial business. The end result proved extremely profitable for both companies. On November 6, 1850, an agreement was signed that the CVRR would be paid quarterly an annual sum of $5,000 for the next ten years to ban all pedestrian, stock and wheeled traffic from its bridge and demote itself entirely to locomotive travel. Both companies enjoyed this transaction so much that it extended long past the original expiration date of 1860.[9]

DEFENDING THE CAPITAL

Harrisburg, with a population of fourteen thousand in the 1860 census, had certainly seen its share of war by the early summer of 1863. Three days after Fort Sumter had surrendered and the war broke out in mid-April 1861, Camp Curtin was established. It soon became the largest training camp in the North.

In the late spring of 1863, General Robert E. Lee and his Confederate Army of Northern Virginia were again plotting an invasion into the Dutch farm fields of southern Pennsylvania after he had been stalled at Antietam the previous fall. His goals included relieving Virginia of the heavy burden of being the eastern theater's main fighting ground, replenishing his army's subsistence with foods at the expense of Maryland and Pennsylvania farms, drawing Federal attention from other sectors and targeting Harrisburg, the capture of which had the potential of greatly embarrassing Federal war efforts. A combination of the above could give Lee a successful campaign and push forth peace talks for the end of the war and ultimately the Confederacy's independence.

Harrisburg was among the most promising of these options. It was, of course, a Northern capital, the capture of which would give the Rebels a major morale boost and an outside chance of foreign recognition. Camp Curtin was located in Harrisburg, which, if captured, would cut off a major flow of Federal reinforcements to the Northern armies engaged in the field. Lastly were the dozens of roads, bridges and railroads emanating from the city, several of which led to Philadelphia, Baltimore and Washington, three cities that would have, if captured or substantially threatened, severely damaged any leverage President Abraham Lincoln still held to continue the war. "If Harrisburg comes within your means, capture it," Lee wrote to Second Corps commander Lieutenant General Richard S. Ewell on June 22.[10] Capturing or threatening Harrisburg could significantly help Lee accomplish his strategic goals.

To protect Pennsylvania's capital, the Federal War Department assigned Major General Darius Nash Couch, a West Pointer and former corps commander in the Army of the Potomac. Born in Putnam County, New York, on July 23, 1822, he was raised with a common school education. He graduated from the highly noted West Point class of 1846 with George McClellan and "Stonewall" Jackson, the latter Couch's roommate. Couch was brevetted for gallantry and meritorious conduct in the Mexican War. In 1855, he resigned his commission to enter the copper fabricating business of his wife's family in Taunton, Massachusetts.

When war erupted in 1861, he became colonel of the 7th Massachusetts. Couch enjoyed rapid promotion when former classmate George McClellan took command. The New York native proved to be a steady and consistent commander as he led a division of the Fourth Corps in the Peninsular Campaign. In July 1862, illness prompted Couch to tender his resignation to McClellan, who refused it and instead promoted him to major general. Engaged at Antietam as a divisional commander, Couch commanded the Second Corps at Fredericksburg and Chancellorsville. He expressed disgust at the behavior of then–army commander Joe Hooker,

Major General Darius N. Couch, commander of the Department of the Susquehanna. *Courtesy of the MOLLUS-MASS Collection, U.S. Army Military History Institute.*

who was largely (and rightly) blamed for the disaster at Chancellorsville. Couch reportedly "told Mr[.] Lincoln that he had served through two disastrous campaigns rendered so by the incompetency of the commanders as he had no faith in any improvement, he requested to be separated[.]" By one account, Lincoln even tendered command of the army to Couch, though he declined it.[11]

On June 9, an order establishing two different departments was drafted; however, evident errors in the order required another edited order, which was released from the War Department the next day. Brigadier General William T.H. Brooks assumed command of the Department of the Monongahela, which embraced those parts of Pennsylvania west of Johnstown and the Laurel Hills, including several counties in West Virginia and Ohio, with headquarters in Pittsburgh. General Couch was assigned to the command of the Department of the Susquehanna, which consisted of the land east of Johnstown and the Laurel Hills, headquartered in Harrisburg.[12]

On June 11, Couch left Washington and entrained for Harrisburg. When he arrived the next evening, he met with Pennsylvania's Republican governor, Andrew Gregg Curtin, and his council of military advisors.[13] All understood the first task at hand was to raise volunteers. Couch proposed a proclamation that began by explaining the emergency. The document went on to detail that "when not required for active service to defend the department, they will be returned to their homes, subject to the call of the commanding general." Couch's order also incorporated a bounty system using the only enticing item he had because the department was desolate of funds: rank. It stated that any person who brought forty or more men would be commissioned a captain, twenty-five or more men a first lieutenant and fifteen or more men a second lieutenant.[14] Instead, many showed up eager to be officers but with no men accompanying them.

On June 12, Curtin issued the first of three proclamations, confirming the rumors of a Rebel invasion and urging citizens to respond to either Couch's or Brooks's General Orders for troops. "The importance of immediately raising a sufficient force for the defense of the State cannot be overrated," Curtin declared.[15]

Colonel Thomas A. Scott, aide and advisor to Curtin, recognized several flaws in Couch's call (which Curtin's June 12 proclamation advocated), namely its appeal to ordinary Pennsylvanians. As Scott's biographer noted, "There was a serious lack of definiteness about the whole arrangement." Volunteers were informed that they would be treated like Regulars while in the field and returned home when "not required for active service." Their terms of service were all up in the air. Couch's call essentially named terms of service within the parameters of at "the pleasure of the President or for the continuance of the war." Additionally, they would receive no bounty (other than rank) and no pay unless Congress (which was currently not in session) authorized so. In the latter, Scott acknowledged "a fatal weakness." Good-paying, fair-wage jobs were, in the words of Scott's biographer, "plentiful throughout the state. To expect men to leave lucrative employment to enter the military service without any prospect of immediate compensation was asking too much."[16]

Even despite Scott's grim (and, for the most part, correct) assessment of Couch's proclamation, the morning

Andrew Gregg Curtin, Pennsylvania's wartime governor. *Courtesy of the Library of Congress.*

of June 13 saw dozens of responses. One man in the 104th Pennsylvania Volunteers requested permission to recruit troops, and many others inquired about the terms of service.[17] Garret G. Ramsey of the 3rd Pennsylvania Heavy Artillery stationed at Fort Monroe requested that he be mustered out of service so that he could recruit a company for state defense.[18]

Many of the respondents were clueless more than anything else. One Philadelphian penned the governor explaining that he wanted "to know how we are to recruit men," as well as what the terms of service are so that "we can tell the men for they all want to under stand the sistem [*sic.*]"[19] It was tough enough to raise an army of fifty thousand men but much more difficult to do so in a span of roughly two weeks. These letters sent to Curtin are the epithet of that struggle. The invasion brought out well-meaning citizens who offered their service for state defense but knew absolutely nothing of military tactics. Requests frequently came for "any orders, or regulations[.]"[20] Others were confused at the terms of service. "If I recruit I want to do it with an understanding as to the length of time the men must serve," one man informed Commonwealth Secretary Eli Slifer.[21]

Many citizens had a distorted view of warfare, thanks largely to newspaper coverage of Confederate partisans such as John Mosby. One Philadelphian proposed to raise one hundred men to serve as couriers and marauders. "We will place ourselves under your immediate command," he added. "I think I can get a fine, intelligent set [of men] between 18 and 21 years of age."[22]

Harrisburg's dire straits also attracted the attention of more experienced men. Lieutenant Colonel George Osborn of the 56th Pennsylvania Volunteer Infantry (abbreviated PVI) in the Army of the Potomac requested to be relieved so that he could command a militia regiment. Osborn reasoned that because the 56th contained only three hundred men, it did not need the standard three field officers. He believed that command of a militia regiment "would render me more beneficial to my State and country."[23]

Another respondent, a man named Jones, had served twelve years as a captain in the Royal Artillery, including commanding a battery in the Crimean War. The Brit had also served more recently in the 8th New York Cavalry and the 19th New York Independent Battery. Discharged from the latter due to ill health, Jones pronounced himself ready to enter a new endeavor.[24] Jones was not the only foreigner whose application appeared on Curtin's desk. Arthur Wolff, a Frenchman with eleven years of active service (including seven in Africa) in the French army under his belt, also offered his services to Curtin. Formerly a field officer of the 1st Zouaves Imperial, Wolff was a member of the French Legion of Honor. "I want to strike one blow before I die for Humanities Freedom," Wolff explained. His résumé included being "decorated" by Queen Donna Maria of Portugal. "I am a Stranger, here without, friends or protectors, but am willing to pass the most strict escamination [*sic*] as to my qualification[.]"[25]

BATTLING WASHINGTON

Couch learned that no more than 250 men, many of them from the Invalid Corps, were ready to defend the state capital.[26] Curtin (doubtless through Scott's influence) did not favor Couch's proclamation and instead telegraphed Secretary of War Edwin Stanton, proposing that the recruitment for three years' service be temporarily postponed "in order to fill up speedily the army corps for General Couch." The message ended with an endorsement from Couch.[27] "I hope you [Couch] had nothing to

Secretary of War Edwin M. Stanton at first did little to ease Couch's and Curtin's difficult situation. *Courtesy of the Library of Congress.*

do with such agreement," Stanton quickly fired back. "The recruiting for three years or during the war should not be postponed an hour."[28] Couch realized that it was useless to continue making proposals to Stanton and it would be best to allow him to simmer down.

Later on June 13, more dire reports arrived from Major General Robert F. Schenck's headquarters in Baltimore. Schenck commanded the force that was intended to deal with the sort of mess accompanying a Confederate invasion, but because his department was stretched across the Potomac from Washington to far out west, it was too thin and practically useless. Schenck informed Couch that Confederates were attacking Winchester and openly doubted his own ability to check any further advance.[29]

By this time, Curtin and Couch must have looked with envy on the situation of W.T.H. Brooks and his Department of the Monongahela. "Pittsburg is busy fortifying, 6800 men (volunteers) have been at work all week, we will not quit till the city is surrounded by formidable works and then we are secure from rebel raids," a young and upcoming Andrew Carnegie claimed.[30]

Curtin knew that calling out the state militia would be hazardous both politically and financially, and even with the Democratic State Convention meeting then in Harrisburg to nominate his opponent for the October election, it appeared as the only answer. Curtin, in poor health, had not eagerly sought reelection. On April 13, Lincoln notified Curtin that he could go abroad "with one of the first-class missions." News of this and that Curtin would likely not run for reelection caused uproar within the Republican Party. The governor eventually succumbed to these pleas and, despite his health, announced his bid for reelection.[31]

Not getting any positive answers out of Stanton, Curtin bypassed the War Department and went directly to General-in-Chief Henry Halleck. Curtin wired, "If the rebel cavalry move across the Potomac, will the cavalry of General Hooker's army pursue them, or be used to retard their movements? My object in asking is to know whether my duty as Executive of this State, under direction of the President, may not require an immediate call of the militia to resist invasion." Not knowing that Curtin had purposely bypassed Stanton, Halleck wired back shortly that the matter should be taken to Stanton and Lincoln.[32]

By June 14, Couch and Curtin decided that Stanton had probably cooled down from his earlier outburst. "We find difficulty in getting our people aroused, but it is now being effected," Colonel Scott informed the fiery secretary of war. "The difficulty about no pay for troops until Congress meets is a serious one, but I think we can arrange to-morrow for the corporate and other moneyed interests of the State to contribute, as a loan, sufficient to pay men until Congress meets. [I] shall leave nothing undone to effect speedy organization of forces."[33] Scott did not receive as much money or the number of volunteers he had hoped for. The city of Philadelphia, however, raised $500,000 for the cause.[34]

Late on June 14, Scott was sent to Washington, arriving at 1:00 a.m. the following morning. Immediately he was ushered into a meeting with Stanton, Secretary of State William Seward and Solicitor of the War Department William Whiting to discuss raising volunteers. Curtin was in a very precarious political situation already, without calling out his state's militia. Therefore, he wanted the president to do so. "On examination," Scott wired Curtin at 2:30 a.m., "it is found that the President cannot authorize a call in the form you suggest, the law in express terms prohibiting, but he will make a demand or call upon Pennsylvania, Ohio, Maryland, and West Virginia for 100,000 men, in view of the threatened invasion…to serve six months, unless sooner discharged by order of the President, the men so called to be provided by the General Government with arms and all usual supplies[.]" Additionally, all men who volunteered would be exempt from the upcoming draft. Scott added an unnecessary but thoughtful precaution, telling Curtin to keep this backdoor political deal "entirely private." Curtin, overjoyed, wired back two hours later giving his approval and stating he would make a call for 50,000 volunteers from the Keystone State.[35]

Later on June 15, Curtin issued his second proclamation, calling for fifty thousand men, but received relatively little response.[36] However, men fit for service were in abundance at the time, as the editor of the *Philadelphia Daily Evening Bulletin* detailed: "The returned regiments of nine months men may furnish a basis for the whole force required, and the experience that they have had in the field will especially fit them for company officers. A half dozen regiments composed of the discharged nine months' men would be more efficient than twice or thrice as many made up of raw recruits."[37]

"In a few of the country towns," explained future Governor Samuel Pennypacker, "there was some little effort to raise men, and in Philadelphia, a meeting was held, the newspaper called on the citizens with glowing words to volunteer but nobody appeared to be willing to shoulder the musket." Pennypacker cited several reasons for this reluctance—first and foremost, many Democrats believed that this was a political scheme hatched by Curtin to save his despairing reelection by keeping them from the polls. Additionally, the previous fall the militia had been called out during Lee's Maryland Campaign but did not prove to be of any use. Pennypacker reasoned that it was "the opinion of most persons that it was a mere cavalry raid which would be settled without much difficulty, and there was no necessity for such a great disturbance or interfering with the transaction of business."[38]

However, Curtin soon noted progress on gathering troops. Secretary Stanton wired Governor Horatio Seymour of New York on June 15: "The movement of the rebel forces in Virginia are now sufficiently developed to show that General Lee with his whole army is moving forward to invade the States of Maryland and Pennsylvania, and other States." Stanton requested twenty thousand militia, to which Seymour responded, "I will spare no effort to send you troops at once." New Yorkers would be defending Pennsylvania, which was fully capable of defending itself but so far showed no intention of doing so.[39]

Major General Charles W. Sandford headed the First Division of the New York State National Guard (NYSNG). Between June 17 and July 3, Sandford sent thirteen regiments to aid the Keystone State, eight of which arrived in Harrisburg, while five others were sent to Baltimore.[40] Under normal circumstances, the Federal government would not have accepted the general officers who accompanied the regiments, namely because they held New York state, not Federal, commissions. But this was different; it was an emergency. Therefore, the government let this pass for the brigadiers who commanded the pre-designated brigades. However, Sandford, who was not well respected as a general officer, remained in New York. The government drew the line there—the major general was too much to handle.

There were many soon-to-be-obvious flaws in these New York brigadiers, many of whom had held their commissions for more than three decades. "During this [prewar] period their duties had been confined to street parades," wrote Corporal George Wingate of the 22nd NYSNG, "with the occasional exception of perhaps an annual brigade drill, when the brigade commander had his orders carefully written out, and put on his spectacles to read them. There were no reports, no inspections and no discipline outside that maintained by the regiments themselves."[41] When noncombatant Isaac Harris of the U.S. Sanitary Commission saw Philip Schuyler Crooke—one of the New York brigadiers—arrive in Harrisburg, he opined that Crooke and his staff "look greener than any of the boys in the Brigade."[42]

From the Garden State came the 23rd New Jersey Volunteers, whose term of enlistment had expired but before being mustered out of service decided to lend a hand in the defense of Harrisburg. Arriving in the city in open coal cars on the afternoon of June 18, Colonel Edward Burd Grubb of the 23rd reported to Couch's headquarters in the capitol building. "He told me there were no organized troops in the town and he did not know when there would be," recalled Grubb.

Couch mentioned a ford near the CVRR Bridge and added "that if the bridges were burned, he thought the enemy would attempt to cross at that place as the river was very low." Couch directed Grubb to post his regiment in Harris Park near this ford on the shores of the Susquehanna "and throw up a demilune rifle pit and to pierce the cellars of all the houses that abutted the river in that vicinity for musketry."

Working the afternoon of June 18 and the following morning, the 23rd established "a tolerably good rifle pit,"

Colonel Edward Burd Grubb of the 23rd New Jersey Volunteers. *Courtesy of the U.S. Army Military History Institute.*

which, according to Grubb, extended "nearly the whole length of the Harris Park and just back of the fence, which was on the river side." The New Jersey colonel left the fence in place "so that the rifle pit was masked from the river." The citizens, however, refused them canteens of water and charged outrageous prices for food goods. A fistfight erupted between civilians and the New Jersey soldiers. The 23rd decided to return to New Jersey after spending only a few days "without regret."[43]

On June 18, the 8th and 71st NYSNG arrived in Harrisburg. These two units were some of the most experienced under Couch's command; both units had been in the thick of the action at First Manassas. On June 19, Couch ordered the duo down the Cumberland Valley to Chambersburg, where they were to delay the Rebel advance by all means. Shortly thereafter, Couch assigned Brigadier General Joseph F. Knipe, a brigadier in the Army of the Potomac, as their commander.[44]

While the flow of men into Harrisburg may have been steady, Couch noted in a June 22 letter to Stanton his command's many obvious flaws: "You will readily understand what kind of a force I have, when a few regiments, with a sprinkling of nine-months' men in them, are the veterans. The New York troops look very well, but are without much confidence in themselves. My little artillery is all raw; my cavalry the same."[45]

Harrisburg Companies

While some Harrisburgers expressed apathy at the Rebel threat, others volunteered their services. On June 24, a drumbeat and a fife shrilled as a unique sixteen-man company marched through the streets of the keystone capital to volunteer. Their ages set this group apart—the youngest was sixty-eight and the oldest seventy-six. They were all veterans of the War of 1812. They bore a "tattered silk flag," formerly the colors of a Pennsylvania regiment at the Revolutionary War's Battle of Trenton. Marching to the governor's room, they expressed their desire to serve in the fort, and "if any other and harder service was required of them, they would cheerfully attempt it." Curtin accepted, though he only used them for guard purposes. These old-timers insisted on being armed with the out-of-date flintlock musket, the model they had used in their fighting days. One reporter detailed:

> It was a grand and inspiring sight!—those old men, scarcely hoping to live
> through the war, their locks white with the frosts of many winters, their

frames bowed by age and long toil in the journey of life, marched as briskly and accurately to the drum and fife, as any of their grandsons could. They seemed almost carried back to the olden time, so inspiriting was the occasion. When they came out of the Governor's room they marched, according to the old fashion, in single file. They were halted on the green. It was curious to modern ears to hear the order of the captain—so different from our tactics. It was; "By sections of two, march;" instead of "file right" or "left" it "right" or "left wheel;" instead of the sharp, short, peremptory "front," it was "left face." So they marched down in the town, carrying the old tactics of the Revolution with them. They kept their places, and kept step and obeyed orders with a precision that showed that the drill they had gone through in those stirring times had gone not merely to the era, but to the heart. Wherever they passed a squad of soldiers they were loudly cheered—"Three cheers for the veterans of 1812," and such lusty shouts as split the heavens you never heard…What an example to the young men of Harrisburg![46]

One noncombatant mused, "It is a funny sight to see these old fellows and how determined they look, as if a good sized 'Johnny' would be only half a mouthful for any one of them; and then the way they carry their muskets is enough to make a dog laugh."[47] Several other companies were also raised within the city. A black company volunteered for six months' service, but they "refused by unanimous vote to be mustered in with white officers."[48]

COUCH'S RIGHT-HAND MAN

While Couch busily attended to administrative matters and the Confederates continued to inch closer, a senior field commander was evidently lacking— someone whom he could trust to lead his men to victory. It was a well-established fact that the New York National Guard brigadiers were inept.

After the disaster at Fredericksburg in December 1862, the Army of the Potomac sulked, and many pointed fingers. Generals William B. Franklin and William F. "Baldy" Smith both criticized army commander Ambrose Burnside's performance. Because of this, the Senate Military Committee never mentioned Franklin's name for promotion and withdrew Smith's name for promotion to major general. Smith, who had by that time risen to command of the Ninth Corps, was ruled ineligible to serve in that capacity as a brigadier general and sent home to New York.[49] The names Franklin and Smith appeared frequently in Couch's correspondence throughout early June

1863. Smith, however, seemed to be the most eager to serve under Couch. "I directed General Franklin to write to General Couch," Smith recollected, "and say I would be glad to join him as a lieutenant if I could be of assistance." Couch accepted his offer but kept Smith at his proper rank of general.[50]

Despite not serving in the department, Franklin nevertheless remained interested in departmental affairs and visited Harrisburg on June 22. While there, he observed tensions among Curtin, Couch and former Secretary of War Simon Cameron, a resident of Harrisburg, who also happened to be an avowed political enemy of Curtin. "There is no good feeling between any two of them," Franklin penned to Smith, who was still in New York at the time. "Cameron abuses Curtin, and Curtin is not quite so open in abuse but is just as bitter as Cameron. Couch does not feel comfortable under the circumstances of course, but I think tries to do his best. If the Rebels soon come he will be in an awful plight."[51]

Born in St. Albans, Vermont, on February 17, 1824, Smith graduated fourth in his class from West Point in 1845. He spent the majority of his prewar years as an engineering officer, involved in countless surveys, and later became secretary of the Lighthouse Board. He served on Irvin McDowell's staff at First Manassas, led a division during the Peninsula and Maryland Campaigns and commanded the Sixth Corps at Fredericksburg. "He considered it a great descent from the magnificent corps in the Army of the Potomac that he had formerly commanded," Wingate wrote, "and he was in that state of mind familiarly known as 'sour.'" Despite his attitude, Smith was very popular among the militia in the department.[52] On June 25, Couch officially assigned Smith to command all the troops belonging to the department west of the Susquehanna River.[53]

Brigadier General William F. "Baldy" Smith was Couch's right-hand man in preparing the defenses of Harrisburg as the Confederates approached. *Courtesy of the Library of Congress.*

Chapter 2

The Defenses of Harrisburg

B y June 14, General Couch realized battling Secretary of War Stanton and his fellow Washington bureaucrats was pointless. The department commander noted a commanding rise on the opposite bank of the Susquehanna that dominated the vicinity. He correctly determined that if the Confederates took possession of these heights, Harrisburg would be defenseless. On June 12, Couch requested a military engineer be sent to assist with construction, but the urgency he conveyed was apparently not appreciated, and the engineer would not arrive until June 20.[54] Couch needed to act now. To do so, he reached all the way to Philadelphia on June 14, requesting that assistant railroad engineer John A. Wilson of the Pennsylvania Railroad Company report at once to Harrisburg to assist in constructing the entrenchments. Wilson and two fellow engineers left at 6:00 p.m. on an express train to Harrisburg.[55]

Bridgeport Heights (also known as Hummel's Heights) lay about 250 yards west of the Susquehanna and about a mile south of Harrisburg. Even though modern construction has practically destroyed the old earthworks that once adorned the hill, one can still see the major terrain features quite clearly. The heights consist of two main bodies: bluffs directly opposite the Susquehanna and an adjacent hill that juts out diagonally in a southerly direction to a small hill on which sat the J. Haldeman farm. On the southern side of the heights was the Carlisle Turnpike, and on the northern side, a steep descent led into a hollow then covered with thick woods and underbrush. Several farms, mostly abandoned upon news of the Confederate invasion, dotted the hillside. Another prominent feature was Bridgeport Station, just west of the Susquehanna beside the CVRR bridge.

A postwar view of the Camelback Bridge from Forster's Island in the center of the Susquehanna River. *Courtesy of the Pennsylvania State Archives.*

Engineer Wilson was "about town" the morning of June 15. About 4:00 p.m., Wilson and Captain Richard I. Dodge of the 8th U.S. Infantry crossed the Camelback Bridge and began staking out the planned works on Bridgeport Heights. At 5:00 p.m., work began, with over one thousand Harrisburgers assisting.[56] It was a joyful assemblage at first, but soon the citizen-volunteers learned that the only tools available were picks and hand shovels.[57] Disgruntlement turned into vehemence when they discovered the heights consisted primarily of shale, which proved nearly impossible to dig.

Wilson soon received help from a large group of workers from the Pennsylvania Railroad and Canal and "a large gang of negroes." He realized the urgency (ludicrous rumors had spread through Harrisburg that the Confederates would be within sight of the town on June 16)[58] and insisted that he would "not stop for anything" by working his ragtag gang all night, even sleeping on the heights himself so he could constantly monitor the work. This work proved too much for some citizens. As it hurt their hands, they figured that the Negro laborers could do the work and left. By 7:00 a.m. the following morning, of the one-thousand-plus white volunteers there the previous evening, only three hundred remained, or as Wilson referred to those faithful, the "true citizens of Harrisburg." The laborers were paid $1.25 per day of ten hours, which would be reduced in July to

$0.75. This work was dangerous. About 2:00 p.m. on June 16, a young man died after falling from a twenty-four-foot-high embankment.[59] About noon that same day, Major James Brady, a Pennsylvania artillery officer, took charge of the construction.[60]

THE PANIC OF JUNE 16

All this hustle and bustle took a toll on the residents of Harrisburg. Governor Curtin's call for volunteers to join the militia and to build fortifications opposite the city threw a toilsome weight on their shoulders. The rhetoric of Washington politicians—and that of Democratic politicians at the state level—could protect them no more; war was coming to Harrisburg. Adding to the uncertainty, farmers from all parts of the Cumberland Valley clogged the roads as they fled with their stock from the Rebels. Rumors flew throughout the town, inaccurately reporting the Rebels to be approaching to within a stone's throw of the city. Posters circulated around the state requested 100,000 men to assist in constructing the fortifications.[61] Noted pianist Louis Moreau Gottschalk described the panic:

> *1 P.M. A mile this side of Harrisburg the road is completely obstructed by freight trains, wagons of all sorts, and in fine by all the immense mass of merchandise etc., which for the last twelve hours has been concentrated near the town to avoid capture or burning by the rebels…The anxiety increases. Can you conceive anything more terrible than the expectation of some vague, unknown danger? Some passengers have sat upon the floor, to be sheltered from bullets in case the train should be fired upon. One hour of anxiety, during which all the women, whilst pretending to be dead with fright, do not cease talking and making the most absurd conjectures…The city expects to be attacked every moment…The clergy (many hundred persons), in a meeting which took place on this subject, have placed themselves at the disposition of the Governor, to be employed for the defence [sic] of the city. Priests, pastors, rectors, ministers of all denominations, are at this moment engaged in wheeling barrows full of earth and in digging pits for the sharpshooters…I see all along the river great clouds of dust; it is from the herds of cattle which the frightened farmers are driving toward the mountains, in hopes of hiding them from the rebels…A thousand absurd rumors are in circulation. The great news for the moment is, that [Major General George] McClellan, who is the idol of the army, particularly*

since the President has taken from him the command, arrives this evening to place himself at the head of the Pennsylvania militia, to crush Lee.[62]

The state capital "has been completely denuded of everything of value," detailed one reporter, "from the portraits of the Governors to the books in the library." The correspondent detailed the "perfect panic" that had overtaken "all classes of people" that morning and resulted "in the grandest demand for railroad tickets ever witnessed in this city…Trunks were piled up at the depots six feet in height for nearly a square."[63] Workers packed the state archives and sent them to Philadelphia.[64] William Robinson of the 8th NYSNG penned in his diary, "The people of Harrisburg [are] scared to Deth [*sic*]."[65]

As news spread of the city's peril, Harrisburg attracted curiosity seekers such as one naïve New York businessman, who remarked, "I thought I should like to see a battle if possible, and I thought if the Rebels pressed too hard I would have a shot at them if I should be allowed the priviledge [*sic*]."[66]

This photograph shows the original state capitol building, built in 1822, present during the invasion before it was destroyed by a fire in 1897. *Courtesy of the Library of Congress.*

HARRISBURG AND ITS DEFENDERS

Despite the potential danger of an invasion, many Harrisburgers were most concerned about making a profit. Corporal George Wingate of the 22nd NYSNG complained that the shopkeepers "put up their prices to 'all that the traffic would stand.' Fifteen cents for a cup of rye coffee, five cents for a glass of water, exorbitant charges for anything that the soldiers wanted, and an apparent general indifference as to which side would be the victors for the impending contest." "It must make those old Dutch down the Valley swear to have their apple butter carted off; but it serves them right," opined Isaac Harris of the U.S. Sanitary Commission. "There is no fight in them…[they] have no gratitude for those who are here to protect them. To charge a man twenty-five cents for a slice of bread smeared over with apple butter and thus expect him to fight for you is a mistaken idea—very! I have seen men sell water on the streets in this city…to soldiers…at five cents a cup-full. And I have also seen the same men have the contents of their buckets poured over them as soon as all the boys had had a drink." "Although the roofs and spires of Harrisburg were in plain sight," added Wingate, "there was but little desire to visit it."[67]

Perhaps the ultimate testament to Harrisburg's greed was the Harrisburg Bridge Company. The company took careful note of every soldier who crossed the Camelback Bridge to defend it, charging six cents a man. Later that year, the company slapped the Federal government with a bill of $3,028.63, which was paid. "This is abominable," one Pennsylvania militiaman opined.[68]

Not only did the Harrisburgers' greed dismay the defending militia, but so did their remarkable absence in the earthworks. New York soldier John Lockwood expected in the entrenchments "thousands of the adult men of Harrisburg, with the rough implements of work in their hands, patriotically toiling to put into a condition of defence [*sic*]…of their capital" but found "[n]othing of the sort. Panic-stricken by the reported approach of the enemy, the poltroons of the city had closed their houses and stores…and were thinking of nothing in their abject fear except how to escape with their worthless lives and their property."[69] Colonel Chauncey Abbott of the 67th NYSNG concurred: "I did not see but one company of the citizens of Harrisburg organized and on duty for the defense of their own city, and that was a small company of Americans of African descent, drilling under some shade trees in front of the capitol."[70]

"The Harrisburghers [*sic*] are a queer people," remarked New Yorker L.T. Hyde. "They walk around gaping at the fine looking New Yorkers. They don't seem inclined to do anything for there [*sic*] own defense."[71] "The residents of the capital itself appeared listless," opined Lockwood. "Hundreds of strong men in the prime of life loitered in the public thoroughfares, and gaped at our passing columns as indifferently as if we had come as conquers to take possession of the city they cravenly submitting to the yoke."[72]

As citizens from the Cumberland Valley ushered their goods northward through Harrisburg and into safe havens east of the Susquehanna, those Harrisburgers who had not departed remained about their business. Many—primarily Democrats—maintained that the whole invasion was a ruse. "We have had another scare here," penned citizen Jacob Spangler. "[T]he Town has been in excitement the most of this week from reports of Rebbel [*sic*] raids…but we have not had the pleasure of seeing any of the Rebbs [*sic*] yet." Spangler went on to call Curtin a "poor man" and added, "I think all this fuss is got up to bring out the men the Dem[ocrats], but the most of them think it is time now for the other Party to come out and go to work instead of laying back and taking all the money[.]"[73]

COLORED TROOPS

During this tumultuous period, several companies of African Americans arrived in Harrisburg to offer their services. One group from Philadelphia arrived but was turned away. "[A]fter referring the matter to some of the chief executive officers of the state," recalled Couch, "I was informed that their presence would cause serious disturbances among the state troops[.]" Secretary of War Stanton had authorized Couch to "receive troops without regard to color" but cautioned, "If there is likely to be any dispute about the matter…It is well to avoid all controversy in the present juncture, as the [colored] troops can be well used elsewhere."[74]

PENNSYLVANIA MILITIA

Governor Curtin's calls had managed to raise a few thousand proud Pennsylvanians determined to defend their homes. Most men came in the form of companies from various individual towns and would be formed into regiments in Harrisburg. However, many of these Pennsylvanians were greatly upset at their reception in their own state capital.

"I recall with considerable amusement," reminisced future Governor Samuel Pennypacker—who at the age of twenty had enrolled with a company from Phoenixville—"the expectation I had formed of what would be our reception. I had supposed…that the Governor would have some officer at the depot ready to receive us, comfortable quarters prepared for us, and treat us as if we were of some consequence. We were, therefore, surprised, and our feelings somewhat chilled, to find that we were left to provide for ourselves and seek accommodation as best we might." Pennypacker spent his first night in Harrisburg on the steps of the capitol building, listening to the "shouting, hurrahing and…inflammatory speeches [of the Democratic Convention], while the pavement, the stone porch, and the floor of the galleries were covered with militia, trying to sleep amidst the din. The thought was enough to anger a saint," recorded an incensed Pennypacker. "[T]he Capital of the State threatened by the rebels…and those who respond compelled…[to] listen to the disloyal yells of the enemies of the country comfortable quartered within."[75]

Pennypacker's experience was not unusual. Some companies (the lucky ones) crammed themselves inside the statehouse.[76] Charles Sayles, a volunteer from Bradford County who arrived around 2:30 a.m. on June 18, penned home to his wife that the company "marched up to the capitol Grounds and spread our Blankets (those that were fortunate enough to have them) some on the side walks some on the roof of the stats [*sic*] house and some…under the Trees[.] I was one of the latter[.] [W]e stretched out for about 2 hours but [got] little sleep[.]"[77]

General Couch issued an order on the morning of June 17 requiring all militia to be mustered in for six months or the "emergency." This considerably angered many Pennsylvanians. Could they trust that the "emergency" would not be changed to six months or the duration of the war? "[T]here is a great deal of disputing about the meaning of Curtin's Call and fears are entertained that we will be retained in the U.S. Service after the rebels are cleared out," detailed one militiaman.[78] Curtin spoke to some Pennsylvanians at the camp that bore his name and "urged them to go and…that any man who would not enlist for the 6 months was a coward[.]"[79] While most refused this six-month term of service, several companies, determined "not to stand on fine points," were mustered in.[80]

While many were bitter at the terms of service, others were just plain ignorant. A volunteer from Northampton County reminisced, "There was much talk about the manner in which the Militia was to be sworn in, of which the writer, however, with a great many hundreds of others, was totally ignorant. Who assumed the authority to speak for the boys is unknown to the writer, but certainly there had been no meeting of the Cos to take action in the matter."[81]

Much of the remarkable neglect of the emergency came directly from the fact that Harrisburg looked little like a threatened city for those who had missed the panic of June 16. "I expected to find every body in a hurry and all the bustle naturally attendant upon a beleaguered city," wrote Henry Wirt Shriver, a Marylander who had enlisted in a company from Hanover, "but there was no excitement visible whatever—people regarded us with as much curiosity as if we had marched tho' [sic] town times of peace—we saw nothing of intrenchments [sic] nor in fact anything indicating war except a few carloads of cannon standing on the RR track[.]" A shocked Shriver could scarcely count seven hundred men within the limits of Camp Curtin. "[T]here seemed to be a poor show for defending the city against a single regiment of Rebels," he observed.[82]

Shriver was not alone in his assessment. E.J. Moore of Allentown arrived in Harrisburg and was forced to sleep under the cover of a tree near the capitol building. Via a gas lamp, he penned a letter home communicating much frustration to his wife on the evening of June 16. "It does not appear here…any danger…[is] now feared," he wrote. "The rebels are not near[.] There is some talk of sending us immergency [sic] men home to morrow." "The fright is entirely over," Moore continued the following evening. "[T]he people here have settled down into their usual quietness, and if you could be here to see the ladies loiter along the different thoroughfares you would not suppose that the Commonwealth of Penna was seeking…to defend their homes from desecration, and our Capitol from dishonor[.]"[83]

With this stalemate over terms of service, most Pennsylvania companies simply laid in Camp Curtin, although a considerable number left for home. Very few of those who remained were mustered in right away. Many who had no blankets and tents of their own began to suffer the consequences, as these would not be issued until the men were mustered in. By one report, Curtin was considerably "annoyed by officers asking for transportation home of Philadelphia volunteers."[84] In camp, rumors spread like wildfire. Maryland native Shriver wrote home that the "most reliable accounts here" indicated that the invading hordes of Rebels had already left. "Hardly anything…[is] said or thought of the rebels," he added.[85]

The most entertainment volunteer E.J. Moore found while in Camp Curtin was when an intimidating lot of Rebel prisoners passed through:

> *Saw a squad of live secesh today at Camp Curtin. As a general thing they are healthy, strong, tough looking. Their physical appearance is excellent. [T]hey have a dogged and sullen look, and what is more they*

[are] *determined men. Their torn and tattered garments are no disgrace to them. As I stood looking at them, noting their scowling eyes, and their utter indifference to the insults that I am sorry to say were cast upon them. I wished our Union Soldiers were as heroic as they are.*[86]

By June 25, Curtin realized that his only chance to raise a large force was to make an independent call for volunteers. The governor knew that would be disliked in Washington—or, as he wrote to his wife, it "would have a most dangerous if not fatal effect" on the wishes of Stanton and many other War Department officials. "It would stop the conscription and I fear any further contributions of men to the National Armies[.]"[87] He nevertheless received Lincoln's approval and the next day issued a stirring third proclamation: "I will not insult you with inflammatory appeals. A people who want the heart to defend their soil, their families, and their firesides, are not worthy to be accounted men. Heed not the counsels of evil-disposed persons, if such there be in your midst. Show yourself what you are—a free, loyal, spirited, brave, vigorous race."[88] This proclamation received a substantially warmer response. Since it stated that men would be mustered into state, not Federal, service, it dismissed many fears of detainment after the emergency was over. Additionally, a ninety-day term, as offered in the proclamation, also served to soothe fears—even if they were detained after the emergency, they would be discharged in ninety days.

During the Maryland Campaign, militia regiments were raised up to the number 25. Only the 20th returned in 1863; therefore, the first new regimental designation was the 26th. Often a matter of confusion, regimental designation for 1863 emergency regiments was determined by what terms the units accepted. Units that accepted "for the emergency or six months" were the 20th, 26th through 31st and 33rd Regiments—eight regiments in total. These units were officially designated as Pennsylvania Volunteer Militia (abbreviated PVM) though referred to often as Emergency Militia. All other regiments were mustered in for either sixty or ninety days and simply referred to as Pennsylvania Militia (abbreviated PM).

Colonel James Beaver of the 148th PVI commanded Camp Curtin during this tumultuous period. When his native state was invaded, Beaver, a future governor who had been badly wounded at Chancellorsville, rushed to Harrisburg en route to rejoin his regiment in the Army of the Potomac for the upcoming campaign. Upon arriving there, surgeons "advised him by no means" should he attempt to rejoin his command. "But he could not remain inactive," chronicled his biographer, and he offered his services to General

Couch. Beaver became commandant of Camp Curtin, "a position," Beaver wrote, "of much vexatious toil. The militia force here is immense and untamed. I have never seen anything equal to it." By June 27, Beaver was able to mount his horse for the first time since Chancellorsville, giving him "great satisfaction." He immediately penned a letter home to his mother expressing his hopes that he could rejoin his regiment soon but was not relieved until July 15.[89]

THE DEFENSES

Work continued on the entrenchments on the other side of the Susquehanna. A traveling New York businessman named Went, who had gone to Harrisburg "to see a battle" and if possible "have a shot" at the Rebels, ascended the dome of the capitol. From there, Went "took a survey from the Cupolo [*sic*] and in the distance on the other side of the river we could just perceive the men in a cloud of dust working on the earthworks." Upon crossing the Camelback Bridge, Went "found quite an extensive work being constructed." He described the scene:

> *Thousands of flour barrels ranged in the form required for the work and bein* [sic] *filled with soil formed an upright breastwork to begin with which was being enlarged by digging outside some 16 or 18 feet throwing the earth to the barrels, and carrying it above them in the centre of the embankment leveling it both ways, but much more outside than on the inside. The work commanded both Bridges* [Camelback and CVRR] *being situated on a hill* [Bridgeport Heights] *I suppose about 100 or 150 feet in height. Beyond the earth work Trees were cut down and an abattis formed of them while the stumps of the trees were being burnt out so that they could not be used a shelter for rifle men approaching the work. A Field battery was there so as to protect them in case the Rebels should come before the work was sufficiently finished, to offer much protection, and the abattis was in front of this battery because that would [be] assailed first.*[90]

On June 19, Couch issued orders naming the earthworks Fort Washington.[91] Upon its completion, Fort Washington was very impressive, considering the time span and circumstances under which it was completed. One reporter termed it "a walled city." The rifle pits were "thrown up beyond the chief parallels, to form a sort of refuge for stragglers and retreating troops."[92]

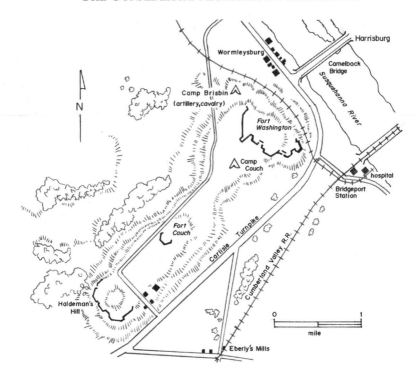

The fortifications on Bridgeport Heights. *Map by John Heiser.*

Troops entering Fort Washington soon noted, however, that it was dominated by part of Bridgeport Heights that extended about one-quarter mile to the west. If the Confederates seized this high ground, the new fort would be defenseless.[93] Major Brady took a portion of the laborers to this spot, while Captain Dodge continued perfecting Fort Washington.[94] What Brady would build was named Fort Couch. It was also known as Fort Henry Clay. If all worked out as planned, Fort Couch would defend Fort Washington, which in turn defended Harrisburg. But few, if any, of its defenders had confidence in Fort Couch. "This [Fort Couch] had been partially intrenched [*sic*], but not enough for effectiveness," wrote one artillery officer.[95]

Most regiments on Bridgeport Heights encamped in the half-mile stretch between Forts Couch and Washington. The 23rd NYSNG named this area Camp Couch (not to be confused with Fort Couch), and dozens of other units followed suit.[96] A regiment of Pennsylvanians encamped in what they called Camp Susquehanna, likely an alias for Camp Couch.[97] Within Camp Couch were separate bivouac sites for both the cavalry and artillery, which was located on a small bluff immediately overlooking the river. The artillery

This modern photo shows the extensiveness and height of Fort Couch, which is almost entirely preserved by the township of Lemoyne. *Photo by the author.*

was placed here so that it would not slide down the steep slopes of Bridgeport Heights. It was an entirely different story, however, to get the artillery up to Camp Couch. One artilleryman recorded in his diary that it took eight horses and twenty men to haul just one three-inch ordnance rifle up the hill. The cavalry camp was adjacent to the artillery park and, until later in June, was also called Camp Couch, but after reportedly "giving much annoyance to persons wishing to find their friends, and many of the letters being sent to the wrong camp," it was changed to Camp Brisbin, named for the late chief of cavalry in the department, Captain James S. Brisbin. On June 28, Major John Estill Wynkoop replaced Brisbin, who took medical leave and was borne to Harrisburg for treatment.[98] Little drill was done, many of the cavalrymen instead lending a hand in constructing the earthworks. One Mechanicsburg native who had enlisted in a cavalry company later proclaimed that he had "helped to Build Fort Washington[.]"[99]

A third fort was also constructed. On June 26, the 28th PVM was moved from its encampment in Camp Couch about a half mile west to Haldeman's Hill, which was then being "surrounded with breastworks." During the entire night and a large part of the next day, the regiment busily dug breastworks with the assistance of contrabands. On Saturday,

This photo from the summer of 1863 was taken by photographer Fred Clark of Harrisburg facing south, away from the Susquehanna River, and shows a camp scene, as well as other buildings. In the background, note the trains on the Cumberland Valley Railroad line. This was later used by Currier & Ives artist Fanny Palmer in 1865 to make a popular print entitled *Cumberland Valley. Courtesy of the Cumberland County Historical Society.*

June 27, even with the works in a state that Charles Smith of Company B termed unfinished, the regiment was ordered to man the breastworks. Early twentieth-century genealogist Jeremiah Zeamer recorded that this fort was "left without a name."[100]

On the morning of June 20, Captain J.B. Wheeler—the military engineer whom Couch had summoned to construct the fortifications more than a week earlier—finally arrived. Wheeler was given the position of chief engineer of the department and then crossed the Susquehanna and examined the forts. He was not impressed. "However faulty they may have been, [they] were not interfered with by me, as so much work had been already done on them," Wheeler reported.[101] Wheeler may not have been the only one to notice faults in the earthworks. Captain Thomas Dwight, a staff officer serving with Landis's Philadelphia battery in the fort, reported:

> *These* [the gun platforms] *were depressed from eighteen inches to two feet below the rampart, which was construct*[ed] *of a soil made up of equal parts of loam and fragments of rock. Had an attack been made*

accompanied with shell, these bits of rock would have proved more destructive than volleys of musketry—a single shell bursting on any portion of the glacis near the gun would have converted hundreds of them into grape and canister, and might have disabled an entire gun detachment and its infantry supports.

Immediately from the ditch, the ground inclined gently to the Carlisle turnpike road. It had been cleared to obtain materials for the ramparts, but clumps of bushes were left in every direction capable of being used as coverts for sharpshooters and skirmishers…

In the rear of the Fort, the bridge had been cut, and arrangements had been made to drop a span on the appearance of the Rebels. Had they assailed in force and gained the high ground in front [Fort Couch], with their guns in battery on it, with the bridges behind us cut, with all the opportunities for riflemen afforded by vicinage, together with the adjuncts of slaughter, sown th[r]ough the body of the parapet in the shapes of small stones and fragments of rock, the tale brought from the scene would have been a short narrative of our simple annals![102]

Another Fred Clark photo of Bridgeport Heights during the summer of 1863; this view shows an encampment in the foreground, Forster's Island in the center background and the city of Harrisburg in the far background. *Courtesy of the Cumberland County Historical Society.*

Private John Lockwood of the 23rd NYSNG voiced similar concerns:

> [T]*he construction of defensive works appeared to some of the unprofessional of us to be extremely faulty. The soil of the place is…known geologically as shale. This being thrown up to form a breastwork constituted, as was thought by some of those whose duty it was to be to stand behind it and deliver their fire when the order came, a source of greater danger to them than rebel shot or shell. A ball striking the parapet near the top would have scattered a shower of stones into the faces of the men standing behind it, thus acting with almost as fatal effect as a shell bursting in the very midst of them…At any rate we were fortunately spared the experimental test of the theory.*[103]

Wheeler also attempted to cut corners and save money spent on wages by assigning detachments of the militia to dig the works. The militia were worse than the citizens who had come out on June 15, either refusing to break a sweat or woefully ineffective in their digging. When Wheeler learned the nearness of the Confederates, he quickly turned his attention from this matter to destroying anything "which would have afforded cover to the

This photograph shows Company F of the 23rd NYSNG while in Fort Washington. Another Fred Clark product, this photo was taken facing Harrisburg and the Susquehanna River, which are obscured by the trees and foliage in the background. In the center is the company's thirty-nine-year-old captain, James Merritt Ives of Currier & Ives. *Courtesy of the U.S. Army Military History Institute.*

enemy." This strategy had been previously instated by Major Brady, and Wheeler seemed apt to intensify it.[104] The "beautiful grove which crowned the crest of Hummel's hill" was cut down. There was "not a stalk of the waving wheat or clover" left on the hill, either beat to the ground "by the tramp of soldiery and the coming and going of horses and wagons" or cut down by order of the engineers. Soon Bridgeport Heights, just weeks ago covered with underbrush, trees and foliage, was barren.[105]

Bridgeport Heights hosted a complex outlay of earthworks. Rifle pits and ditches lined the descent down the eastern side. The main earthworks of Fort Washington were about two hundred by six hundred yards in length— about two hundred facing west and nearly six hundred yards continuing eastward to overlook the Camelback Bridge. The entrance, located near the easternmost edge of Fort Washington, was described as "a wagon road winding up the hill from the rear."[106] "Some hundred or so feet in front of the fort down the slope, two lines of rifle pits had been dug," recalled one Pennsylvania militiaman.[107]

A turn-of-the-twentieth-century view of the entrance to Fort Washington. *Courtesy of the Historical Society of Dauphin County.*

CAMP LIFE ON BRIDGEPORT HEIGHTS

"Our stay at Bridgeport Heights was so brief," recalled New Yorker John Lockwood, "that the daily recurring camp duties had not time to crystallize into wearisome routine. Each day was enlivened by some novelty or amusing incident or other, which served alike to break the monotony of our work, and to hurry forward the hours with pleasing animation."[108] Another factor distracting the men was the vista. "The scenery from my tent is magnificent," penned L.T. Hyde of the 13th NYSNG. "I see a distance of thirty miles across the river[,] and the view from the rear is also very fine."[109] Maryland native Henry Wirt Shriver wrote home, "The view from [the] highest part of the fort is most extensive—probably 15 miles on all sides and the river forms a most beautiful feature in the picture Harrisburg too with the trees and houses well mixed is almost under us."[110] Lockwood further detailed:

Toward the river the hill descends by a double slope,—the upper gentle, the lower abrupt. The camp was spread upon the former,—the company streets looking off toward Harrisburg and terminating at the brow of the bluff. The latter was covered with timber, but so thinly toward the top as not to intercept the view. Looking down from the crest of this bluff the eyes rest upon a ribbon of land one hundred feet below, dotted over with small white houses and little plots of garden, and divided lengthwise by a country road. Beyond is the river, in the midst of which lie four or five wooded islands. One of these stretches up and down for a mile or more, and is made picturesque by cultivated fields and a farm house nestled among the trees. The river is moreover broken in the present stage of the water by innumerable shallows where tall grass grows. These green islets appear to be Meccas to the neighborhood cows; for you may see them daily in solemn file making pilgrimage thither by the fords. The opposite shore spreads out in a plain on which stand Harrisburg clustered about its looming capitol. The landscape up the river is bounded by the Blue Ridge, five miles off, which melts away behind the city in the far distance…From the summit of the camping ground the view down the river is even more charming. There the eye wanders over an immense region warm with repining wheat fields and white farm houses, and cool with hills, woods and water.[111]

Lockwood and others would sit under trees at the foot of the camp "and catch the cool breeze as it crept up the bluff." Here they read the newspapers, ate their rations and read and responded to letters from home, using their plates as desks. They also discussed the cowardly citizens of Harrisburg—conversations that, not surprisingly, involved significant amounts of profanity.[112]

While the view might have been striking, there were drawbacks. "We can show no fancy appearance of Camp," complained New Yorker L.T. Hyde, "as it is on the summit of a very high hill about two hundred feet high above the Susquehanna. There is not a level spot in it, and every parade drill or sentry walk has to be [done] with one foot much lower down than the other."[113] Maryland native Shriver was forced, undoubtedly like many others, to place a piece of cordwood secured by stakes, against which he propped his feet "and slept very well that night without the disagreeable sensation of slipping down the hill all the time, as it was the night before."[114]

Another frequent task was guard duty, taking "charge of the gate," as it was dubbed. "That was much more agreeable than walking around the parapet and beside relieved us from the necessity of going on picket," recalled Samuel Pennypacker. "Two large marquee tents were arranged with board seats in them and other conveniences for guard quarters, and being just within the entrance to the fort, formed a very pleasant and capacious retreat for the reliefs off duty. My turn to go on guard came around once in every three or four days and I had no particular objection to it, save that it rained nearly every night and I was consequently very often soaked."[115]

Fort sutlers sold small comforts—including delicious, ice-cold lemonade—at inflated prices. Another merchant near the Camelback Bridge was known for selling quality butter. Much of the reason men would buy from the sutlers was their sheer disgust with their issued rations or homesickness for some little comfort. "How vividly home scenes come up before me during this distasteful life," penned one soldier. "[E]very little thing has a double charm now—it seems like ages since we left [home.]" If the soldiers did not buy from the sutlers, they could always buy from random sellers. Frequently, "county people" came into the fort and attempted to sell fruits and berries to the soldiers. Some soldiers were reluctant to eat the fruits but either gave in or regretted it, considering the standard rations weren't much better.[116]

Harrisburg's Fire Engine and Hose Company, under Chief Engineer George C. Fager, used hoses more than one thousand feet long to supply the fort's garrison with water. They pumped water from the Susquehanna into large hogsheads, which had recently contained coal oil. Therefore, the water had the "taint of oil, and was exceedingly disagreeable."[117] Crews stretched a line of telegraph wire between Harrisburg and the hill for speedy communication.[118]

"A large quantity of filth had accumulated about the fort, rendering it unpleasant as well as unhealthy," recollected Pennypacker, "and the time

This view from the summer of 1863 is one of the best in existence today. Taken from Bridgeport Heights, visible at right is one of the few known photographic images of the Camelback Bridge during the invasion. In the left background is the capitol building. Forster's Island is in the middle of the river. *Courtesy of the Historical Society of Dauphin County.*

we spent in it was very disagreeable to me." To cleanse themselves, the militiamen washed in the river; a group of New Yorkers made use of an old rowboat that they took possession of and were frequently seen "sailing about in." Soldiers filled the entire shoreline every morning and during the afternoons. For those who became sick, a hospital was established in the brick Railroad Hotel near Bridgeport Station.[119]

Feuds and rivalries abounded between the rural Pennsylvania regiments and the urban New York and Philadelphia regiments. "We are treated very meanly here," complained Maryland native Shriver, part of a company from Hanover in the 26th PVM. "The Fancy New York and Phila Reg'ts are fed on fresh beef—have good tents plenty of fire wood &c while we get salt middling (which we have to boil off two or three times to get it palatable) and army crackers [hardtack] and coffee. If we only had good cooking arrangements 'twould do well enough but we must borrow kettles and almost everything from other companies and of course wait till it suits them to lend."[120] It also didn't help, however, that the 26th had threatened to shoot the New Yorkers with their leftover cartridges from their June 26 skirmish at Witmer's farm near Gettysburg.[121]

During the occupation of Fort Washington, the small town of Bridgeport suffered mightily. Bridgeport (now Lemoyne) was a small, hardly noticeable town on the western bank of the river named for its proximity to the Camelback and CVRR bridges. In 1863, the town scarcely numbered a dozen buildings plus the Railroad Hotel, which was bustling as the fort hospital. The Bridgeport lumberyard would suffer considerably; by the end of the summer, it would be entirely denuded of wood.[122]

Meanwhile, defending Harrisburg from the west was Brigadier General Charles Yates and his brigade of the 5th and 12th NYSNG, positioned around Marysville in Perry County. "Various detachments from time to time were sent with ax-men, to obstruct and guard the mountain gaps," reported Yates. Otherwise, little activity occurred.[123]

CAMP COX

On the morning of June 20, Brigadier General John Ewen's New York brigade arrived in Harrisburg. After meeting with General Couch in the capitol, Ewen marched his three-regiment brigade of the 11th, 22nd and 37th NYSNG to the opposite side of the river. They crossed the Camelback Bridge, which Private John Irvin Murray of the 22nd NYSNG described as a "large clumsy structure of wood resting on Stone Piers…it is built like an old Barn in appearance and smells very strong with manure &c."

Ewen selected a campground for his brigade, about three-quarters of a mile southeast of Bridgeport Heights. He detached a portion of the Negroes working on the entrenchments at Bridgeport Heights and had them dig rifle pits in front of his camp. Rain began falling, and the New Yorkers, not yet having been issued their tents, crowded into a barn "like sardines—so tight, in fact," recalled Corporal George Wingate of the 22nd, "that those who found themselves under one of the many leaks in the roof had to remain quiet under their 'douche,' and 'take it coolly' for the night." Private Murray remarked that it "required careful plotting to keep from treading on the men." The 11th fared even worse—they were forced to sleep in the woods without any cover.

The men emerged from the barn on Sabbath day, June 21, and moved to an adjoining field, where they pitched tents. They named the site Camp

Cox in honor of Major James Farley Cox of the 22nd. One tent in Company A was named the Otis House after its captain, James Otis, and designated by a wooden board containing the name pinned to the tent. A regular camp routine was established, with frequent drills, often with many spectators from the nearby village of New Cumberland.[124] Private Murray recorded:

> [E]*very Co*[.] *had its own street about 10 Tents in each—the officers tents occupied a long and wide street the length of the encampment…each Co*[.] *had their Camp fire for cooking…the Barn was also used by the Negroes, Horses &c. The Commissary Dept*[.]*—the field was* [a] *very large one the encampment occupying about half of it, leave sufficient room for the whole Regt Drill and Maneuverer therein—they sloped from the tents toward the river Susqua* [sic], *a Wagon road* [and] *railroad passed along in front of the field on the banks of the river…we also have a fine view of the City of Harrisburg and the river from some miles up and down—also the Harrisburg Bridges—a range of the blue Ridge mountains and the whole Country for miles on the opposite side.*[125]

Camp life in Camp Cox bore a striking resemblance to that on Bridgeport Heights. Drill was regular, and detachments would go on picket every few nights. Murray continued:

> [E]*ach Co*[.] *furnished a quota of members for the Guard—the guard tents are close to the Road in front of our camp*[.] [W]*e took our overcoats and blankets &c. having to stay on guard 24 hours the relief Guard placed their Rifles against the fence in their proper places, numbered, I belonged to the 4 Relief—2 hours on and 4 off—there were rumors that the advance of the Corps of Gen Ewell was imminent and we felt very watchful that night—at 10 PM one of our guard perceived some person on the road who did not answer his challenge, the Guard fired his piece… this caused quite an alarm…A portion of the Guard fired their pieces also and the bullets flew around* [so] *that the guard was unable to tell* [if] *an enemy was firing upon us or not*[.] [T]*he guard was ordered to fall in and to get ready for an attack, we hurriedly formed in line momentarily expecting a volley poured into us, by this time the camp was thoroughly alarmed and some of the Cos were forming in their streets on the arrival of Col Aspinwall and other officers, a squad of our men were ordered to reconnoiter through the road and vicinity no enemy was found and the camp soon became quiet again.*[126]

Ewen's purpose at Camp Cox was more than just to lighten the load of regiments packed on Bridgeport Heights; also, his "command should check the advance of the enemy by the York road, and, if hard pressed, retire to the fort, where a more effectual stand could be made." Ewen had detachments of Negroes and soldiers completing the rifle pits and clearing the woods in front, similar to what was being done under Captain Wheeler's instruction on Bridgeport Heights.

On June 22, Ewen fell from his horse in the camp of the 11th NYSNG and was taken to Harrisburg. He remained there until June 24 and the following day took command of the division of militia west of the Susquehanna for a day because Brigadier General William Hall, the temporary divisional commander, was sick. Ewen supervised the digging of Fort Washington and, fortunately for the sake of the Northern cause, did little else in his one-day tenure as divisional commander.[127]

Back in Camp Cox on June 27, Companies C and G of the 22nd NYSNG established a picket line south down the York Road. The other eight companies marched to the rifle pits, relieving the 11th NYSNG, which was dispatched to the front lines a short distance in front of Bridgeport Heights. "The men had been a good deal annoyed by the conversation of the proprietor of the farm upon which they were camped," recalled Corporal Wingate. "His politics were of a pronounced 'Copperhead'… and had allowed them to affect his common sense so much as to lead him frequently to declare 'that he did not believe there were any rebels in the State and that the whole affair was an election dodge of Andy Curtin.'" His rhetoric gave the New Yorkers "quite a satisfaction" to dig a rifle pit through his garden.[128]

Chapter 3

Southern Invaders

Spearheading the Confederate advance northward was the 1,200-man cavalry brigade of Brigadier General Albert Gallatin Jenkins. One of the lesser-known brigadiers in the Army of Northern Virginia, Jenkins was a native of Cabell County in what is now West Virginia. Born on November 10, 1830, he graduated in 1848 from Jefferson College in Canonsburg, Pennsylvania, and two years later from Harvard Law School. Jenkins practiced law at Charleston, Virginia, until he was elected to the U.S. Congress in 1856. He resigned his seat upon the outbreak of the war and soon rose to the colonelcy of the 8th Virginia Cavalry. However, Jenkins did not serve long in that post, rejoining his political life when he was elected to the First Confederate Congress. He resigned his seat in August 1862 when he was commissioned as a brigadier general and given command of a brigade of Virginia cavalry that roamed the western portion of his native state. Jenkins was arguably best known for his skill in conducting raids independently, including one in which his men trekked five hundred miles into western Virginia and even into parts of Ohio.[129]

By the spring of 1863, Jenkins's brigade consisted of the 8th, 14th, 16th, 17th and 19th Virginia Cavalry Regiments, as well as the 34th, 36th and 37th Virginia Cavalry Battalions.[130] However, not all these units would accompany the brigade north. Jenkins's brigade was part of the Army of Southwestern Virginia, commanded by Major General Samuel Jones. Jones needed some of the units to harass Northern efforts in that rather small but nevertheless vital theater of war.

In what was probably the first actual troop movement of the Gettysburg Campaign, Jenkins reported to the Shenandoah Valley in May with the

8th, 14th, 16th, 17th and 36th in anticipation of Lee's upcoming invasion. The 34th was on duty with Brigadier General William "Grumble" Jones's brigade in the Jones-Imboden Raid through western Virginia and would rejoin the brigade in June before it crossed the Potomac. Sam Jones held back the 19th Virginia because they were the only troops on the Huntsville Line, one of Jones's many fronts under his responsibility. The loss of the 19th significantly hampered Jenkins's manpower, considering that it was—as of May 25—the largest regiment in the brigade. The 37th would also remain with Jones's small army.[131]

By the beginning of June, Jenkins's reduced brigade was located near New Market, Virginia, in the upper (southern) end of the Shenandoah Valley.

A wartime photograph of Brigadier General Albert Gallatin Jenkins, who commanded a brigade of Virginia Cavalry that served as the main menace to the Keystone state capital. *Courtesy of the National Archives.*

Morale was high, and the men rejoiced in the spring weather, especially after a grueling winter. "I am much pleased and think that this country is much preferable to operate with cavalry than Western Va," wrote First Lieutenant Thomas Lewis Feamster, commanding Company A, 14th Virginia Cavalry. "The Valley is the prettiest section of country I ever saw and well may it be said that it is worth contending for[.]" By early June, the brigade had moved to the vicinity of Staunton, farther north down the valley. Many of the men began to receive their horses, which due to forage shortages had been sent farther south during the winter. "We have the finest and fastest lot of horses I ever saw," bragged Feamster. "Our men are all well and in fine spirits[.]"[132]

The 36th had the unique honor of arriving in Lexington, home of the Virginia Military Institute, on May 15—the day of Stonewall Jackson's funeral. Two companies of the battalion under Lieutenant Joseph Coleman

Alderson borrowed mourning badges and joined in the procession.[133] Lieutenant William "Billy" Thomas Smith, captain of Company F, 14th Virginia Cavalry, commanded all the cavalry participating in the procession. He gave the command for a salute to be fired across the general's grave.[134]

Complementing the brigade were two batteries of horse artillery—Jackson's Kanawha and Griffin's Baltimore. Jackson's battery had been one of the few Virginia units sent west early in the war. The majority of the battery was captured at Fort Donelson in February 1862. Paroled, Captain Thomas E. Jackson re-formed the battery in the spring of 1863. The outfit was equipped with four howitzers and two Richmond-made three-inch ordnance rifles.[135] Griffin's battery, on the other hand, had a much more decorated war record—involved in the 1862 Valley Campaign, Second Manassas Campaign and Antietam, the latter where the battery claimed the honor of opening the battle on the Confederate side. However, since the battery had been re-formed into a horse artillery unit, it had not seen much active service.[136]

On June 3, Lee began moving units of his army west from Fredericksburg toward the Shenandoah Valley. On June 9, the Battle of Brandy Station occurred. Northern cavalrymen caught legendary Confederate cavalry commander Major General James Ewell Brown "Jeb" Stuart sleeping and stormed across the fords near Brandy Station. By the end of the day, Stuart had barely staved them off, with his command still intact but his reputation permanently damaged. But even more important than Stuart's hefty ego—the affair sent shockwaves throughout much of the North—the Confederate advance was no folly.

EWELL AND HIS INFANTRY

As Jenkins concentrated his brigade in the Shenandoah, the lead elements of Lee's foot soldiers began to reach the upper end of the valley. After Stonewall Jackson's friendly-fire mortal wounding at Chancellorsville, Lee reorganized his army and formed a third corps, composed of elements from both of the former. The First Corps remained under Lieutenant General James Longstreet. To fill Jackson's shoes in command of the Second, Lee promoted Lieutenant General Richard Stoddert Ewell, and at the helm of the newly fashioned Third Corps, he placed a fastidious and promising divisional commander, Ambrose "Little Powell" Hill.

Born on February 8, 1817, Dick Ewell graduated from West Point in the class of 1840 as a dragoon and a talented waltz dancer. He spent a brief period at the Carlisle Barracks before spending the large majority of his antebellum career in the Southwest, winning a brevet for gallantry in the Mexican War. Resigning in May 1861 at the outbreak of the Civil War, he had risen to major general in the Confederate army by January 1862 and commanded a division under Stonewall Jackson. He played a minor role at First Manassas but figured prominently in Stonewall's 1862 Valley Campaign, the Seven Days' Campaign and the Second Manassas Campaign, in which he lost a leg at Brawner's farm.[137] Old Dick was given a wooden peg leg and, throughout the Gettysburg campaign, would be limited to a carriage for most of his travels. In May, Ewell was both married and promoted to corps command.[138] He knew he would have big shoes to fill.

Lieutenant General Richard Stoddert Ewell, commander of the Confederate Second Corps. *Courtesy of the Library of Congress.*

Ewell's corps consisted of three divisions: Edward "Allegheny" Johnson's, Robert Rodes's and Jubal Early's. All but the latter would participate in the approach on Harrisburg; Early was detached to march eastward, toward York, shortly after entering Pennsylvania. Rodes was relatively new to divisional command but was seen by many as a rising star in the Army of Northern Virginia—he had spearheaded Jackson's flank march at Chancellorsville and performed well. Johnson had so far proven himself, having fought well during Jackson's Valley Campaign, in which he was wounded. His assignment to command of Stonewall's old division, however, drew vastly different responses from within the ranks. "Johnson is a good general and a brave man, but one of the wickedest men I ever heard of," opined one Virginian.[139] Another Virginian had a more favorable view, stating, "Johnson is our Major General now[,] the man that whipped the yankees at Aligany [sic] Mountain[.]"[140]

Since Chancellorsville, the corps had fared quite well in camp near Fredericksburg. "We are getting along very well now," penned Samuel Dunbar, a member of the 4th Virginia in Johnson's division. While Lee may have been dangerously short on rations, the men of the 4th certainly did not feel so. "[W]e are now getting a half pound of bacon for a day's rassions [*sic*]," Dunbar wrote. Additionally, the men could purchase food goods from sutlers. "[W]e can get from the sutlers dried peaches $1.00 per quart[,] dried apples at .75 per quart[,] beens [*sic*] at $1.00 per quart[,] paper such as this at $5.00 a quire[,] envealops [*sic*] from $1.00 to $3.00 a pack [of] allspice at $2.00 per pound we make some pies occasionally but it will not do to have them all the time it is too hard when we only get $11.00 per month."[141]

As Ewell's corps prepared to pave the way for the rest of the Army of Northern Virginia, it mustered roughly twenty-one thousand battle-hardened soldiers.[142] Not only was its size enviable, but morale and self-confidence were also extremely high. "[W]ith what confidence we entered into our enemy's country; how we believe[d] we could surmount every obstacle; that there was no foe we could not defeat; such was our faith in our Commanders and in our powers to do," recollected Lieutenant Colonel David Zable of the 14th Louisiana.[143]

From June 13 to 15, the largest battle yet in the campaign occurred at and around Winchester, known as the Second Battle of Winchester. Major General Robert Milroy's Yankees had long overstayed their welcome in the valley and were defeated by Ewell, who easily flanked and drove back Milroy. Afterward, Confederates boasted of the ease with which they had routed the luckless Milroy. "We had not much hard fighting to do to get the town of Winchester," boasted Virginian Daniel Sheetz.[144] While the Confederates basked in their victory, many Yankees attempted to highlight a few bright spots of the affair. "We have to record another reverse or defeat in the Valley," wrote Pennsylvania cavalryman George Daugherty. "The rebels have overpowered and driven out Millroy [*sic*], but not until he had slain them by the quantity. It is glorious to hear of men so gallantly defending their country. Had we more of them…by Heavens direction would this rebellion go down."[145]

Chapter 4

Carlisle Falls

Carlisle, the Cumberland County seat, has an extremely rich history. In October 1794, the town, situated at the county's center, became a major concentration center for the forces assembled under President Washington to suppress the Whiskey Rebellion. Washington attended what he termed "a political sermon" at the First Presbyterian Church on the town square. After spending eight days in town, the first president continued westward.[146] By the time of the Civil War, Carlisle was an important regional railroad and trade center. It also was home to the U.S. Army's Carlisle Barracks, an important training facility.

Brigadier General Joseph Knipe and his 8th and 71st NYSNG, recently returned from a brief, roundabout trip down the Cumberland Valley to Chambersburg, prepared for a Confederate advance at the county seat. On June 19, the duo of regiments had departed Fort Washington under the leadership of Colonel Joshua Varian of the 8th but were soon joined by Knipe. On the evening of June 21, the command happened upon outspoken abolitionist Congressman Thaddeus Stevens, who informed them of a strong Rebel presence south of Chambersburg. "The road was thronged with…[African Americans,] white folks—cattle, sheep and horses and Dutch wagons, all on the skedaddle for Harrisburg," recorded Isaac Harris of the Sanitary Commission, who had temporarily attached himself to Knipe's staff. Later that evening, Knipe reached Chambersburg, with his command described as "about used up."

Early the following afternoon brought word that Major William Boyd's detachment of the 1st New York Cavalry was skirmishing with Rebels. Boyd's troopers and a company of Jenkins's 14th Virginia Cavalry met near

Greencastle at the William Fleming farm. There, Corporal William Rihl became the first Union soldier to be killed by enemy fire on Pennsylvania soil. "This caused some excitement," detailed Harris, "and the Militia who had arrived worn out, suddenly became very fresh to march[.]" Knipe personally informed Harris that "if the enemy advanced his orders were to fall back slowly upon Carlisle and H'bg and that he should probably do so about dark as they were in considerable force and 'sassy.'"[147]

The right wing of the 71st was detached and placed in the rear of Varian's 8th, which was on the Valley Turnpike, farther south on which the skirmish had occurred at the Fleming farm. Shortly afterward, Couch telegraphed Knipe instructing "the rolling stock of the road to be withdrawn, even if it involved the abandonment of the men and stores[.]" News of this order quickly spread, and panic broke out. Varian's 8th and the right wing of the 71st scurried to the depot, where they packed themselves into the trains. However, orders never reached Colonel Benjamin Trafford and the left wing of the 71st. Trafford "was in ignorance of this movement until he saw all but it entrained." Trafford quickly attempted to rectify the situation by requesting orders from Knipe. He received orders to pull out as soon as

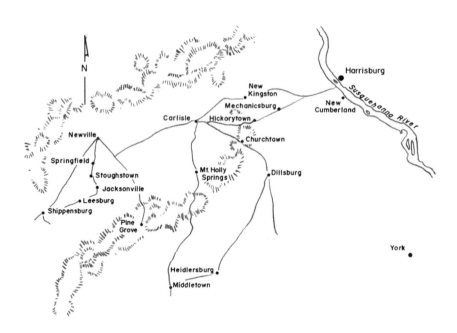

South central Pennsylvania in 1863. *Map by John Heiser.*

possible, as well as to detach "a small force" as a rear guard. After he had given orders to his battalion, Trafford made sure the rear guard was set and proceeded to the depot, only to find the left wing nowhere near there.

With no idea where his battalion was, Trafford roamed the area until he found the battalion nearly six miles away, marching—it had taken the wrong road to the depot. By that time, the train with the rest of the brigade onboard had long since departed. Traveling by foot, the disgruntled New Yorkers arrived in Shippensburg at 2:00 a.m. The regiment boarded a train, which arrived around 10:00 p.m. at Carlisle, where they joined the rest of the command at the Carlisle fairgrounds, north of town.[148]

KNIPE PREPARES TO DEFEND CARLISLE

Joseph Farmer Knipe was in many respects the most qualified brigadier in Couch's department in late June 1863. Formerly a brigadier in the 12th Corps, he had served as colonel of the 46th PVI and had named Camp Curtin. A veteran of the 1862 Valley Campaign, Cedar Mountain (where he was wounded) and Antietam, Knipe left the army temporarily after Chancellorsville because of failing health. Without other duties, he tendered his services to Couch, who welcomed him with open arms.

Going from wielding brigade command in the seasoned Army of the Potomac to the raw Department of the Susquehanna did not please Knipe— namely, he did not respect the New Yorkers under his command as he had the men of his brigade in the Army of the Potomac. He later scorned the militia when he returned to his 12th Corps brigade later that summer. His divisional commander later penned home that Knipe "tells most amusing stories of the crack New York regiments which were under his command."[149]

On the afternoon of June 24, the New Yorkers moved from their camps at the fairgrounds to Rocky Ridge, a stony outcropping a mile west of the town square, where two companies of home guards raised in Carlisle had set up a line of works, along with the nearby colored population. "Now that they have drafted the blacks to work they ought to draft the whites to fight," sarcastically remarked young Carlisle citizen John Sullivan.[150]

Charles F. Himes, after the war a professor at Dickinson College, remained at his house in Carlisle "during our troubles here preferring to look the Johnnies in the eye and see for myself what they look like and how they felt[.]" He later reminisced that as the entrenchments were being dug, "considerable commotion" overtook the town, with "minister[s], physicians, lawyers, and all ranks of people running about with muskets and cartridge boxes[.]" Those shopkeepers who had not already shipped away their goods to places of safety did so immediately. Himes withdrew his personal fortune of $10,000 from his bank and departed south toward his home in New Oxford, despite warnings from Knipe's officers as to the strong Rebel presence in that direction. Undeterred, Himes proceeded home unscathed and without having met a single Confederate.[151]

While Carlisle's citizens were all hustle and bustle, Knipe's two regiments prepared to man the earthworks. Colonel Joshua Varian's 8th NYSNG held the left across the Walnut Bottom Road, while Colonel Trafford's 71st occupied the right, astride the turnpike, or High Street as it became upon entering Carlisle. Four pieces of Captain Elihu Spencer Miller's Philadelphia Battery were split, two guns supporting each regiment. The men were ordered to "load at will, and fire low." After several hours, however, they were permitted to thrust their arms, bayonet first, into the ground so as not to be a disturbance. "[E]verything indicated that resistance would certainly be offered," recalled one Carlisle citizen. The men of the 8th "stack[e]d arms and slept close by our muskets without tents[,] expecting to have a fight before morning."

Brigadier General Joseph Farmer Knipe, a native of Mount Joy and later a resident of Harrisburg until his death in 1901, led New York National Guard troops during the Gettysburg campaign. *Courtesy of the Library of Congress.*

June 25 dawned with reveille at 4:00 a.m. As one New Yorker mused, "Rebels or no rebels, we must have breakfast." Because the knapsacks had been sent to Harrisburg after their hasty withdrawal from Chambersburg, the nearby homes "supplied" the New Yorkers. Throughout the day, "all hands were busy building barricades, and digging entrenchments." By noon, the rifle pits were described as adequate, while Miller's guns were "well protected." Along the pike, the 71st masked its section of defenses with treetops, while the men also enjoyed the cover of the large boulders and rocks for which Rocky Ridge had received its name. Miller's men had "commenced the work of digging rifle-pits" for his pieces since daybreak. Instead of doing the latter, the 8th drilled until noon and, after lunch, formed in line of battle. Large contingents of the 8th were detailed as sharpshooters.

This work continued most of the day, and toward evening, the Yankees began to turn in for the night in the entrenchments. At the end of this day of hard work, the New Yorkers felt much safer with their rifle pits "enlarged" and the earthworks "strengthened." In case of a battle, two men from each company were detailed to carry off the wounded, and a house was established as a field hospital behind the line. In the 71st, Colonel Trafford walked in front of the regiment's line and remarked that the enemy was near and not to let them pass. At sunset, "every military precaution was taken. The pickets were increased, the lines lengthened and advanced, and the men ordered to be ready at a moment's warning."[152]

Word soon reached Knipe of large Confederate forces close by. "Genl I have the most positive information of the enemy's advance," he wired Couch. "I shall fall back to Kingston tonight. The enemy passed through Chambersburg on the morning of 24th...they are on the Pike and Walnut Bottom roads, I have ordered [the home guard] citicens [sic] to hide arms and go to homes. My cavalry will keep to the front and watch for movement of enemy."[153] Captain Daniel H. Hastings, the Carlisle Barracks post commandant who had a garrison of roughly 250 men and four pieces of artillery, followed suit that evening, evacuating the post and "bringing with me all the munitions of war and moveable public property."[154]

Knipe's New Yorkers were still at the rifle pits, some "sleeping soundly" while others chatted quietly. Shortly after 9:00 p.m. came the command, "Fall in, boys! Not a word!" The order was first received by the 71st. The majority of that regiment was already "fast asleep," but in several minutes, they were back on the march. Two pieces of Miller's battery were placed in railroad cars. The 8th was the last to receive the order. By 10:00 p.m., Knipe had cleared Carlisle.

The brigade continued to retreat until it reached New Kingston around midnight. "[T]he night had been very dark, and heavy clouds, which had been threatening, soon poured down their contents," recalled one New Yorker, "and officers and men were all soon drenched to the skin." Knipe ordered his column to halt in the road while he searched for accommodations. The soldiers made themselves comfortable in the road, and soon the column began to sing. As one Yankee mused, "A soldier will sing under all circumstances, comfortable or uncomfortable." Several soldiers quartered themselves in the parlor of David Strohm, also feasting on some of his "delicious ham." The 71st camped in a wood nearby. As the rain continued, the regiment stumbled upon a "country church," which sheltered "all that could crowd into it." The men packed into the aisles. Soldiers crowded into many other nearby houses, barns and shops. Captain Miller roughed out the night near the upper end of town by the side of a fence, where he slept on an overcoat and an army blanket, wrapping his "personage" in the blankets. On June 27, Knipe advanced a short distance and formed on Ironstone Ridge, now traversed by the Appalachian Trail. However, reports from Boyd's cavalry that Jenkins was lurking nearby prompted Knipe to retire from this position toward Harrisburg, bivouacking for the night less than three miles from the city.[155]

On Friday morning, June 26, Carlisle residents expected to awake to Confederate occupation but instead found only rumors of picket fire— reports that soon proved true. Despite Knipe's withdrawal, small Union picket detachments still occupied the town. That afternoon, a thirty-four-man contingent of Captain Frank Murray's Curtin Guards, a mounted militia unit raised in Harrisburg a week prior, was ordered to proceed southwest on the Walnut Bottom Road from Carlisle. It was an especially dangerous task for such a small group of men. The area several miles west of Carlisle was infested with Rebel pickets, skirmishers and ambush parties.

The patrol was commanded by Lieutenant William A. Fisher, with orders "to push south," locate and, if practical, attack the Confederate picket lines. Fisher's detachment followed the Walnut Bottom Road toward the Stone Tavern.[156] This tavern, built in 1788 by wealthy farmer James Moore and still standing, is located at a road fork where the Walnut Bottom Road continues northeasterly to Carlisle and the York Road branches off to the east to Boiling Springs. One traveler who visited the tavern in 1810 was pleased with his stay. "I got coffee, bread and butter, eggs and excellent honey in the comb," he detailed, "for which I was charged only nineteen cents. My landlord presented me one of the largest and finest apples I had ever seen: it was the produce of his own orchard."[157]

The eighteenth-century Stone Tavern. This was the site of an engagement between a detachment of mounted Pennsylvania militia under command of Lieutenant William A. Fisher and Jenkins's cavalrymen. *Courtesy of the Cumberland County Historical Society.*

When the patrol neared within a quarter mile of the tavern, Fisher detached three men to reconnoiter. They first questioned a man who claimed to be a farmer standing in front of a farmhouse. They inquired whether there were any Confederates ahead, and the "farmer" replied that there were none. The trio continued a short distance farther. As they approached the tavern they were surrounded by Rebels and taken prisoner. One of the group, Private John Bates, shot and killed two Confederates with his revolver before being dragged into the inn and captured. The other thirty-one men of Fisher's group had by then approached to within one hundred yards of the tavern, and nearly one hundred Confederate cavalrymen swarmed from both sides of the road and successfully cut off ten Pennsylvanians. The remainder of Fisher's troop scurried away. The elated Rebels fired a volley at the retreating group, one shot striking Sergeant James Cosgrove's thigh. Despite his painful wound, Cosgrove managed to limp off and elude capture. Pennsylvanian William Rudy was seen to fall from his horse and be captured—erroneously reported killed in the Harrisburg papers. Fisher fell back to rejoin Murray and the rest of the company.[158]

By 8:00 a.m. on Saturday morning, June 27, all business in Carlisle was suspended, and the pickets had been ordered into town. Two hours later, Major William Boyd's detachment of the 1st New York Cavalry passed through, leaving the town defenseless, save the ill-trained Carlisle Barracks cavalry detachment of Lieutenant Frank Stanwood. As word of the Rebels nearing the town reached Stanwood, he determined to open fire on the enemy. Soon Stanwood could see the 1,200-plus troopers of Brigadier General Albert Jenkins's brigade fast approaching. He fired his pistol to no effect, wheeled his horse around and galloped out of town as fast as possible, his command not far behind.[159]

JENKINS OCCUPIES CARLISLE

Jenkins had indeed arrived at the town's western outskirts. Leading the vanguard of Lee's army, the Virginians had crossed the Potomac at Williamsport on June 15. Passing through Hagerstown and crossing the Mason-Dixon line into Pennsylvania, they entered Chambersburg in a ruckus near midnight. Remaining there throughout June 16, the brigade withdrew the following day around noon in a panic after Jenkins became mistakenly fearful of a Federal advance, riding back until midnight to Hagerstown. The brigade of Virginia cavalry remained in that vicinity until June 19, while detachments raided the Pennsylvania countryside. On June 22, part of the brigade engaged cavalry under Major Boyd near Greencastle, where Corporal Rihl became the first Union casualty on Pennsylvania soil. On June 23, they reentered Chambersburg and remained there until the following morning, when they headed north to Shippensburg.[160]

Boyd's cavalrymen, closely followed by Jenkins, fell back into Shippensburg about 1:00 p.m. on June 24. "Within a half hour their [Jenkins's] advance guard rode into town more like so many devils yelling like h—l-hounds," penned Eunice Stewart of Shippensburg. Boyd's New Yorkers darted out of town. Jenkins proceeded through the town to its eastern edge, where he deployed the four Parrott rifles of Griffin's Baltimore battery. Boyd's men hung around just outside the range of Griffin's guns. Jenkins and Griffin tried for the next hour to induce Boyd to put his cavalrymen within the range of the Parrotts. The Baltimore artillerymen stood attentively at their guns like eager fishermen patiently waiting for their catch. Boyd wisely kept his distance.[161]

Shortly before midnight, Jenkins had one of his all-too-frequent panics when Boyd's troopers fired on his pickets on the Walnut Bottom Road outside

Shippensburg. Jenkins sent a courier galloping to Chambersburg to find Ewell, who responded by dispatching the doubtlessly grumbling North Carolinians composing the brigade of Junius Daniel, who were aroused from their slumber shortly after midnight and arrived in Shippensburg around 5:00 a.m.[162]

Jenkins's men were fatigued from the constant marching and foraging. "[W]e wasnot [*sic*] allowed to unsaddle our horses or sleep with our shoes off," complained Isaac Reynolds of the 16th Virginia Cavalry. "We were riding day and night while we was in their [*sic*] and fighting nerly [*sic*] evry [*sic*] day more or less." Not all aspects of the Keystone State were undesirable. "We could get anything we wanted in the eating line while we was in yankeedom [*sic*]," raved Reynolds: "lemmons [*sic*], oranges, figs, rasins [*sic*] nuts of various kinds, cheap as dirt too. Penn was the prettiest country I ever seen or ever expect to see. Mostly dutch, though. The Dutch never knew anything of the war until we invaded them and fought all round them and stoled [*sic*] their horses and cattle."[163] Nathaniel Harris, another member of the 16th Virginia and future governor of Georgia, later reminisced:

> [W]e subsisted almost entirely on provisions gathered from the enemy. In most cases these were paid for in Confederate money. But the people who had contributed felt that they had gotten very little in return for what we took…Every family in Southern Pennsylvania seemed to own a bakery and likewise kept a supply of apple butter on hand. We slept along the fence corners or in the open fields or under the trees in the forests, if we got any sleep at all. There was a ceaseless call on all the energies of every soldier in our ranks. When our horses would give way on the forced marches we would swap them for horses belonging to the citizens, very rarely paying any difference; sometimes leaving only a few dollars in Confederate money, so that the transaction might not be classed with the usual foraging business…
> In Pennsylvania the horses that we found were generally of large bodies and exceedingly large feet. They were undoubtedly draft horses of Percheron-Norman breed. We swapped a great many of our Virginia horses for these large animals, but soon found out that they were almost worthless for cavalry purposes. They could not stand the exposure, and the marches on the pikes, especially in the winter time, soon put them out of the running.[164]

By June 27, Jenkins had finally crept from Shippensburg to the outskirts of Carlisle. From his position just west of the county seat, he saw the Union banner "defiantly flying from the public buildings" and, supposing the Yankees to be in force, prepared for an attack. Placing two pieces of Griffin's battery in position to fire down the main street, Jenkins was about to demand the surrender of the town when a deputation of citizens, including Colonel William Penrose and Assistant Burgess Robert Allison, approached him. Penrose assured Jenkins that no resistance would be made. Carlisle had surrendered.[165]

About 11:00 a.m., Jenkins's cavalry entered the town on the west end of High Street at a trot, every man carrying his gun "in a position to use it on the instant, with his hand on the hammer." Continuing through the town to the intersection of the York and Trindle roads just east of Carlisle, part of the brigade proceeded to the left (north) and encamped at the barracks, where Jenkins made his headquarters,[166] while the remainder dismounted for several minutes at the intersection before returning to the town square. There, Jenkins requested the borough authorities. Chief Burgess Andrew Ziegler, along with several town council members, met the general, who informed them he wanted 1,500 rations and corn for his horses delivered to the Market House near the square in one hour. Ziegler and a group of citizens went door to door through the town, informing the families of Carlisle of the requisition. Jenkins also added that if the request was not completed, he would allow his men to help themselves. The requisition was readily complied with. After lunch, Jenkins permitted his men to walk around town, visiting the garrison, gasworks and other leading buildings.[167]

EWELL ARRIVES

About 5:00 p.m., Jenkins's cavalry let out a shout as Ewell's infantry appeared. On June 18, Ewell's corps had crossed the Potomac into Maryland. On June 22, Rodes's division crossed the Mason-Dixon line into the Cumberland Valley of Pennsylvania. The Rebels had at their disposal a beautiful but repetitive sight. As one 1788 traveler complained, "The country…is universally of limestone formation, and watered with living springs."[168] "This Cumberland Valley would be just the place to tie up for a life time," opined one Union officer, "but that everybody eats bread and apple butter and apparently nothing else."[169] "[The] farms are larger, from 200 to 400 acres, half of it cleared, the other in woods, with house, barn, etc…The farmers keep too much woods," sneered a traveler in 1794, "they are always afraid of not having enough, either for their fire, field-fences, or buildings."[170]

President Washington, also in 1794, observed, "From Harrisburg to Carlisle the lands are exceedingly fine, but not under such cultivation and improvement as one might have expected. From Carlisle along the left [Walnut Bottom] road…the lands are but indifferent, until we came to within a few miles of Shippensburg. The first part being of a thin and dry soil succeeded by piney flats…For a few miles before we arrived at Shippensburg the lands were good but uncultivated. The improvements along this road were mean. The farms scattered, the houses but indifferent, and the husbandry apparently bad. Along the road [the pike] which the Troops marched both lands and the improvements, I was told, are much better."[171]

On June 24, Ewell's infantry occupied Chambersburg and vicinity. Early on June 26, the column proceeded northward and entered Shippensburg. "This morning our eyes and hearts were pained again at the sight of some ten or twelve thousand of our assured foes pass through our streets accompanied by Gen. Ewell who was strapped on to his horse," confided citizen Eunice Stewart. "Every Street and Alley in town is guarded and we are Prisoners in our own homes."[172] "Shippensburg is a place of considerable length, being built along on each side of the road," opined Sam Pickens of the 5th Alabama. "It is a common looking place and is inhabited by common looking people—principally Dutch."[173]

Half of Pickens's regiment was dispatched a mile out of town on the Walnut Bottom Road on picket duty. They were some of the first Confederate infantry to get a taste of the bounty of Cumberland County. "We were quartered in a large barn where there was a plenty of straw with which we made very comfortable beds," wrote Pickens. "There were a great many cherries and one large tree of black hearts which were the finest I ever tasted." A "good many hens" crowed in the barn, but in a few minutes, they roamed no more. Many of the Alabamians simply took the fowl, but others "who happened to have a little U.S. currency" paid for them.[174]

At Shippensburg, Ewell made his headquarters at the H. Craig home in the eastern portion of town, while "Allegheny" Johnson established headquarters at the Samuel Nevin farm northwest of town.[175] Staffer Henry Kyd Douglas remembered their host as "a clergyman who was extremely civil and gave us good entertainment." The following morning, Douglas wrote,

before breakfast, I went to the stable to look after my horse and came upon a scene of merriment as the servants were busy taking out from the hay a new set of harness, saddles, bridles, and other things which had been hidden there. At breakfast I told our host that he was not as thrifty as the proverbial Yankee, or he would not let his valuable goods lie around in such places as to give dyspepsia to horses. By that time he had found out that we were not on a plundering expedition and joined in our laughter at his feeble attempts at concealment.[176]

On the morning of June 27, Ewell's infantrymen (save the half of the 5th Alabama) got their first good look at the Cumberland County countryside en route to Carlisle. Several days earlier, they had received notice of Lee's General Orders No. 72, which prohibited disruption of civilian property while in the enemy's country. The temptations to break this were strong—especially considering how Federal troops had treated civilian property in Virginia. Overall, the Southern soldiers behaved remarkably well but at times violated Lee's orders. "Our Boys could not resist the temptation offered by the sight of ripe cherries growing on large trees…on the side of the road," recalled a Southern artilleryman. "The Boys were like birds flocking to the trees…often pulling off great bunches and strewing the road with boughs." So much so, he remarked, that the trees took on "the appearance of having passed through a…hail storm."[177]

Rodes's division proceeded out of Shippensburg on the Walnut Bottom Road, arriving at Carlisle around 5:00 p.m. The band at the head of the column was playing "Dixie" as it entered town. The column turned north on South Pitt Street to arrive on High and then proceeded north on Hanover until it took a right onto North Bedford Street, arriving at Carlisle Barracks.[178] "Some had chickens under their arms, some loaves of bread, some onions, and some eggs in their pockets, captured in the fat valley of Cumberland," recalled Dickinson College professor S.D. Hillman. "Some were quite jocular—'Say, strangers,' said a jolly red-faced fellow, 'we are back in the Union now, and we like it mighty well.'"[179] John Sullivan, then a young boy in Carlisle, recalled:

When the infantry came along they presented nothing very strange to our eyes in their appearance. They might have been recruited along the seventy miles from Carlisle to Baltimore…Where were those "ragged uniforms?" those "half-starved stragglers?" that "army in a plight?" Our newspaper prophets of a speedy Confederate collapse through its army's miseries must have been talking about some other army! The passing uniforms undergoing our inspection were if not new, newish; there was no showing of torn coats and badly frayed trousers…Knapsacks and haversacks, the whole personal kit, was in order; arms were at every man's command. A significant touch as to neatness was a tooth-brush at hatband or button hole—an odd sight to some of our hardy youthful townsmen…The officers' uniforms were of a light-gray cloth, the garniture a brilliant gold gallon; the privates' a

Brigadier General George Doles commanded a brigade of Georgia troops in Rodes's division. *Courtesy of Gettysburg National Military Park.*

Colonel Edward Asbury O'Neal led Rodes's old brigade of five Alabama regiments. He later served as governor of Alabama. *Courtesy of Gettysburg National Military Park.*

dark gray with a few martial frills. Further opportunity for inspection of cavalry, infantry, artillery and the transportation service confirmed my first impression of a fit, well-fed, well-conditioned army.[180]

Doles's brigade encamped on the Dickinson College campus, where General Doles established his headquarters in a tent. Residents recounted unconvincing rumors that fifty thousand militia were awaiting them at Harrisburg.[181] Ramseur's, Daniel's and Iverson's brigades all encamped at the barracks, while the 53rd North Carolina of Daniel's brigade was detached as provost guard in the town. "I got satisfide [*sic*] talking with the Union People," penned Lieutenant James Green of the 53rd in his diary, "that they believe they will [n]ever whip us from there [*sic*] talk. They treated me and all my guard with kindness here, fed us all we woul[d] eat and charged nothing, but they are real Union."[182]

O'Neal's Alabama brigade turned right (south) as it entered town and followed the Baltimore turnpike, encamping for the duration of the occupation in a large orchard about two miles south of town. Most of the Alabamians fancied themselves with their plentiful and pleasurable supply of water. "The pond is 4 or 5 feet deep in places and yet the water is so beautifully clear that every thing on the bottom is seen as distinctly as if it were on the surface," raved Alabamian Sam Pickens. "There are large springs around the edges and some boil up in the bottom, and the water is so cold that it made my feet ache to keep them in it a few seconds."[183]

THE OCCUPATION

Ewell ordered Jenkins forward to Mechanicsburg, making his and Rodes's headquarters at the vacant quarters of Carlisle Barracks post commandant Captain Daniel Hastings.[184] As Ewell rode to the barracks with his aide, Campbell Brown, they saw citizens carrying "plunder of all sorts" from the barracks. "One enterprising couple had a sofa—many had chairs, tables &c.," Brown recalled. One Irishwoman even went so far as to attack Confederate staff officer Thomas Turner, who had found a "handsome fox-skin robe." The woman "came near to securing it," but after a "sharp tussle," Turner retained the prize. Ewell, arriving at the barracks, characterized the situation to his aide as a "mere mob" and ordered the plunder to be stopped at once.[185]

Old Dick was no stranger to the barracks. More than twenty years earlier, in 1840 as a young dragoon, he had served several months there, where he

In this circa 1861 view of Carlisle Barracks, a cavalry guard mount receives instructions before going on duty. *Courtesy of the U.S. Army Military History Institute.*

also learned in his pastime that "the ladies of Carlisle never waltzed." Dick commented that "there are some very pretty women among them" and "if it were not for an insurmountable prejudice I have to everything which has the smallest claim to be called Dutch I should certainly fall in love with some of their pretty faces." After the Mexican War, Ewell returned to the barracks in 1849 as a recruiting officer. It was a fairly easy and enjoyable job, and when not on the job, he often hunted partridge and fished for trout in nearby forests and creeks. During evenings, he was entertained by Carlisle's social elite. Later in 1850, Ewell was transferred to duty in Baltimore. He would call on several of these acquaintances during his unwelcome 1863 visit.[186]

It is unlikely Ewell's past experience at the barracks played any role in his decision to spare the Yankee outpost from the torch. Odds are he made the decision on two factors. First, as Ewell reported, he felt it was agreeable "to the views of the general commanding[.]"[187] Additionally, the facilities provided his troops the most comfortable quarters many had enjoyed in over two years. John Coghill of the 23rd North Carolina raved in a letter home about the conditions at the barracks—houses, water and ice, rarities for the past two years of the war, were in plentiful supply. "Everything is comfortable," recorded another North Carolinian. "We have plenty of supplies of every diescription [sic]. I fear that we will not remain here long, but I hope we will." Brigadier Alfred Iverson occupied the same quarters as when he had served as a lieutenant of cavalry at the barracks before the war. During the occupation, Iverson went through Carlisle on "a visiting tour among his old friends."[188]

Not only did Ewell's men enjoy the barracks, but they also took strolls around the town. "This is a very handsome place, much more so than any town of like size in the South," remarked one Alabamian.[189] Others complained the citizens were antisocial. "[T]he inhabitants...appeared gloomy and dejected, and showed no disposition to converse with us. This condition, however, did not disturb or distress [us]," remarked one Confederate, "as we were not paying the city a social visit."[190] Captain Robert Park of the 12th Alabama journeyed to the National Hotel for dinner, where he was met by "an unfriendly and scowling crowd of rough looking men in the office...the dinner was quite a poor one, and was rather ungraciously served by a plump, Dutchy looking young waitress."[191]

"An hour after their arrival the town was filled with officers who thronged the hotels, and rode quietly through the town," recalled Cumberland County Deputy Sheriff Simpson K. Donavin, formerly a West Virginia news reporter who had witnessed John Brown's raid and execution.

> *The most of them were gentlemen in manners, evidently educated, and carefully guarded against any expression calculated to evince the real bitterness which they felt for our people. Occasionally one...laid aside his restraint and was unmeasured in his abuse of Northern people...It was only necessary to use the slightest insinuation that they were intruders to elicit a glowing, in some instances eloquent description of the desolation which had swept over parts of the South...They could not find language base enough to speak of Butler, Milroy and one or two other Union Generals and without exception threatened instant death to either of them.[192]*

Ewell had scarcely settled into his new quarters when several ministers inquired whether they could open their respective churches on Sunday. "Certainly," replied Ewell, "I wish myself to attend Church." The ministers departed but soon returned to ask the general whether he would object to a prayer for President Lincoln. "Not at all," he smartly replied, "I know of no man who is more in need of your prayers."[193]

Ewell then submitted another requisition for Carlisle's civic leaders through Major Wells J. Hawks, his commissary chief. If the goods demanded were not collected in front of the courthouse by 6:00 p.m., stores and houses would be searched.[194] Hawks demanded twenty-five thousand pounds of bacon, 1,500 barrels of flour, three thousand pounds of coffee and sugar, one hundred sacks of salt and 25 barrels of potatoes, dried fruits and molasses.[195] Failing to receive this absurd requisition, squads of mounted cavalry accompanied by foot soldiers searched several houses and buildings. One store was searched seven times, but the Confederates could not manage to find any food.[196]

On Sunday, June 28, many of Ewell's corps attended services. Staffer Sandie Pendleton and Dr. Hunter McGuire—the doctor of the late Stonewall Jackson—attended services at the First Presbyterian Church on the square, where the preacher added prayers "for the dear ones *we* had left at home [emphasis original]." "One of the preachers here prayed that God would bless those he was in the habit of praying for," penned Ewell's mapmaker, Jedediah Hotchkiss.[197]

Johnson's Division

Edward Johnson's division was a short distance behind Ewell and Rodes. It was not the first time Old Allegheny had visited the Harrisburg area— during the summer of 1850, Johnson had spent three months in the vicinity on recruitment duty for the antebellum army.[198] His division broke camp shortly before 8:00 a.m. and soon cleared Shippensburg, leaving that town on the Valley Turnpike. After a seven-mile trek, the column passed through Stoughstown.[199] In 1802, Nicholas Stough of Dauphin County had purchased roughly two hundred acres, on which he built the Sign of the Indian King Tavern. After Nicholas's death in 1816, his son John took over. From John, Stoughstown reportedly took its name. It was reported that Stough "did a business quite sufficient" and was "considered one of the best, in point of accommodations and generous fare along the road."[200] The tavern was conspicuous along the roadway, and Johnson's men must have noted it with special interest. One Confederate artilleryman simply noted the settlement as a "log village."[201]

A turn-of-the-twentieth-century photograph of the Sign of the Indian King tavern. *Courtesy of the Cumberland County Historical Society.*

After departing Stoughstown, the division continued along the pike, which in 1863 ran nearly straight from Shippensburg to Carlisle, except that about half a mile from Stoughstown it turned north to the village of Springfield on the Big Spring Creek and then southeast, where it once again became a straight line to Carlisle. This was due to the fact that attempts to place the road in a straight line were "met with complaints from people living along the [Big Spring] creek."[202] Johnson's division continued to Springfield, where they encamped about 7:00 p.m.[203]

In 1863, Springfield was quite the blossoming community. Seventeen years earlier, it had consisted of fifty dwellings, a store, a tavern and a schoolhouse. The Civil War greatly benefited the town's industry. By the end of the war, it housed two wagon and saddle shops; both of the latter produced saddles for the Federal government. One of the saddle makers, John Troup, held the claim of being "the best horse collar maker in the United States." Barrel factories, blacksmith shops, an assortment of mills, two schools, a church and five distilleries composed the thriving town in the 1860s, with nearly two hundred homes. One nineteenth-century historian ventured so far as to say that Springfield "presented a strong claim to the county seat."[204]

"The men are very much fatigued, and there is some straggling," logged Lieutenant Thomas Tolson of the 1st Maryland Battalion in his diary. Tolson and others went into the tiny village for supper. "The people treated us all very kindly, giving away their last loaf of bread." Lieutenant Randolph McKim, aide-de-camp to Brigadier General George H. Steuart, entered a shop in Springfield to purchase items. "The surprise of the storekeeper when an officer of the terrible Rebel Army desired to purchase copies of the New Testament may be imagined," McKim later mused. While near Springfield, the Big Spring Creek provided water for Johnson's division.[205]

Located at the head of the Big Spring was McCracken's mill—one of the most prominent buildings about Springfield—dated from about 1784. Namesake William McCracken, a former captain in the Continental army, also owned a nearby tavern. One 1794 traveler expressed his displeasure with the inn. "Bad lodging, isolated on the road," he complained. Johnson's Confederates reportedly gave the mill, owned in 1863 by William Keller, a "sacking."[206]

Springfield was able to secret some of its bountiful stock of flour by concealing it in a large hole cut in the haymow of a neighboring barn owned by a miller. Local folklore holds that Johnson's men stormed into

Major General Edward "Alleghany" Johnson commanded one of the three divisions in Ewell's corps. Johnson had been wounded in the ankle at the Battle of McDowell in May 1862, from which he took a full year to heal. He commanded Stonewall Jackson's former division, among which was the famed Stonewall brigade. *Courtesy of the Library of Congress.*

the house of the miller, where they found a man clad in preacher's robes. The "preacher" insisted they erred in their belief of stores secreted in the barn. The Confederates, believing the preacher to be honest, searched other buildings. Not until the Rebels had left did the "preacher" remove his robes.[207]

The next morning, Johnson's division marched at 7:30 a.m., proceeding along the pike as it curved southeastward from Springfield. Johnson bivouacked three miles west of Carlisle near Cedar Spring Run, now Alexander's Spring Run, a short distance south of the pike. The Southern soldiers found water near their camp at "a fine large spring flowing from the massive solid rock."[208]

"[A]t reveille [on June 29] every man was promptly at his post, and prepared, nay impatient," recollected William Goldsborough of the 1st Maryland Battalion, "to resume the march to Harrisburg, which town we cherished the fond hope of reaching that day." Goldsborough continued:

> But hour after hour sped by and no order to "pack up" was given. What could it mean? For days we had taken up the line of march at sunrise. Twelve o'clock, and no order. One, two, three o'clock, and an aid was observed to dash up to brigade headquarters, and in a few minutes the welcome command to "fall in" was heard throughout the vast encampment. All was bustle and excitement, and many were the speculations indulged in by both officers and men, as the companies formed, as to the cause of our delay and our probable destination that day. "It is my impression," observed one, "we will go no farther than Carlisle, where Rhodes [sic] is encamped, join him, and make the attack upon Couch's forces about midday to-morrow." "There is where you are mistaken," was the reply of a comrade… "we will make a forced march to-night and begin the attack at daybreak in the morning."… Entertaining such opinions pretty generally, great was the surprise of all to observe the head of the column, upon reaching the turnpike, file abruptly to the left instead of the right, and we found ourselves retracing the steps of the day before.[209]

Departing Cedar Spring Run at 12:40 p.m. on June 29, the division marched roughly a dozen miles before bivouacking just southwest of Stoughstown. "The evening's meal was moodily discussed," recollected Goldsborough, "and all went sulkily to sleep."[210] After sunset, Confederates hunted chickens in a nearby barn, using torches for illumination. By sunrise, all but an old rooster were missing. "We were satisfied to have the chickens gone," wrote John Sharpe, a young boy who lived on that farm, "for they were dying of chicken cholera. The campaign cleared our place of chicken cholera and we never had another attack." However, the Confederates also took an entire crib of corn to feed their horses.[211]

OUTSIDE CARLISLE

Many Confederates hunted for any Negroes who had not fled to Harrisburg and beyond. Nettie Jane Blair, then a young girl, recalled, "All the Negroes who had ever worked for grandfather had come down the mountains with their belongings tied in bed quilts[.]" After being fed, they were "piled into big Conestoga wagons drawn by mules. Another wagon was stacked with food and then the whole outfit including the stock started for Harrisburg." Crossing the Susquehanna, the group went as far as the Chester Valley for protection. Little Nettie and her family watched as gray-clad cavalrymen hunted concealed Negro servants. "They went all over the farm," she remembered. The horsemen even watered their horses at the springhouse, while a young female Negro servant watched from inside in pure terror.[212]

Pennsylvania was infested with "Copperheads," a term the Northern public gave to Southern sympathizers. However, many Confederates expressed disgust at disloyalty. In one instance near Carlisle, ten citizens met Jenkins and "assured him that they were friends to the Southern Confederacy." They pleaded for paroles so they could not be drafted into Federal service. Jenkins reasoned that "since they were such friends to the Southern cause, they were of course willing to fight for it" and placed some of them into his ranks. The citizens begged to be released, and Jenkins did so with the reprimand, "Such men in the South would be shot, without judge or jury."[213] One Cumberland County citizen informed Confederate soldiers where his brother had secreted a team of horses. After capturing the animals, the soldiers returned to the betrayer and "went in his mill and took a hundred barrels of flower [sic] from him[.]"[214]

Captain Frank Bond's Company A, First Maryland Cavalry, had accompanied Ewell's corps into Pennsylvania. He was authorized "to make occasional scouts in the vicinity, to replenish our larder or pick up something good for the boys." He set out to do just that on June 29. After proceeding several miles out, Bond came to "quite a village about noon" and "determined to stop for dinner." The townsmen had fled, and only "hostile" women remained. Taking ten cavalrymen into the largest house (while he sent squads of six or eight into other homes), Bond "was reluctantly allowed to enter, and with very bad grace the good lady set about getting us something to eat." "At first the old lady was rather reluctant to obey our Captain's command," recalled trooper John Gill. "She did not relish working for a lot of rebels, but seeing that we meant business and intended to have the dinner, she finally got to work."

Bond continued, "We did our very best to put her at ease, and in a short time we sat down to a comfortable meal." While eating, Gill spotted "some very pretty girls in the kitchen, doubtless the daughters of the old lady, squinting at us from time to time, but whenever perceived that we could see them, they 'skedaddled out of sight.'" After assurances that they were not barbarians and that they "should be very glad to see the young ladies," the old woman "opened a door leading down into the basement and called out, 'You girls may as well come up here, for I do not believe these men will hurt you!' and with much trepidation and crowing…at least a dozen girls came into the room and stood up close to the wall around us. We were objects of great curiosity to them," Bond wrote. One girl was heard to remark, "Well, I declare! if they ain't just like our men!"[215]

On June 27, as Johnson's division camped at Springfield, a scouting party rode north into Newville. "Some fifty Rebel cavalry entered town to-day," penned resident Will McCandlish. "One a brother of Mrs. Wm. Reifsnider, of town. Another had been a scholar of one of our citizens, while teaching in Virginia a few years ago…Capt. Priest, of Mississippi, commands,—quite a gentleman [*sic*] who stood on one of our street corners, talking politics with one of our citizens, until nearly midnight." The unwelcome guests camped southwest of town in Davidson's clover field at Newtown, a suburb. There, in the knee-high clover, they held "the large herd of horses and cattle," which they had captured.

For quite some time, Newville residents had braced for an invasion. Many buried valuables. "[S]ome of the men of the farm had dug large opening[s] in the ground and put several wooden boxes down and the folks filled one with cured meats and the others with the best bed clothes and what they thought would be taken of the most valuable articles of clothing," recalled one citizen. "The boxes were covered with earth…making it look like a little garden patch, setting it out with young beet plants." On June 28, McCandlish saw "very few people at church." That morning, Priest's cavaliers left Newville with "some 350 head of cattle." No significant force would return, but June 29 found several Rebels still "prowling around."[216]

Confederates also occupied Churchtown, a hamlet two miles south of the Trindle Road roughly halfway between Carlisle and Mechanicsburg. They established headquarters at the C.B. Niesley farm. Niesley, a resident of Mechanicsburg, complained that they are "using things as they see proper. The mills are all put to work grinding and teams hauling away."[217]

On June 28, Ewell sent another reconnoitering party north toward Sterrett's Gap, on the Cumberland-Perry County line. The Southerners approached the gap via Carlisle Springs, then "a famous summer resort, capable of accommodating 400 people," where its proprietor, Nathan Woods, told them fifty thousand men were defending the gap. The Confederates continued north. At the Joseph Miller farm at the base of the gap, several children sat under a cherry tree eating fruit when, according to one lad, John Miller, they were "startled as a Union soldier mounted upon a fine sorrel horse gallops rapidly past us evidently intent upon arriving at Carlisle Springs, one mile farther on." Learning of a Rebel advance, the Yankee hastily retraced his steps.

As the blue-clad rider disappeared from view, twenty Rebels with pistols in hand simultaneously appeared. One Southerner dismounted and chatted up the children, while the others stood idly by. After a brief conversation, the riders determined it was not advisable to advance any farther— perhaps deterred to a degree by the absurdity told to them by Woods. It is doubtful there were more than one hundred Yankees defending the gap. The force was primarily local farmers, as one Newville citizen mused: "The Perry county people have the gaps in the mountain blockaded with felled trees and 'defended' by themselves, with shot guns old muskets etc." This was the farthest north any Confederate military force reached during the Gettysburg Campaign.[218]

Liquor at Carlisle

"It wasn't often that our boys got a chance at liquor, and when they did, they made good use of it," recalled one North Carolinian. "I've never seen so much liquor in a country as we struck there in Pennsylvania[.]" Much of this liquor Ewell's soldiers found at Carlisle. At one point, the drinking in Carlisle escalated so much as to nearly cause an intoxicated battle between the 23rd North Carolina and a regiment of Doles's Georgia brigade.[219]

Ewell confided to aide Major Campbell Brown that the Confederate flag should be raised over the barracks "for the benefit of the ignorant

Major General Robert E. Rodes was at the helm of Ewell's largest division, numbering over eight thousand men. He would be killed at the Third Battle of Winchester on September 19, 1864. *Courtesy of the MOLLUS-MASS Collection, U.S. Army Military History Institute.*

citizens." Several tailors were secured, and as Brown recalled, "in an hour or two we had a handsome flag ready for hoisting." The troops gathered around the flagpole as the new Second Confederate flag design was unfurled. The 32nd North Carolina later would carry this banner into the Battle of Gettysburg.[220] General Rodes stepped forward from the balcony of his and Ewell's quarters and spoke briefly, followed by Brigadier General Junius Daniel and then Major General Isaac Trimble, who, just arrived, had no assigned command other than to assist Ewell as a supernumerary. Trimble gave a few remarks that were "not so very neat." The enlisted men shouted for somebody else, to which staffer Ben Greene stepped forward, "blandly smiled, waved his hand, introduced himself and began but was utterly incoherent." A friend pulled him back by the coattail, and he returned a few minutes later but was "a worse exhibition than before, when pulled down a second time and put to bed."

The cause of this sloppy display was a keg of lager beer found by Rodes's staff. "The beer was the strongest I ever saw," commented Campbell Brown, "I must add by the way of excuse—probably mixed with whiskey—and Greene was indiscreet enough to take a glass of brandy on top of it." Brown wrote that it was the first and last time he ever saw Rodes intoxicated. "Quite an animating scene," mapmaker Jedediah Hotchkiss penned in his diary. Ewell did not partake in the spoils. He was suffering from a severe headache at the time and was lying down in his quarters after giving a few brief remarks at the ceremony.[221]

Perhaps adding to Ewell's headache was the overly aggressive Isaac Trimble, who told Ewell when he arrived that if he gave him one brigade he would capture Harrisburg.[222] Trimble was not alone in his ardor to capture the state capital. "We were within twenty miles of Harrisburg," wrote Georgian Henry Thomas, "and were elated with the hope that we would have that city before the setting of another sun."[223] In the camp of the 8th Virginia of Jenkins's brigade in Greenbrier County, West Virginia, word had arrived that their brigade was near Harrisburg. "I hope that is true and that he will succeed in taking and burning that hotbed of abolition," wrote one Virginian.[224] To General Rodes, taking Harrisburg was "a step which every man in the division contemplated with eagerness."[225] Now it was up to Jenkins's cavalry to reconnoiter and report back whether Harrisburg could be taken.

Chapter 5

Preparations at Oyster's Point

Nearly three miles west of the Susquehanna River lay a point or fork in the road where the Harrisburg-Carlisle Turnpike, then little more than crushed stone and oil, and the dirt-paved Trindle Springs Road once met. At this intersection lay a popular tavern or hotel built by Abraham Oyster of Abbottstown. In 1814, Oyster had purchased thirty-nine acres of land in the vicinity, where he built his brick tavern. For this reason, the intersection was known as Oyster's Point and the inn the Oyster's Point Hotel.[226] Private John Irvin Murray of the 22nd NYSNG visited Oyster's Point on June 30. "New Yorkers would suppose that a place called Oyster Point was at the seaside or a place for selling oysters by wholesale," he remarked, "but it consisted of one [water] pump [and] one old brick house."[227]

The area around Oyster's Point in 1863 was known as White Hall (now Camp Hill). Roughly sixteen buildings composed the hamlet. About three hundred yards east of the hotel was a tollhouse. Opposite of it and just south of the pike was a limekiln and a farm lane that led to it, known as Limekiln Lane. Also included was Professor David Denlinger's store, the business path he had embarked upon earlier that year after closing his White Hall Academy for the time being. Marking the eastern boundary of the village was the Church of God. South of the pike, in the vicinity of the limekiln, was a large, dense forest known as Oyster's Woods.[228]

A circa 1900 view of the Oyster's Point Hotel. The equivalent of a modern bed-and-breakfast, the tavern served thousands upon thousands of travelers until it was razed in 1969. *Courtesy of the Cumberland County Historical Society.*

GENERALS HALL AND SMITH DEPLOY THE MILITIA

Before Baldy Smith arrived to take command, Brigadier General William Hall had been assigned temporary command of the fortifications opposite Harrisburg. Hall, more than sixty years old in 1863, had begun his service as colonel of the antebellum 8th New York Militia and was later elected brigadier. Hall was known for his bad temper, which would be "severely tried" during the Draft Riots the following month.[229]

On June 20, Hall arrived in Harrisburg, where Couch assigned him to command of all units detailed to the fortifications on Bridgeport Heights. Hall established headquarters in a home in Wormleysburg and set to work immediately. His first order of business was to establish a picket line, deploying for that purpose the 693-man-strong 37th NYSNG.[230] Hall's picket line began just north of White Hall and continued south down Church Street, now 21st Street in Camp Hill, where it crossed the Carlisle Pike and continued south along a fence line to where the Lisburn Road crosses over Cedar Spring Run, just northeast of Slate Hill. At the latter place, a detachment of cavalry deployed on the crest, anchoring the southern flank of Hall's picket line.[231]

In late June, New York and Pennsylvania militia began to arrive by the thousands in Harrisburg. After being mustered into service, most would cross the river and be deployed by Generals Hall or Smith, depending on when they arrived. "Under Couch there was much to do in attending to the defenses…opposite Harrisburg, and the general overhauling of the command," reminisced Smith.[232]

One such regiment, the 33rd PVM or the "Blue Reserves" of Philadelphia, arrived in Harrisburg in two halves on June 19 and in the predawn hours of June 20. On June 24 the regiment, about seven hundred strong, was mustered into service for six months or the emergency. Two days later, the regiment received forty rounds of cartridges before marching from Camp Curtin into Harrisburg. "The Colonel…left us standing patiently in the rain while he went into the Capitol to receive orders," wrote Private Joseph Boggs Beale of Company D. "None of us were allowed to were [sic] our gum blankets and had our overcoats rolled up on our knapsacks for uniformity."

Marching across the Camelback Bridge, they paused after reaching the west shore in a drenching rain that soaked the men. The regiment then double-quicked a short distance on the pike before halting and lying down in ankle-deep mud. Soon the command "Attention Battalion" roused the men, and the regiment marched up the entrance to Fort Washington. The drenched column halted for half an hour in the rain until it resumed its march west through the entrenchments, upon receiving orders from General Ewen, and spotted the unfinished Fort Couch. The 33rd would continue west and bivouac about a quarter mile behind Limekiln Lane, naming the site Camp Taylor after its colonel. The Philadelphians set up their shelter tents, which they called doghouses "because we have to creep in them on our hands and knees." The men of the 33rd were impressed with the importance of their situation, considering they could eye the capitol dome in Harrisburg from their camp. The Philadelphians also posted guards past Oyster's Point Hotel. These men took position behind fence rails with their muskets loaded. The countersign was Solfirino.[233]

On the evening of June 26, Colonel William Everdell's 23rd NYSNG was ordered out of Fort Washington to the defenses at Oyster's Point. A native of Brooklyn, Everdell has been credited with "introducing" colored printing.[234] "We marched out of the fort with very uncertain feelings," recalled Private John Lockwood. "The rain was falling, but we thought little of that: the roads were heavy—that troubled us more." The head of the column halted when it reached Oyster's Point. A few yards in advance of the point, the 23rd erected a barricade of barrels, farm wagons and all the fences north and south of the pike and whatever else they could find across the two roads. They posted pickets while the rest of the regiment searched the neighborhood for any empty or unoccupied barns or structures in which to sleep. This was the 23rd's first time on picket, and soldiers spent an eventful night in which they

Colonel William Everdell of the 23rd NYSNG was a prominent citizen of Brooklyn until his death in 1912. *Courtesy of the U.S. Army Military History Institute.*

ordered many tree stumps to halt. Their barricades remained at Oyster's Point longer than they did. After one night, Everdell's regiment returned to the fort.[235]

Saturday, June 27, was a day of preparation and anticipation at Oyster's Point. In Camp Taylor, a large contingent of the 33rd PVM was detached to Fort Couch, where it helped three to four hundred Negroes dig "the deep pit in front of it." The 33rd was notified that in case of a retreat, it would fall back to Fort Couch. In the afternoon, a squad of Negroes began digging a line of rifle pits an eighth of a mile west of Camp Taylor (near modern 27th Street in Camp Hill), following lines laid out by army engineers. Guards were posted at a fence at the edge of the camp to keep the eager Philadelphians from interfering with the work on the nearby rifle pits. Another squad of Negroes was ordered to cut down a nearby three-acre wood. "It was moonlight, and white men helped the others; citizens as well as soldiers dug and chopped, and at daylight the woods was gone, every tree was down and the rifle pits finished," recorded Private Beale.[236]

Meanwhile, wagons of all kinds were passing through Oyster's Point "as fast as the horses would bring them." John Mater, tenant of Dr. Joseph Crain's farm on Limekiln Lane, recalled that a large contingent of militia was encamped in Oyster's Woods, south of the hotel. "There was about two acres of woods," recalled Mater, "and they were full of our own soldiers." "There were lots of New Yorkers here," recalled then eight-year-old Charles Rupp, who lived just west of the point. "Why, I saw the pike covered with them, just like droves of cattle."[237]

The evening of June 27 brought the arrival of General Knipe's 8th and 71st NYSNG and Miller's Philadelphia battery at Oyster's Point, where they found the 11th and 23rd NYSNG. The 23rd retired later that night to Fort Washington, while the 8th, 11th and 71st remained at Oyster's Point. Knipe's two regiments and Miller's battery encamped in Holler's Field, north of the hotel, without tents and in "very heavy dew." Miller's battery reportedly "slept with our guns in position[.]" The 33rd PVM remained at Camp Taylor about a quarter mile east of Limekiln Lane, the 11th near the hotel and the 30th PVM north of the pike.[238]

THE MILITIA AND THE CITIZENS

The locals around Oyster's Point did not have favorable opinions of the Yankee militia. "They turned out to be our worst enemies," wrote White Hall resident Zacheus Bowman. "They killed our hogs, chickens, and so on."[239] William Gorgas, then fourteen years old, reminisced:

In many of the houses not a single piece of furniture could be found; preserves and apple butter were used to decorate the walls, doors broken, chaff and feather beds cut open and their contents thrown around the floor, and everything in much worse condition than had there been a battle. The contents of the store of David Denlinger…were strewn along the picket line…Packages of tea, coffee, muslin, calico could have been obtained from the pickets with but the asking for them.[240]

One New York captain, drinking liquor from a flask, impressed a farmer who was driving an empty hay wagon into Harrisburg and instead forced him to make several trips to Camp Couch with his men's baggage.[241]

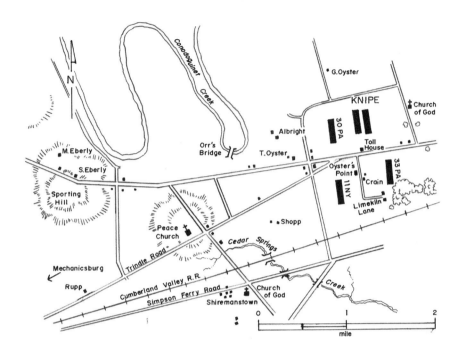

Union deployments at Oyster's Point on the evening of June 27. *Map by John Heiser.*

At Holler's field north of the point, the New Yorkers took fish, apple butter, meat, blankets, bed clothing and much more. They also targeted hogs. One soldier stuck a bayonet in one and carried it to the Oyster's Point Hotel. Simon Dresbach, the owner, and Holler, the tenant, saved the rest of their hogs by moving them to their nearby wheat field, obscuring them from view.[242] John Mater, who tenanted the Crain farm on Limekiln Lane, lost all but about a dozen of his chickens to the New Yorkers. Mater put the remaining fowls under a mortar box that he had used for building the barn, turning the box upside down in an orchard where the grass was fairly high. Several New Yorkers, guns in hand, stood on the mortar box while they strained to spot the chickens. "I remember distinctly how it worried me," recalled Mater's seven-year-old son, George. "I guess the chickens knew it and kept quiet," surmised the elder Mater.[243]

The soldiers also took linen and a large supply of unfashionable hats from old Polly Oyster. Soon, many soldiers were prancing around, sporting the oddly shaped high hats. "They would make a nice mark to shoot at," sniped one citizen.[244] In reference to the damage, one Pennsylvania militiaman wrote home:

There was an old woman and a man staying at this home the rest of the family being across the river—I had several talks with the old woman who seemed to be aggravated even by the sight of a soldier at first, but I finally converted her opinion to a more favorable one of our Company at least— and she cooked me the best coffee before we left the post that I drank since in the service—She said that the soldiers who behaved so badly were the 30th Pa [Militia] Reg't who were enlisted in that very locality in fact a hired man who had lived with them and had enlisted was their guide to thro the premises—They broke open the desk expecting to find money which luckily the farmer had taken out the day before—destroyed or carried off all the eatables, Killed all the chickens, carried away even the books which the man said he would not have taken 50 dollars for—Their officers either could not or did nothing to restrain them—She said if the Rebels had come, and behaved that way every body would have made the greatest fuss about their barbarity but here our own men did it which was worse, and nothing was done—a regiment of New Yorkers were equally as rascally—the farmers told me that in a field which he pointed out they shot a fine steer dead leaving him lie to rot in the sun and at a neighbors house they shot several of his hogs from pure wantonness, and in defiance of his remonstrance— Had I read accounts of these things in the Southern Papers of Baltimore, I would have considered them malicious lies to injure the cause; but that it is really and truly the case.[245]

"It seemed as if our soldiers thought they were in an enemy's country," remarked young Gorgas.[246] Albeit, the stage was set for June 28 to be a decisive day in the struggle for Harrisburg.

Chapter 6
Jenkins Captures Mechanicsburg

G eneral Jenkins and his brigade left Carlisle at about 3:00 p.m. on June 27, marching toward Mechanicsburg. Three miles out, the brigade halted to feed horses and then proceeded onward for another two miles before encamping near the small village of Hickorytown.[247]

It was the duty of Captain Frank Murray's Curtin Guards, who had retired to Mechanicsburg after their misadventure at Stone Tavern on June 26, to delay and harass Jenkins as much as possible. General Couch knew that behind Jenkins were the 15,000 soldiers of Ewell's corps in Carlisle and that if Ewell attacked the works on Bridgeport Heights, it was only a matter of time before the Keystone capital fell. Therefore, Couch's goal was to keep the Confederates from reaching Bridgeport Heights. Murray's sole objective was simple—delay Jenkins as long as possible because every minute counted. This, however, was easier said than done. Murray could scarcely count 100 men. Jenkins, on the other hand, mustered roughly 1,200 cavalrymen.

The 1,900 citizens of Mechanicsburg and its surroundings began to realize that they would likely be occupied within the next twenty-four hours. One witness wrote:

> *On Saturday* [June 27], *all excitement had pretty well subsided, and our people settled down into a state something like a person might be supposed to assume who was expecting visitors, and had put the finishing touch to all the preparation for their reception and then patiently awaited their arrival. There was this marked feature, however, that all our citizens appeared to be expecting visitors at the same time, and from the remarks made, none appeared to be overjoyed at the expected arrival. Our citizens retired*

Saturday night—but fully assured from the reports of Capt. Murray's cavalry, that the morning would bring the rebels.[248]

Murray's men spent the night harassing Jenkins's pickets, making for an unpleasant slumber for the Virginia cavalrymen.[249]

The following morning, Jenkins prepared to seize Mechanicsburg. Murray again used the harassment technique, which had fair success, bringing on a skirmish with Jenkins's advance somewhere between Jenkins's bivouac site and Mechanicsburg, which escalated enough to prompt Jenkins to unlimber a piece of Griffin's battery. One shot caused Murray's Harrisburgers "to beat a hasty retreat," in the words of one Marylander.[250] About 8:30 a.m., Murray bolted into town to the telegraph office, where he sent one last telegraph, cut the wire and sent the operators to Harrisburg on a hand-operated railroad car, arriving there about 1:00 p.m.[251] The main body of Murray's company retreated through the town.

Jenkins continued his march on Mechanicsburg, frequently skirmishing with Murray's rear guard. However, as Jenkins approached the town, he observed freshly dug lines of what appeared to be entrenchments. Additionally, the Stars and Stripes dominated the skyline over Mechanicsburg. Jenkins took these as signs that Federals were somewhere in the vicinity, perhaps preparing an ambush. Jenkins prudently sent two bearers with an improvised flag of truce—a stick with a soiled white rag tied to it—into Mechanicsburg. What Jenkins had thought were entrenchments were actually newly dug pathways through the Chestnut Hill Cemetery.

Murray's rear guard was still in town. At about 8:45 a.m., Jenkins, his advance guard and two truce flag-bearers entered the town. Jenkins met Murray at the western edge of town. Murray later told a reporter that he "had the pleasure of shaking hands" with Jenkins, who politely instructed him to "get out of the way as soon as convenient, as he was in strong force and we could look out for hot work before long." Murray immediately took his rear guard, about a dozen men, and fell back through town.

While Murray and Jenkins were shaking hands, residents had taken down the flag at the suggestion of several of Murray's Harrisburgers who were idling near the town square. The flag was hidden at the home of Burgess George Hummel at 312 East Main Street. By 9:00 a.m., the two bearers of truce had made it to the town square, while Jenkins and the rest of the advance guard anxiously waited outside of town. In the square, the duo questioned a citizen for the civil authorities and was informed where Hummel lived. The two galloped "rapidly" down Main Street to his home, all the while "still holding their flag aloft." Hummel answered their knock and was told that if the flag was not turned over, the town would be shelled. The beleaguered burgess reluctantly surrendered the flag and watched in what must have been mortification as a Confederate placed it below his rump as a saddle cushion. The unwelcome guests felt it would be a shame to leave the flagpole in the town square bare and, in turn, hoisted the Confederate banner.[252]

In Mechanicsburg

In order to cover both the Carlisle Pike and Trindle Springs Road, Jenkins divided his force, sending part north on the Hogestown Road, which conjoined with the Carlisle Pike. This force, the 34th Virginia Cavalry Battalion and Jackson's Kanawha Battery, was commanded by Lieutenant Colonel Vincent Addison Witcher of the 34th.[253] The remainder of the brigade—the 14th, 16th and 36th Virginia, along with Griffin's battery—would remain with Jenkins.[254] As Witcher and his battalion proceeded north, Jenkins and the seven hundred some men of the units remaining with him began what one citizen termed "the grand march" down Main Street.[255] One witness recalled:

> Some were clad in the butternut uniforms, while the majority had no uniform on at all, many…having nothing but shirt, pants and hat. A few we noticed…looked very much like Pennsylvania farmers…They were armed with all sorts of weapons. Some with carbine, pistol and sabre, though the majority had nothing but muskets, while a few had double barreled fowling pieces. Their horses were generally very good, having been stolen from farmers in the upper end of the valley. The men were with a few exceptions, a stout looking set of fellows—picked men for hard service and would have done some good fighting had they been attacked. They were, as a body, pretty well behaved, considering the cause they were in…who have no ideas above eating, sleeping, stealing and fighting.[256]

Jenkins's men bivouacked in the fields immediately east of town. Jenkins and his staff returned to Mechanicsburg, where they visited the Ashland House Tavern, a sublet of the Railroad Hotel, located just south of the town square alongside the Cumberland Valley Railroad. There, Jenkins ordered the host around "as if he intended paying him for what he got." The general ordered a pitcher of water and elevated his heels on the table while he read a

The Railroad Hotel played host to Jenkins. No longer standing, the hotel was located just south of the town square alongside the Cumberland Valley Railroad. *Courtesy of the Mechanicsburg Museum Association.*

Northern newspaper "with apparently great interest." With all the splendid accounts of the Federal defenses of Harrisburg, Jenkins likely received the equivalent of a dozen scouting reports. One or two of his aides, who evidently did not order water, became drunk. Before leaving, Jenkins offered proprietor "Colonel" Irvin payment in Confederate scrip. Irvin informed Jenkins that it was worthless in the North, but Jenkins replied that it was all he had.[257]

While there, Jenkins sent for Burgess Hummel, to whom he issued a requisition for 1,500 rations and horse feed to be delivered at the town hall— also known as Washington Hall—in ninety minutes, strikingly similar to his demand in Carlisle the previous day. If his demands were not met, Jenkins threatened to allow his men to find the food themselves and even went so far as to place part of Griffin's Baltimore Battery at the western edge of town to perhaps intimidate the citizens into complying. A little boy was given a bell to spread word of the order to the citizens.

"It was very humiliating and yet amusing," penned resident C.B. Niesley, "to see persons walk up with their baskets of ham, bread, butter and whatever else they choose to bring." "It was rather a novel spectacle in town," reported another citizen, "to see a large number of citizens wending their way to the Town hall, on a Sabbath day, carrying baskets of provisions for a band of rebel invaders." At town hall, several citizens kept track of which families had contributed food. One reporter visited town hall as the rations were being collected. He strongly believed that more rations were gathered than were needed due to the panic to fill the requisition in time.

Meanwhile, a group of hungry and impatient Confederates dragged back and forth down Main Street an old hay wagon they had stolen farther down the valley, eagerly awaiting their lunch. The Confederate cavalrymen also established their hospital at Thomas B. Bryson's grain warehouse (now the

An 1892 view of Washington Hall. In 1863, part of the building served as a town hall. Since then, the building was torn down due to inferior brick and rebuilt on the same site. It now serves as the Washington Fire Company. *Courtesy of the Mechanicsburg Museum Association.*

Simpson Public Library). Horse feed was appropriated from the warehouses of Brandt and Company and Johnson and Sons, with payment made in Confederate scrip. "Almost everything in the provisions line fit to be eaten (and a good deal that wasn't) from a little onion to a Western ham, was taken to Washington Hall," recalled one citizen. Mechanicsburg had more than filled Jenkins's requisition, and within the prescribed time. The hungry Confederates took most of the provisions to their main camp just east of town, while some ate at Washington Hall. One citizen chided that Jenkins's men "recklessly wasted" one-third of the rations. "We…were treated by the citizens to a delicious dinner," recorded Lieutenant Hermann Schuricht of the 14th Virginia Cavalry. "Probably the frightened people gave up to us the meals prepared for their own table."[258]

Witcher's command received some of the food as well. "Yesterday 1500 rations were required of the Mayor of Mechanicksburg [*sic*] which he furnished in one hour," penned Lieutenant Micajah Woods of Jackson's battery. "[E]ggs, ham, beef, apple butter—pies, and vegetables of every description."[259]

After their requisitioned lunch, numerous clusters of gray-clad soldiers returned to see what the town's stores had to offer. The selection for the Southern cavalrymen was limited considering that most sellers had either fled or shipped away all their valuables. One citizen estimated that, in total, $300 of Confederate scrip was circulated through Mechanicsburg, part of which was allegedly counterfeit. "However, that is equally as good as the genuine," mused a Mechanicsburg reporter.[260]

"During their stay in town our enemies were quite friendly toward us (doubtless because we fed them well)," detailed one citizen, "doing no damage to property, with the exception of cutting the telegraph wires[.]" Citizen M. Richard commented that Jenkins's cavalrymen "did not do a great deal of damage" save that they "stole every horse they could get." The not-so-welcome but nonetheless respectful guests did venture into Richard's home, though they only "asked for bread[,] some for water, but dident [*sic*] disturb enything [*sic*]," despite Richard's reputation as a "good Union man[.]"[261]

Often the Southern soldiers "traded" with the town's population. If a gentleman wore a hat they liked, the butternut-clad cavalrymen would without a word remove the desired hat, place their own "tattered beaver" in return and gallop off. "It did not usually take long to make a trade," detailed a Mechanicsburg reporter, "the rebel riding up to a man whose hat pleased him, would remove it from his head, hand him down his own in return, which he might wear or not, as he choose." Reportedly, most citizens opted not to wear the worn Southern hats.[262]

Chapter 7

The Skirmish of Oyster's Point Begins

W itcher's command left Mechanicsburg, marched north on the Hogestown road, reached Hogestown and continued east on the pike "without being halted." As Witcher's Virginians came within sight of the small hamlet of Hogestown, situated where the Hogestown road conjoins the pike, resident Jacob Otstot destroyed his forty-five gallons of brandy at the wise request of the citizens so that it would not fall into Rebel hands.[263]

After reaching the pike, Witcher continued eastward to the Salem Church, just east of Silver Spring Creek. Once there, he spotted a brigade of Union militia in position nearly two miles beyond at Sporting Hill. Witcher ordered unlimbered two pieces of Jackson's battery near the church to fire on the Yankees.[264]

This blue-clad force was Joseph Knipe and the same trio he had during his expedition to Chambersburg and operations around Carlisle—the 8th and 71st NYSNG and Miller's Battery. With these three mildly experienced units, Knipe could count roughly one thousand men. Shortly after their Sunday services at Oyster's Point, Knipe ordered his three units to advance to Sporting Hill and form a battle line in an orchard. By the time Witcher arrived about noon, the defenders were growing exceedingly impatient. "This performance of 'laying for a fight' which never came, had by this time grown tame, in fact intolerably stupid, and I for one was growing tired of sitting in silence," reminisced one New Yorker, "when boom! crash! a cannon shot in front of us, the smoke visible too, curling above the woods, and showing how near it had been fired. A smothered 'Ah!' and 'Now you've got it, boys,' went through the ranks. It was no humbug this time. The rebels were shelling the woods as they advanced."[265]

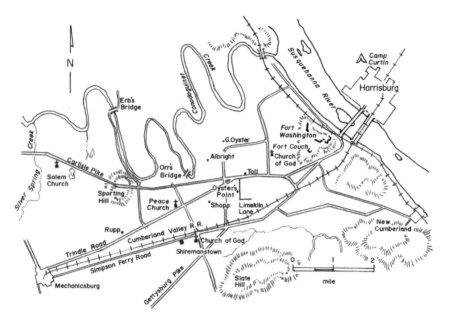

The Harrisburg area in 1863. *Map by John Heiser.*

"[O]ne of Lt. Blain's Howitzers and my rifle 3 inch piece were ordered to the front," penned Lieutenant Micajah Woods of Jackson's battery, "and I took position with my guns…and opened fire with shell[.]" This began what Woods termed "a severe fight" when Miller returned the favor. General Jenkins stood by his gunners, intently observing the engagement from his mount.[266] "[T]he enemy's guns opened upon us from so great a distance," reported Miller, "that they produced no effect."[267] With Miller's battery at Samuel Eberly's farm near the crest of Sporting Hill and Jackson's at Salem Church, the opponents were separated by just over a mile of ground, stretching the artillery pieces to their utmost range.

After about half an hour, Knipe determined to withdraw. Most likely Knipe had been alerted to the presence of Jenkins's main command moving east on the parallel Trindle Road and feared he would be flanked. "But it appeared we were not to receive them at that spot," penned one New Yorker, "for suddenly we were ordered off again, and marched across lots, to the destruction of many a bushel of wheat[.]"[268] There are some discrepancies on how the retreat took place. "[T]he retreat was made cooly [*sic*] and at common time," a man of the 71st reported. However, a local citizen disagreed in an 1897 newspaper article: "They [Knipe's men] were fired on by rebel pickets or imagined they were, when they all took to their heels dropping blankets, knapsacks, canteens, guns and haversacks never looking back till within the fort." While both accounts are exaggerated, it appears the retreat caused slight commotion. One bystander at Oyster's Point noted that Knipe's men retreated "as fast as they could walk."[269]

This was the first engagement of Jackson's battery as a re-formed organization after having been for the most part captured at Fort Donelson, and in Woods's view, it "proved eminently successful and efficient." The only confirmed casualty on either side was a horse serving the Confederate guns.[270]

SOUNDING THE ALARM

As Jenkins's brigade entered the newly captured city of Mechanicsburg earlier that morning, the Southern cavalrymen heard church bells clanging from nearby Shiremanstown. This was not any ordinary ringing of the bells on a Sabbath by the Shiremanstown Church of God but, rather, several soldiers of the 11th NYSNG warning of the Confederate approach. The previous day, a detachment had been placed there under orders to ring the bell on sight of the Rebels and then skedaddle down the steps of the church and sprint back to their regiment.

On the morning of June 28, the guardsmen successfully executed these planned actions. However, shortly after the Confederates entered Mechanicsburg, several rode into Shiremanstown "in hot rage against the innocent residents," alleging they had sounded the contentious bells. When told that New York soldiers were responsible, the Southern cavalrymen (according to the New Yorkers) did not believe "that the pickets of the Yankee militia could have shown such audacious enterprise." Apparently this incident disturbed Jenkins enough to prompt him to place an artillery piece by the church, which by the recollections of one citizen was unlimbered one hundred feet east of the church aimed at Harrisburg. The lone cannon remained there only a short while.[271]

ADVANCE ON OYSTER'S POINT

About 10:00 a.m., Mrs. John Neidig saw Jenkins's Rebels riding east on the Trindle Road from her house a mile and a half east of Mechanicsburg. Closing the shades and peeping through a small crack below the shade in the kitchen, she watched as a large portion of Jenkins's command bivouacked immediately opposite her home. Several Confederate officers demanded sleeping quarters, and she allowed them to sleep on the floor of the parlor. The Neidigs were quite surprised at their guests' good behavior. The soldiers greatly enjoyed the presence of the Neidigs' four-year-old boy, who gave Jenkins's cavalrymen "fond memories." Mrs. Neidig remarked that the cavalrymen "were very well behaved and were strictly disciplined by their officers."[272]

As Jenkins's main command proceeded east shortly before noon, his men raided houses and barns along the Trindle Road. They denuded the farm of John Reeser, about two and a half miles east of Mechanicsburg, of a two-year-old sorrel mare and appropriated an estimated 125 bushels of corn.[273] Meanwhile, Witcher's command reached the Samuel Albright farm on the Carlisle Pike, within a stone's throw of Oyster's Point, where Witcher unlimbered two pieces of artillery.[274]

War Comes to the Peace Church

So far, it had been a quiet Sabbath morning at *Die Friedens Kirche*, or in English, the Peace Church. Sixteen-year-old local William Cromleigh observed as eight hundred Southern cavalrymen emerged, trotting eastward on the Trindle Springs Road, and occupied the vicinity of the church. In 1863, before modern construction altered the landscape, this church, dedicated to the cause of peace, ironically enough presented a great tactical position for an army. Lieutenant Herman Schuricht of the 14th Virginia termed the eminence on which the church sat "a dominating hill."[275] On this "dominating hill" the Confederate soldiers set up camp and deployed four pieces of Griffin's battery in a diagonal, southwest line on the southern side of the church.[276]

Before rejoining his command at the Peace Church, Jenkins had been on the pike with Witcher. About noon, he had left Mechanicsburg and ridden north, where he found Witcher scrapping with Knipe at Sporting Hill and intently observed the engagement from his mount.[277] After that minor affair terminated, Jenkins trotted eastward on the pike with Witcher's four-hundred-man contingent as it took position at the Albright House. White Hall resident Zacheus Bowman observed Jenkins and staff watering their horses in the spring on the banks of the Conodoguinet Creek at Orr's Bridge.[278] Afterward, he rode south on St. John's Church Road and rejoined his command at the Peace Church.

Jenkins stood in front of the church, gazing east with his field glasses, when he gestured for young Cromleigh to peer out of his glass. The sixteen-year-old later recalled he was "afraid, and yet as pleased as could be." Jenkins informed the youth that he believed Federal pickets were about in the woods in front of the church. After looking through Jenkins's glasses, Cromleigh expressed his opinion that what Jenkins saw were fence posts. "He swore at me like everything when I told him I didn't think they were soldiers," remembered the youth. Whatever they were—fence posts or soldiers—Jenkins soon became convinced they were advancing and ordered Cromleigh to go to his family's cellar, which was directly opposite the church, and take cover. Fifteen minutes later, Cromleigh peeked out but saw no sign of Jenkins or his men until glancing at the cemetery wall, where he observed the muskets of Jenkins's cavaliers shining in the sunlight.[279]

Jenkins's force was reduced at this time when four companies of the 16th Virginia Cavalry under Major James Nounnan departed the Peace Church en route to hunt up horses and other goods from farms in northern York County. On June 29, they turned over their loot to Ewell's quartermaster in Carlisle. The group spent the night just outside Carlisle and did not rejoin Jenkins's brigade until the evening of June 30 in Carlisle.[280]

TENSE TIMES AT OYSTER'S POINT

Federal cavalry pickets stationed near Oyster's Point reported the advance of the Rebels, and the infantry were ordered into line. In Camp Taylor, it was 11:00 a.m. when reports of the Southern advance interrupted the 33rd PVM's lunch. "Before we got through with our hot dinner," penned Private Beale, "we were ordered to fall in line of battle in fighting trim without haversacks, some even forgot their canteens." By noon, they were in the rifle pits on the edge of camp that they slightly enlarged but otherwise "laid there roasting in the hot sun all the afternoon[.]"[281]

The 30th PVM north of the point and the 11th NYSNG immediately south of the hotel formed in line of battle. Supporting columns, skirmishers and flankers were thrown out, "and then came a long wait for the foe." The 30th's Captain Nicholas Rice of Company D, who unlike most of the militia officers gathered around Oyster's Point was a veteran of the Army of the Potomac, wondered whether the Yankee militia could "stand the fire and charge of Lee's veterans[.]" Rice looked along his regiment's line of battle and noted the "nervous, suppressed excitement amoung [sic] them[.]"[282]

About noon, the militia at Oyster's Point heard cannonading in the direction of Sporting Hill and shortly after saw Knipe's brigade retreating on the pike "as fast as they could walk." When these troops arrived at Oyster's Point, Knipe was ordered to Fort Washington to take command of the garrison, along with the 8th and 11th NYSNG. Colonel William Brisbane, commanding several regiments of Pennsylvania Militia, assumed command of all troops in the Oyster's Point vicinity. Brisbane had formerly served as the lieutenant colonel of the 49th PVI, which had been in Baldy Smith's division of the Sixth Corps. Knipe's 71st NYSNG remained in reserve near the Church of God on the eastern edge of White Hall. Miller's Battery was placed between the companies of the 33rd PVM in the rifle pits near Camp Taylor.[283]

Shortly after this commotion, Murray's cavalry detachment from Mechanicsburg was seen "dashing to the rear" on the Trindle Road, "closely followed" by Jenkins's Confederates. Murray led his company back to the Camelback Bridge, where he finally halted. Witcher's Confederates on the

Colonel William Brisbane was in command of all Yankee troops in the Oyster's Point vicinity. *Courtesy of the U.S. Army Military History Institute.*

pike became visible to the 30[284] PVM, whose line of battle was almost directly opposite the Albright House.[284]

The 28th PVM arose on Sabbath morning in Fort Washington to orders for seven of its companies (Companies A, E and H were detached) to fall in with forty rounds of cartridges and go on picket at Oyster's Point. With their colonel, James Chamberlin, leading them, the companies marched up the Carlisle Pike in a column of fours. As the vanguard neared the tollgate, it received a greeting from Jackson's guns at the Albright House. The shell missed the Pennsylvanians, noted Robert Vaughan of Company I, "but ricocheted alongside the regiment and was our introduction and good morning from our visitors." "We could plainly see the discharge of the gun every time it was fired while we were on the pike," observed Vaughan, "which was only for a short time, for the Colonel gave orders for the leading companies to deploy as skirmishers." Companies C and I deployed to the south of the pike on Limekiln Lane and covered a line from the pike to the Cumberland Valley Railroad. Company B formed as a reserve in the rear of the Oyster's Point Hotel, while Company F of the 33rd PVM was posted in front of the hotel and advancing slowly. Companies D, F, G and K of the 28th, under Colonel Chamberlin, picketed north of the pike and in front of the 30th PVM.[285]

Because the 11th NYSNG had retired with Knipe to Fort Washington, Oyster's Woods was devoid of defenders. Confederate skirmishers on the Trindle Road advanced into the woods and area just in front of the point, even occupying a young apple orchard immediately in front of the hotel. Some of the gray-clad skirmishers even took cover behind the barricade just west of the hotel made several days prior by the 23rd NYSNG. Meanwhile, the Southern skirmishers pushed deeper into Oyster's Woods, all the while "yi-yi-ing and firing," according to Vaughan. The two companies of the 28th had just deployed, and the Rebel advance scattered the Pennsylvanians in seconds. "[A]way went Company I," Vaughan later recalled, "back over a small Wheatfield to the farther fence, where they stopped and looked around them in wonder to see what struck them." Captain Joseph Hutchinson reprimanded the company for the panic and then led it back beyond Limekiln Lane where it reestablished its line in Oyster's Woods.

Company I occupied the Rebels in front while Company C slipped around their flank. Outflanked and outmanned, the Southerners fell back through Oyster's Woods into a cornfield belonging to Samuel Shopp, opposite the woods and south of the Trindle Road. The two Pennsylvania companies then advanced to the western edge of Oyster's Woods, where

Private Peter P. Bubb of the 28th PVM. Bubb also served in the 23rd Pennsylvania Militia during the 1862 Maryland Campaign. Note his gray uniform and shako-style hat. *Courtesy of the U.S. Army Military History Institute.*

they formed a more stable skirmish line, despite being under the fire of Griffin's battery at the Peace Church.[286] A contingent of the gray-clad skirmishers, eager to find a safer place to respond, retired to Shopp's farm about eight hundred yards away. There they knocked the gable end out of the barn so they could fire at the Pennsylvanians at a fairly useless long range, while the rest of the Rebel skirmishers continued short-range skirmishing in the cornfield nearer the Pennsylvanians.[287]

In reserve behind the hotel, Captain William Post's Company B, 28th PVM, fared much better than the other six companies of the 28th, considering that the Confederate artillery fire was concentrated to its right and left; however, reported one Pennsylvanian, "the shells [still] fell sufficiently near for the music to be more exciting than captivating[.]" Company B's worries were further lessened when the pesky Rebels occupying the apple orchard and behind the barricade in front of the hotel were forced to fall back as the Yankee picket line gradually advanced.[288]

Company F of the 33rd PVM was having its own troubles near the center of the skirmish line. Rebels had occupied Tommy Oyster's home, located nearly five hundred yards west of the point and on the north side of the pike. The house was deserted, as Oyster had opted to flee to Harrisburg. "Directly in front was the rebel line of pickets and skirmishers," Corporal Robert Welsh of Company F recalled. "They soon let us know they were about, as occasional shots came from them, to which reply was always made. The first excitement gave way to a feeling of annoyance. This sniping was useless and vexatious."[289] Welsh continued:

> *Right where we were stationed, was an old stone farm house...The family had fled in terror and the house being easily defensible and affording much comfort to the tired and ragged gentleman from the south land they had taken full advantage of the situation. The weather being very warm they had conveyed the beds to the lawn; also chairs, lounges, etc. Evidently there was a piano player among them, for an old piano had also been lugged out of doors. Where being an Union piano and therefore refusing to satisfactorily render "Dixie" and "Maryland, My Maryland" or that the played being rusty became angered at want of skill will never be known. But something happened for the works of the instrument were scattered upon the ground and the case badly shattered. An attempt had been made to burn one leg, not very successfully.*[290]

Company F sent forward a line of skirmishers that moved through the orchard in the rear of the house, which the Confederates hastily vacated for fear of being flanked. However, the gray-clad skirmishers gained the pike before the rest of the company could cut them off and took position on the same ridge where the Albright House sits. "It looked dangerous," wrote Welsh, "we didn't know what was behind that hill, so [we] contented ourselves with strictly obeying orders[.]" Establishing headquarters at the newly recaptured home, they formed a skirmish line about two hundred yards out at the edge of Tommy Oyster's orchard and behind a stone wall, straddling both sides of the pike. "Both sides fired an occasional shot to let the opponents know all was well," Welsh mused. He added:

> *As our Johnie [sic] friends had burned all the fence[s] in sight we resorted to what they had left of the old piano. It burned solely but surely and a gang of*

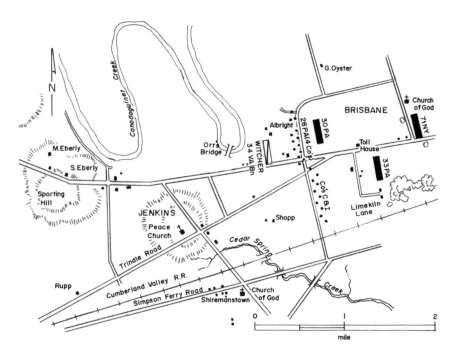

The opening salvo at Oyster's Point, June 28, 1863. *Map by John Heiser.*

the boys were boiling coffee in their tin cups soon after dark, when bang, bang, bang came several shots at the conspicuous spot. A ball smashed through the tin cup of Corporal Jim Loo and he had no coffee. Billy Helm was stooping at the fire lighting a splint for his pipe when a minie [sic] ball hit a piece of the burning wood and knocked a lot of ashes into his face, filling his eyes. He saw very little for an hour, but sat in a safe place bathing his eyes with water out of a canteen and saying anything but his prayers. He was all right in the morning. After this the fire was voted a bad place to sit by.[291]

These movements, essentially the opening salvo of the Skirmish of Oyster's Point, lasted less than two hours in the early afternoon. The fire of Jackson's battery at Albright's began to slacken. "We were expecting an attack every minute and all had our 40 or 39 rounds of cartridges ready and lots of boxes of 1,000 rounds at hand where we could see them," recorded Private Beale of the 33rd PVM. "Several Generals have been riding about here," he continued. "The signal corps is at work on a hill to the right of us, and we are the extreme advance placed here to be cut to pieces or retire before the

Fort can be attacked behind us." Beale and his fellow Philadelphians could look up from their rifle pits and "see the Rebels in large force in the distance on the mountains moving toward us with long trains of wagons shining in the sun."[292]

AT BRIDGEPORT HEIGHTS

If heads were not already turned within the forts when artillery fire was distinctly heard from Sporting Hill about noon in "rapid succession," they must have when the noisy skirmishing began at Oyster's Point.[293] Regiments were drawn up in line of battle and assigned positions at the entrenchments. "There is great activity on every hand to perfect the defences [sic]," wrote Private Lockwood of the 23rd NYSNG. Trees and any form of cover were cut down by squads of men traversing the hill. Religious services were held in Camp Couch.[294] Lockwood continued:

> It is an animating sight to watch from the parapet all these various operations going on. The crackling of branches draws attention to yonder tree which comes tumbling to the ground with a crash—others follow rapidly and the axmen's blows resound on every side. On you yonder knoll a company of mowers are rapidly leveling the tall wheat. Here inside the fort an artillery officer is drilling a squad in artillery firing: and there a gang of contrabands, now for the first time, very likely, receiving wages for their labor judging by the spirit they throw into their work, are putting the finishing touches on the ditch and parapet. Outside yonder a squad of men is tearing in pieces a twig hut which workmen have built for their tools. And so the final work of preparation goes on with great spirit, and is soon completed. There are still no signs of the approach of the enemy except what we observe about us in a sort of expectant air among the officers.[295]

At Camp Cox, the 22nd NYSNG assembled around Colonel Lloyd Aspinwall's tent for religious services. The chaplain assembled the men, distributed prayer books and had risen to speak. He was about to do so when Colonel Aspinwall rode into camp at full gallop and shouted, "Go back to your company 'streets' and strike tents at once." The chaplain, who apparently thought himself as important as God, jumped into a wagon, rode into Harrisburg and was never seen again by the regiment. In a few minutes, the entire camp was struck, tents being loaded into wagons and all as if the

New Yorkers had never been there. "O what a change in the appearance of the encampment," penned Private Murray of the 22nd. "[I]n place of the snowy white tents Standing in rows were now Soldiers packing up their knapsacks for the march and the debris tent floors, Pails, tinware, kettles." None of the New Yorkers realized that they had slept their last night under cover for an extremely long time.[296]

The 11th and 37th NYSNG were in the rifle pits that had been dug across the Copperhead's garden about a mile south of Bridgeport Station, near New Cumberland. The following day, two pieces of artillery would be emplaced between the New Yorkers for support. Several companies of the 22nd were held in reserve. At one point, these companies were marched into a wood nearer Bridgeport Heights, where they formed line of battle for an hour, expecting a Rebel attack. Back at Bridgeport Station, Companies A and I of the 22nd proceeded to barricade the engine house of the CVRR with beams, barrels of earth, sandbags and other nearby materials. By 10:00 p.m., George Wingate of Company A remarked that they "had converted the engine-house...into a loop-holed and casemated battery, to protect two howitzers of Miller's battery placed there to command the railroad." Sandbags masked the two howitzers from view. The New Yorkers should not claim all the credit; much assistance came from Negroes who had been working on the entrenchments at Bridgeport Heights.[297]

THE SKIRMISH DIES DOWN AT OYSTER'S POINT

Meanwhile, at Oyster's Point, the next phase of the skirmish in front of Harrisburg began as the firefight began to simmer down. Jenkins established a more formal main line and skirmish line and soon infested the surrounding area with scouts. The northern end of Jenkins's line began just north of the Albright House and ran south from there to the Peace Church. From there, it arced southeastward to the Samuel Shopp farm (occupied by Confederate skirmishers), about 1,200 yards southeast of Peace Church and 800 yards west of Oyster's Point. "The enemy holds a position almost describing an arc of a circle," read a surprisingly accurate newspaper report in the *New York Tribune*. "The extremes rest on two main roads, cross the railroads, and extend through wheat and corn fields and some small woods. He has pickets out in all valuable positions, and has artillery commanding and intended to sweep the roads and protect his front and flank."[298]

Jenkins's duty in front of Harrisburg was, in the words of General Rodes, to make "a thorough reconnaissance of the defenses of the place [Harrisburg], with a view to our advance upon it[.]"[299] Jenkins was not attempting to capture Harrisburg himself but, rather, report to Ewell whether his fifteen thousand men could capture the city. Because Jenkins was severely wounded later in the campaign and left no official report (and neither did any of his subordinates), one of the few ways to know what areas Jenkins thought worth looking into is the reported positions of his forward scouts. On June 28, John Bigler, William Hemminger and Israel Boyer—all citizens of Lower Allen Township, southeast of the Peace Church—reported horses and/or other property damaged or stolen by Jenkins's men that afternoon and into the evening. One man of this township—Edward Rodgers—upon fearing that his horse would be captured by Jenkins's men, rode his mount to Siddonsburg, York County, where it was taken by the Louisiana Tigers of Major General Jubal Early's division.[300]

Most historians acknowledge that Confederate scouts reached as far south as Slate Hill, just over two miles south of Jenkins's main position at the Peace Church. However, Israel Boyer, who claimed that his eleven-year-old bay horse was taken by Jenkins's cavalrymen on the afternoon of June 28, lived over two and a half miles south of Slate Hill, near what is now the Lower Allen Community Park. His farm was roughly four and a half miles south of Jenkins's main position at the Peace Church.[301] This documentation demonstrates that Jenkins was considering options over four miles south of his right flank.

Interestingly enough, there is also evidence that General Couch knew of or feared such. On June 30, he ordered the four-hundred-man 68th NYSNG to move to Highspire, a suburb of Harrisburg on the east shore that extended farther south than Camp Cox or any other Federal defenses on the west shore. His orders to the unit's colonel, David Forbes, were:

Find out about the ford there, and others in the vicinity down river. Keep your men in hand to resist any attempt at crossing. In no event must an enemy cross. Use the canal for rifle-pits. There will be no difficulty in your work. In connection with the cavalry, you will take command and patrol and watch well down the river, seizing all boats; allow no communication with the other side. Arrest all suspicious persons, and, in general, watch, guard and protect the people. Allow no marauding.

Forbes took all the precautions outlined by Couch, though no Rebel advance was ever attempted in that sector.[302]

During the timeframe that Jenkins's brigade occupied the area, it managed to impress upon the civilians whose land it occupied that its men were significantly better behaved than the Yankee militia. "I only talked to a few of the rebels," recalled Samuel Shopp, in whose barn Rebel skirmishers anchored the right of Jenkins's line. "They were not very sociable. I heard one of them say they 'got into Pennsylvania, but didn't know how the devil to get out.'"[303] Overall, Jenkins's men respected civilians and their private property much better than the Yankee militia. This was in line with the maxim Jenkins had proclaimed earlier in the campaign: "We are not thieves."[304] Only one account exists where Rebels actually injured a citizen. A man was driving his cattle east along the Carlisle Pike, away from the Rebels, when he was overtaken by a group of gray-clad horsemen a short distance west of Oyster's Point. "He pulled out at the top of his speed," read one report, "but stumbled and fell upon his face in the road." Before he could recover from his fall, one Southerner drove his bayonet into the man's backside, imposing a painful but not overly dangerous wound. The Confederates took his cattle, but he was able to walk to Harrisburg. "The lesson to be drawn from this affair is," mused one newspaper editor, "under like circumstances, to give up the cows unless you are iron-clad."[305]

Rebel scouts on Slate Hill encountered Charles Flemming of Mechanicsburg. Unbeknownst to them, Flemming had been commissioned as a spy by General Couch. He was trekking through the fields from Mechanicsburg toward the Susquehanna, where he would have a boat and someone to row him across between the Camelback Bridge and New Cumberland. At one point during his journey, he sat on a fence for a momentary rest when several gray-clad scouts appeared. Flemming informed the soldiers he had come to the hill to "look around." The soldiers asked Flemming if he had seen any Rebels, to which he replied no. "Do we look like rebels?" they inquired, to which he responded, "I don't know, you are all strangers to me." They took Flemming back to the Peace Church, where the group encountered citizens Lewis Bricker and Levi Balmer, also captured. Flemming found them "scared half to death, especially Mr. Bricker." Balmer lived near the Salem Church on the pike, and Bricker lived about two miles south of the Peace Church. Flemming chuckled at their scared state. The trio joined other civilians being held in the church overnight.[306]

It was about 4:00 p.m. when Jenkins retired his brigade just over one mile west to near the Neidig farm, approximately one mile east of Mechanicsburg. There the Southerners encamped for the night, dispatching skirmishers to Oyster's Point to harass the Yankees throughout the night. Witcher bivouacked in a wood on the hill above Orr's Bridge.[307]

As darkness shrouded Oyster's Point, Companies C and I of the 28th PVM received orders to retire from Oyster's Woods to Limekiln Lane. Colonel Chamberlin of the 28th received orders to deploy his entire regiment as pickets in the woods north of the pike. About 10:00 p.m., Colonel Brisbane called the 71st NYSNG out of reserve and ordered six companies to relieve the 33rd PVM in the rifle pits near Camp Taylor so the Philadelphians could rest. Brisbane also ordered Colonel Benjamin Trafford of the 71st to deploy the other four companies as pickets. While Jenkins may have retired, his picket parties kept Trafford's New Yorkers busy almost constantly throughout the night. One of the climactic moments in this ongoing scrap occurred about 4:00 a.m., when a gray-clad party attempted to break through the Yankee picket line, causing a brief flare of gunfire resulting in the first confirmed human casualty of the West Shore area—the wounding of Private John Manly of Company G, 71st NYSNG, in the thigh. His wound was dressed by the regiment's surgeon, Dr. Edgar Birdsell, and he was transported to his home in New York City.[308]

The actions in the Harrisburg area that day had garnered the attention of the commander in chief. At 4:00 p.m., President Lincoln telegraphed Couch with anxious concern, "What news now?"[309]

Night Reconnaissance

Earlier on June 28, Smith had wired Couch, informing him that he "intends to send out two reconnoitering parties of infantry…one on each road leading to Carlisle."[310] Shortly before midnight, the 22nd and 37th NYSNG were roused from their work at Bridgeport Station and from the trenches at Camp Cox. The New Yorkers were told they were to make a reconnaissance toward Oyster's Point. Because of his seniority, Colonel Charles Roome's 37th took the advance. While marching, the men "observed a large fire burning down the Susquehanna." While they did not know it then, this flame was the Columbia Bridge near Wrightsville, in York County, which was burned by its defenders to prevent a Confederate crossing.

The column marched until it reached the Trindle Springs Road. After several miles, the men were ordered to throw away their tin cups to prevent any noise. "We proceeded very cautiously with our pieces at half cock and expecting the rebels to pour a volley into us every moment," recorded Private Murray of the 22nd. "We all felt we were going to be engaged in a fight…

and I believe many of the men said their prayers."[311] New Yorker George Wingate later recalled:

> *It was an imposing sight to see the long column dimly and silently stealing down the roads and through the varying shadows of the night. Not a sound was heard; orders were given in a whisper; and as the troops drew near the position supposed to be occupied by the enemy, the silence was so profound that the heavy breathing of the men was distinctly audible to their comrades. After a march of five miles, whispered orders were passed down the line, and, amid a death-like silence, the regiments halted and formed line of battle, fixing bayonets and freshly capping their pieces in readiness for instant service. Every eye was strained, through the darkness, to discern the patrols of the enemy in the wavering shadows of the woods and fields, and every ear was stretched to its utmost tension to catch the expected challenge.*[312]

Murray claimed to see distant lights in the Southern camps. After waiting in line of battle for "some time," whispered orders were passed down the line to march back to Bridgeport. "The movement was well managed, and only wanted one thing to be a magnificent success," reflected Wingate, "that was an enemy. 'As there wasn't anybody to be captured, we could not capture anybody.'" The two regiments arrived at Bridgeport Station just before sunrise and, in what was left of the predawn hours, lay down beside the railroad tracks "to catch a brief rest."[313]

About midnight at Oyster's Point, the men of the 33rd PVM, which had only been relieved from the rifle pits two hours previous, were awakened and formed into line of battle. Colonel Brisbane rode along the line, impressing upon them "not to speak, not even to whisper, and be perfectly silen [*sic*], that he would show us some fun before morning." The regiment, all with loaded muskets, right faced and marched about two miles west on the Carlisle Pike toward the Albright House. The men were informed they were "sent out to capture 600 Rebel Cavalry in a wood." A short distance beyond the Albright House, a dog barked at the regiment's advance. Witcher's cavalry—their target—was nearby, slumbering until now in the wood above Orr's Bridge. The men heard "the tramp of feet and the cartridges rattling in the boxes sounded like Cavalry moving." Soon afterward, a bugle call sounded, and the Confederate cavalryman fell back to safety. Brisbane realized there would be no pursuit when he called the regiment to attention and found most of the men asleep. "The fun was over so we were ordered back," mused one Philadelphian.[314]

Jenkins's Council of War

While the Yankee militia stumbled through the dark, Jenkins had called a council of war at his headquarters at the eighteenth-century stone mansion of John Rupp about two miles east of Mechanicsburg. With his family, Rupp had fled to Lancaster upon word of the invasion.[315] At this council, the audacious Lieutenant Colonel Witcher proposed a solid plan to his oft-overcautious and conservative brigadier. Witcher recognized that the brigade had to find a way to reconnoiter the fords and defenses of Harrisburg while suppressing Union interference. His plan involved a heavy cannonade concentrated on Oyster's Point, giving the appearance of preparations for a large attack. Then, Witcher's cavalry would "demonstrate" against the Federal skirmishers. This had the possibility of occupying the Yankees' attention at Oyster's Point while Jenkins could find suitable ground from which to observe Harrisburg's defenses.[316]

This was a solid plan. However, Jenkins objected, and well past midnight they debated the plan until the brigadier finally consented.[317] The question then turned to locating the best place for Jenkins to overlook the city's defenses. Jenkins must have been informed by either a subordinate or directly from his scouts of the position to do just that: Slate Hill, just southeast of Shiremanstown. There can be no debate that Jenkins's scouts had been to Slate Hill considering the multitude of stolen horses and the capture of Charles Flemming, and they must have passed up through the chain of command how Slate Hill provided a dominant view of the capital city and its defenses. The next day, Jenkins would observe Harrisburg's defenses, and barring unforeseen circumstances, Ewell's infantry would begin the march from Carlisle to capture Pennsylvania's capital.

Chapter 8

Spies, Scouts and Traitors

Many reports of spies spread throughout Harrisburg and the West Shore during the invasion. Thomas Wilson, a resident of Middletown, just southeast of Harrisburg, and his companion Shaffer were arrested in a boat on the evening of June 28 just below the Half Way House, believed to be sounding the Susquehanna River for a Confederate fording. Union pickets fired at them, forcing them to come ashore on the Harrisburg side of the river, where the soldiers surrounded the suspicious duo and took them prisoner. Soldiers discovered an "excellent"-sounding lead and a signal whistle on Wilson, along with a long, thin pole. Wilson claimed he was taking his father home; however, some onlookers alleged that other men in the boat had jumped ship and waded across the river before the boat was pulled aside. The two were jailed "for further examination[.]"[318]

Another incident occurred near the river in the predawn hours of July 2. A detachment of Captain F. Asbury Awl's Harrisburg Company manned picket lines in Harris Park on the eastern banks of the river. Twenty-seven men had been detailed from the company, nine on picket at a time, while the others quartered themselves in what was then a schoolhouse on the northwest corner of Front Street and Mary Avenue. About 3:00 a.m., one of the pickets whispered, "What's that floating down the river?" One man believed it was a log, but Private Cornelius DeHart soon remarked, "There's some thing on it moving." Another private then shouted to DeHart, "Corney, call out to halt; and, if they don't halt, shoot!"[319] Another picket, Henry Demming, later recalled:

I thought I saw a man standing up on what in the darkness seemed like a floating log. Instantly the order was given to have the party halt and come ashore, or else to shoot, and to be careful to hit. In quick response Private DeHart shouted "Halt;" but there was no effort made to stop the floating obstacle and Dehart fired. Another picket fired at the same time. The man quickly dropped, apparently not hit, as I heard the bullets whizzing over the water toward the opposite shore. At this juncture the craft, about 200 feet from land, ceased to float down the river. I ran northwestwardly down the bank to a skiff lying partly on the shore, and attempted to push it off. Then I saw it was fastened by a chain and lock and staple to a large stone. After trying to break the skiff away, and failing, I made an effort to lift stone and chain into the bow of the boat. Finding the stone too heavy for me, Sergeant Simon Gratz ran down and helped. Then we pushed the boat off. I took the bow, with my rifle ready cocked in my hand, and Sergeant Gratz a position just back of midships, where, laying down his rifle, he pushed the boat into the stream. Rapid progress was made toward what we now saw was a large sand flat and I peered ahead to note how many were crouched down inside. At first, to my great surprise, I saw no one. Then, as we got nearer, I saw one man stooping down at the south eastern end of the flat. He sprang up quickly, and Sergeant Gratz called to him to surrender. Instead of surrendering, he seemed ready to shoot. In a very few words, which I do not now remember, I made him understand that if he did not surrender immediately I would shoot him, having my rifle carefully aimed at his head. He dropped a hatchet that he had in one hand, and said "I surrender." I did not observe what he held in the other hand; but on searching him afterwards I found it was a Sharp's "four-shooter" revolver.[320]

Demming took his prisoner to the provost marshal's office the next morning, where the captive was released—though not for long. He was recaptured shortly afterward while attempting to cross back into Confederate lines. He was temporarily detained in the Dauphin County prison until being transferred to Fort Delaware. Demming later penned that he found a map in the man's boat that contained all the fordable places from Marysville to where he was captured. Demming additionally claimed that twenty years later he was approached by a veteran of "General Stuart's Black Horse (Va.) cavalry," who told him the true definition of an absurdity. He claimed that if the man Demming had captured had succeeded in crossing the river, he would have levied half a million dollars in cash and provisions from Harrisburg. The name of the Confederate

Demming had captured was J.H.M. Weitbrecht, who was apparently known as a "dare devil" within the Confederate army.[321]

Spies—or alleged spies—also thronged the West Shore in the week before the Confederate forces reached Carlisle. One man who visited Fort Washington claimed to be a phrenological lecturer from Clinton County, but after being examined by several militiamen, he "knew nothing about that locality" and "was very unlike his profession," prompting his arrest.[322]

The most authentic reports of Southern emissaries available come on June 28, immediately after Jenkins arrived in the Harrisburg area. One alleged spy dressed as a woman was sent to Oyster's Point, where she (he) was given water. This "woman" described to one citizen "the whole route from the time they left Virginia," also claiming that her husband and sons were in the Confederate army but "lost." This is strikingly similar to an incident at Chambersburg earlier that same month when Jenkins was approaching that town.[323]

John Mater of Limekiln Lane also had an encounter with a suspected spy shortly before noon on June 28. Mater recalled:

In the forenoon my brother-in-law, Snyder, and I went down through Mr. [William] Sadler's farm [at the end of Limekiln Lane]. Had walked through there, and coming back there was a gentleman followed us up through Sadler's farm, and asked us if there were any soldiers around through here. Of course, we knew there were. Then we stood on a work-bench at our home, right in front of our house, and I showed him where the soldiers were,—about two hundred yards away, and I asked him whether he was going out to our fellows. He pretended to be one of our men,—a Union man. He wore black clothes, splendid black frock coat, and was [a]bout five feet ten inches in height, and slightly built. A fine looking man. He had a straight knife on his belt…It was about that long. (Indicating about eighteen inches.) It hung below his coat two or three inches. I asked him if he was going out to our fellows. He said "No, the dumb devils would just as soon shoot their friends as their enemies." He told us he came from Harrisburg that morning. He was a spy. We knew he was a rebel. He wasn't there long until he turned and went back in his same tracks. It wasn't long till the Sergeant came down to our place. He had seen him, the rebel spy, standing here and he told me I should "never do a trick like that again." I asked him what, and he said they "came near shooting all three of us."[324]

Chapter 9
Jenkins Reconnoiters Harrisburg

At Oyster's Point, the "warm, sun shiny day" of June 29 began when reveille sounded as usual at 5:00 a.m. "We have pretty high living now," penned an enthusiastic Joseph Boggs Beale of the 33rd PVM, who described the vicinity that morning:

> All the farm houses are derted [sic] and fresh bread, pots of apple butter, buttermilk, fresh butter, chickens, pigs, potatoes, molasses, etc. etc. are brought in by the boys who go out foraging. Old hats, bonnets, and cloths and pieces of furniture have been brought into camp. One old man in our company captured a side saddle at an empty farm house, after which he deserted taking it with him, and his equipments, knapsack, and even his musket he held onto. Guards have been stationed at these, formerly unprotected houses. Of course they live on the fat of the land, if there is any left. We now see nobody but soldiers, all citizen have cleared out, and it is said when two farmers go to cross the Bridge to Harrisburg the guard there captures one to work on the entrenchments…The fences here are broken and the cattle are running at large over the country…There does not seem to be any excitement here, and all are happy and full of fun. [325]

Company I of the 71st NYSNG moved from its picket line of the previous night to near Limekiln Lane. A cobbler's stall became headquarters, and the company split in two, with half skirmishing with the Rebels in Samuel Shopp's cornfield while the other half went foraging. "Pigs and chickens were captured, and cooking began in the kitchen of a deserted house close by," recalled one New Yorker. "Apple butter, too, the prevalent institution in Pennsylvania was found in plenty." The company continued that process, one half relieving the other after a short amount of time, until Griffin's artillerists at the Peace Church crashed their picnic with a few well-directed three-inch shells, "which shrieked and crashed through the branches, bursting over us, round us, and many of them altogether too near to be pleasant[.]"[326]

To make matters worse, the New Yorkers were fired upon by other Yankees in their rear, which, though it caused no injuries, was not agreeable. A flag of truce (a handkerchief hoisted by a ramrod) soon rectified the situation. The men of the 71st were under strict orders to fire only three or four volleys during the skirmishing, as an engagement (small or large) was expected that day and they should reserve ammunition for it.[327] The skirmishing became heated, not only through gunfire but also when several Yankee pickets who were close enough to exchange words with their Southern counterparts caused a ruckus with some profanity, which led to more firing and a shell landing within thirty feet of a group of fleeing civilians.[328]

Baldy Smith decided to make the first substantial move on June 29, sending forward Lieutenant Frank Stanwood's cavalry detachment from Carlisle Barracks. Stanwood engaged and drove in the Confederate pickets on the pike, nearing the Albright House, but "was obliged to retire under a fire of artillery which was opened upon him."[329]

Within the Confederate lines, General Jenkins was busy redeploying his brigade. Griffin's battery was firing at a rate one observer described as "occasionally," under orders from Jenkins to do their best to harass enemy pickets at Oyster's Point. It was not until about noon that Jackson's battery unlimbered at the Albright House. W.H.H. Smith, a Union soldier on furlough (who had managed to convince General Jenkins himself he was discharged after being captured by Confederate scouts) and a relative of the Oyster family, observed that the Rebels concentrated their fire on the area south of the tollgate, principally Limekiln Lane and Oyster's Woods, which they shelled "completely." Smith observed one shot pass completely through Tommy Oyster's house, going through the upper drawer of his bureau and out the other side before landing in his garden.[330]

"During all the Engagements [near Harrisburg]," wrote Lieutenant Micajah Woods of Jackson's battery, "our Battery played a conspicuous part, and especially the rifled gun in my section, which was called upon more often than the other pieces, because of greater range. The Enemy brought little artillery to bear against us hence we had a fair chance to make good shots with comparatively little exposure."[331]

Witcher's plan was to make the Yankees believe a full-scale assault was imminent. "There was every appearance of an impending engagement," reported an officer of the 71st NYSNG. Panic ran through the Northern lines. "If there is a fight it will be a big one," confided one concerned enlisted man in his diary. Northern pickets noticed unusual stirring in the Rebel lines. Brisbane requested reinforcements from Fort Washington, where rumors circulated that the Rebels were "advancing in force to attempt to storm the works." Regiments were ordered "to be prepared to fall in at a moment's notice." Even General Couch was excited, writing Secretary of War Stanton that he expected a "determined attack."[332]

It was shortly before 1:00 p.m. when Brisbane began rearranging his regiments. He marshaled three regiments from his command and deployed them in a wheat field "hidden from the view of the enemy by a little hill and a woods," north of the pike. This line was near modern 24th Street in Camp Hill, about five hundred yards east of the tollgate. The 33rd PVM was moved from Camp Taylor to the extreme right of this line, with the seven companies of the 28th PVM in the center and the 30th PVM on the left with Miller's battery. Along this line was the Signal Corps, which was hard at work. Forty men of Miller's battery, armed with breech-loading carbines, formed a skirmish line in front of their position. In this concealed line, the four Pennsylvania units stacked arms and awaited news from the front on the coming engagement.[333]

More support came in the form of a 150-man detachment under command of Lieutenant Colonel John Elwell of the 23rd NYSNG. General Knipe had ordered Elwell to assume command of a detachment composed of fifty men each from of the 8th, 23rd and 56th NYSNG. As Elwell approached the point, he heard "heavy cannonading at intervals of from five to ten minutes." Fearing he would be too late, he hastened to the scene and deployed his detachment as skirmishers. He posted the contingent from the 8th to the south, with its left resting on the Cumberland Valley Railroad, and the detachment of the 23rd north of the pike, while he kept the fifty men of the 56th as a reserve. The lieutenant colonel advanced his line to near the hotel, driving back Confederate skirmishers but exposing himself to a "constant fire of shot and shell from the rebel batteries." There Elwell remained, along with the skirmishers of the 71st NYSNG and Company F of the 33rd PVM, who were in and about Tommy Oyster's house.[334]

The diversion to be made by Witcher finally came early that afternoon after nearly two hours of heavy and constant shelling from Jackson's battery. Jenkins's orders to Witcher strictly outlined that the impudent lieutenant colonel was only to advance skirmishers and entertain the Federals. At first, Witcher did just that. An officer of the 71st NYSNG reported that after the cannon fire ceased, the Rebels advanced in what appeared to him to be "infantry in skirmishing order." "[General Jenkins ordered] me to simply demonstrate whilst he was gone with Gen. Lee's engineers, [but] finding the position could be carried, I made a successful direct assault," Witcher later wrote.[335]

Witcher's cavalrymen galloped down the pike from Albright's. Elwell's skirmishers, along with those from Company F of the 33rd PVM and the 71st NYSNG—the latter from the cover of the limestone quarry on the west edge of Limekiln Lane—opened fire on the approaching Rebels. Yankee sharpshooters also took pot shots from behind the chimney on the roof of William Sadler's house at the end of Limekiln Lane. The first casualty came after the charge had only proceeded several hundred yards, when a Rebel was shot from his horse by a sharpshooter in Oyster's Woods opposite the J.G. Rupp farm, about four hundred yards west of the point and still standing at the 3300 block of Camp Hill. The aggrieved Confederate fell off his horse but was forcibly placed back on by his comrades and taken to the rear. The Southern column continued, proceeding right (south) and then up the Trindle Springs Road to Oyster's Point. In the process, the gray-clad cavalrymen galloped over the barricade made three days earlier by the 23rd NYSNG.[336]

Just before reaching the point, a second Southerner was shot, and he, too, was taken to the rear by his comrades. Eighteen-year-old Isaac Wolf of West Fairview, who was at the hotel, estimated that the Rebels numbered about fifty, some mounted and some dismounted. "It was pretty hot about that time," recalled Wolf, "and they [Federal soldiers] told us we had better get out." The Confederate cavalrymen easily pushed back the frightened and numerically superior Yankee skirmish line beyond the tollgate and advanced to Limekiln Lane, where they took position and began skirmishing with the retreating militia.[337]

Back several hundred yards at Brisbane's main line, this ruckus did little to soothe the nerves of the Pennsylvania militiamen, especially when scattered groups of pickets were seen running back, "very much frightened and out of breath as if they had been chased." "[In] the [Oyster's] woods…some of our fellows were spread out as skirmishers and I could see the Rebels firing their cannons at our pickets and hear the shells whistle or hum in the air as they came over toward us and burst," penned Private Beale of the 33rd. "They [the Confederates] were not more than a half mile off, as we could see the men distinctly at the Oyster Point Tavern and hear every musket shot or volley of muskets. Some of our regiment [Company F] were in the engagement, all of us expected to be…The firing is pretty steady and keeps getting closer."[338]

A group of four or five mounted Rebels advanced to the tollgate and seemed to be observing the Yankee lines. While there, a Yankee from a knoll near the Zacheus Bowman home one hundred yards in advance of Brisbane's line opened fire upon the group, wounding one in the left knee, making for a total of three wounded Southerners. His comrades dispersed and left him there to be captured. After the affair was over, he was taken to Zacheus Bowman's barn in the rear of Bowman's home, where Dr. J.D. Bowman of White Hall treated his wound. It was reported that he "never winced."[339]

William Sadler, who lived at the end of Limekiln Lane, witnessed the firefight. "They [the Confederates] came down to the road, and when our men fell back they came down…" described Sadler. "We had a nice view there to look over the whole business, and we could see both our men and the rebels…when we put our heads out of the window they fired at us, and we had to put our heads in. At the east end our men would fire at us, and at the west end the rebels would fire. We had to be careful."[340]

A piece of Jackson's battery remained unlimbered opposite the Oyster's Point Hotel on the Trindle Road. Perhaps Witcher brought this to see if he could reap some more havoc, but it was never unlimbered. The 71st NYSNG was relieved by the 11th a short while later. "As we retired in full sight of the rebels, the rascals yelled at us, and gave us several volleys," recalled a man of the 71st, "from which it is wonderful that every man escaped." Zacheus Bowman, who watched the skirmish from his attic between the two lines and heard bullets spatter against the walls of his home, recorded that the Confederates remained in position for over an hour before retiring with the gun and its crew. "After the rebels fell back," recalled Bowman, "the New Yorkers were as thick as hawks."[341]

Jenkins's Reconnaissance

Jenkins, with three of Ewell's engineers—Captain Henry B. Richardson, Major John J. Clark and Captain Samuel R. Johnson—and their escort, Company D, 14th Virginia, led by Lieutenant Hermann Schuricht, had meanwhile conducted a successful reconnaissance. The group of about sixty had trotted south on St. John's Church Road from the Peace Church and ascended the slope of Slate Hill. They did not tarry long before selecting a place near the crest from which they carefully observed Harrisburg and its defenses.[342]

The brigadier and his entourage then proceeded down the hill on the Lisburn Road and were unknowingly observed by fourteen-year-old William L. Gorgas, who was on the roof of his father's nearby home. After they had proceeded about a half mile from Slate Hill, they emerged from "a bunch of woods in the southwest corner of the farm then owned by Martin Zimmerman," observed Gorgas, who was particularly intrigued that the group "was in sight and within three quarters of a mile of our picket cavalry near Cedar Spring [Run]…This body was, in an air line, within three and one-half miles of Harrisburg." After fifteen minutes of observation and discussion, Jenkins and company left their observation post at the northern base of Slate Hill and turned back to the Peace Church, where Gorgas watched Griffin's battery pound away at the Yankee positions. "The flash and smoke of the cannon were plainly seen by me from the roof of my father's house," recalled Gorgas, who was ordered off the roof by his father, who feared young William might make the house a target.[343] Jenkins sent back word of his reconnaissance to Ewell at Carlisle.

This modern photograph, taken from Jenkins's approximate location while on Slate Hill, shows approximately his field of vision. Removing the non-historic trees and large postwar buildings provides a fair view of Bridgeport Heights and Harrisburg, also considering that Jenkins would have had field glasses at his disposal. *Photo by the author.*

"Jenkins' report of the 29th was encouraging," wrote Lee biographer Douglas Southall Freeman. "The new month must yield a new prize," reasoned Freeman, "the handsomest the Confederacy yet had won." Harrisburg, according to Freeman, was the "new prize" he spoke of.[344] Marching orders were issued, and shortly before 1:00 p.m., the men of Rodes's division lined Carlisle's streets prepared to march for Harrisburg. "All was redy [sic] to march," penned Lieutenant James E. Green of the 53rd North Carolina. "[We] had taken down our Blankets and [were] in line, and the orders was countermanded, so we put up our Blankets again and Remained here till Morning."[345] Ewell had received urgent orders from Lee to join the rest of the army at Cashtown, eight miles from Gettysburg.[346]

EWELL LEAVES CARLISLE

Shortly before 6:00 a.m. the following morning, Ewell with Rodes's division began the march southward on the Baltimore Pike. After proceeding about six miles south of Carlisle, the column came to the Kempton and Mullen Paper Mill in Mount Holly (also known as Papertown). Mr. Mullen, who was present, did not seem pleased at his $5,000 sale of forms and letter paper to General Ewell himself, perhaps considering that Ewell gave him a Confederate requisition. Crossing the South Mountain into Adams County, the column halted at Heidlersburg for the night after a march of some twenty miles.[347]

The last part of Ewell's corps to leave Carlisle was Bond's Company A, 1st Maryland Cavalry, which was under orders to "remain in Carlisle until two hours after the last of the troops had left, then to release one thousand prisoners who were under guard in the market-house, and to overtake the army and report." However, Bond's company scarcely mustered one hundred men. As he wrote, it "became very interesting when they realized that there were but one hundred cavalrymen to hold them in check. I remember I thought of Cortez in the City of Mexico with Montezuma as his prisoner, and felt that I was in for a worse fix." When a conflict "seemed inevitable," Bond announced that, if attacked, he would "retaliate to the utmost." Many of the older prisoners "counseled peace" and allowed Bond to "depart in peace[.]"[348]

Chapter 10

The Battle of Sporting Hill

In Tommy Oyster's house on the morning of June 30, the men of Company F of the 33rd PVM found their situation quite disturbing; their gray-clad counterparts had not fired a single shot all morning. Several scouts found the courage to steal down the pike and discovered, to their astonishment, that the Confederates were gone. A farmer proceeding east on the turnpike spoke to several men in the company: "I guess them graybacks are going back home. There seems to be a lot of them marching off down the road." Mounted scouts were sent down the road, and it was confirmed—the Confederates were no longer in their front.[349]

Couch learned in the early hours of June 30 that Ewell had retired from Carlisle, a fact then unknown to Ewell's subordinate, General Jenkins. "Scouts report a force of rebels having left Carlisle this morning by the Baltimore pike," the major general telegraphed Secretary of War Stanton.[350] Couch directed Baldy Smith to organize a reconnaissance to find and cut off Jenkins's line of retreat to Carlisle.[351] Leading the reconnaissance would be the New York brigade of John Ewen.

A New York native, Ewen trained in the art of a civil engineer and worked in many different engineering positions. He was a strong Democrat, save his vote and ardent support of Lincoln in the 1860 election. In 1836, he began his militia career when he was elected lieutenant colonel of the 8th Regiment and, in 1847, brigadier general of militia.[352] Very few had confidence in the fifty-plus-year-old brigadier—including Baldy Smith, who issued orders directly to Ewen's regimental commanders, bypassing and showing his distrust of Ewen.[353] While Ewen had never seen a battle before, he was eager to lead men and prove himself, though he did neither well.

Ewen received orders early on the morning of June 30 to reconnoiter out the Carlisle Pike, and, if possible, locate, engage and cut off Jenkins's cavalry. After some haggling with Smith, Ewen gave the orders to two of his regiments—the 22nd and 37th NYSNG—to prepare to march after their breakfast of hard tack and a little fat pork. Showing a not-so-subtle hint of leniency, Ewen decreed any man who felt unable to march was invited to drop out and report to the surgeon, though none did. Ewen's order also stated that they would march with only their canteens, arms and ammunition and no haversacks, an order that would draw more postwar controversy than Ewen's poor performance in the battle to come. "If he had possessed any practical experience," complained New Yorker George Wingate, "he would have at least required his men to carry their haversacks[.]" This subsequently cost the New Yorkers their lunch and dinner or, as Wingate termed missing the latter, "great suffering."

By 10:30 a.m., the brigade (the 37th leading) began its march, one mile along the Susquehanna from Bridgeport Station and then up Bridgeport Heights, where they halted momentarily at Baldy Smith's headquarters. There, Smith joined the column, along with Pennsylvania Railroad engineer John A. Wilson, who had been busy working on the fortifications, and Curtin's aide, Colonel Thomas Scott. The column continued through the fields over Bridgeport Heights to its southern side, where it joined the Carlisle Pike and marched to Oyster's Point. After noting the brick Oyster's Point Tavern with especial notice, the column proceeded another mile to the W. Stephen clover field, immediately west of the Albright House.

Here the New Yorkers formed into line of battle, laid down in their places in line and dispatched Lieutenant Frank Stanwood's cavalry detachment to go forward and find Jenkins's brigade. They had been there slightly longer than an hour when Smith decided to return to Bridgeport and ordered Ewen to follow him. It was now about 1:00 p.m. Ewen's men got a drink from a nearby well and made the return march singing merrily, knowing they would be in camp in time for dinner. "The men were in fine spirits," penned Private Murray. It appeared as if their work for the day was done.[354]

JENKINS AT SILVER SPRING CREEK

Meanwhile, Jenkins had gathered his forces around Silver Spring Creek, about two miles west of Sporting Hill. Jenkins's main body on the Trindle Springs Road retired west of Mechanicsburg shortly before 10:00 a.m., assuming positions west of Silver Spring Creek.[355] Witcher did the same on the pike. By one account, the Confederates retired "with so much precipitancy that in some cases provisions had been left uncooked," and their artillery "had gone through Mechanicsburg at a fast trot."[356]

Silver Spring Creek was perfect for Jenkins's purpose on June 30, which was to conceal his brigade, as he, oblivious to Ewell's leaving Carlisle, expected the advance on Harrisburg to occur later that day. The creek also offered a good water source for both men and their mounts. Jenkins enjoyed a strategic view of the vicinity from an overlooking bluff about six hundred yards east of the creek, where the Salem Church is situated. He posted his main picket line near the church. An advance picket post was situated with its headquarters at the Henry Snavely home two miles distant on the western edge of Sporting Hill, and pickets were stationed in Snavely's Woods, which surrounded the home.[357] Jenkins placed his remaining men in bivouac via detachments on the sides of the pike, all in the vicinity of Silver Spring Creek.[358]

From the outpost in Snavely's Woods, men were detached to scout the nearby area. Shortly before noon, a corporal and five men under his command came into the outpost and declared "that he and his men had scouted into within full sight of Harrisburg." The Confederate officer who commanded the outpost "knew that the man told the truth, but nobody else would believe that any human being dared to do such a thing, or could do it." To prove this was correct, this Southern officer and Charles Leland, a member of Landis's battery, met after the war. Leland had seen men scouting the defenses, which "fully prove that it was done."[359]

A large contingent of Jenkins's Confederates occupied the twenty-six acres of grass belonging to Daniel Coble west of the mouth of the Silver Spring Creek and immediately north of the Conodoguinet. Coble's heirs later filed a damage claim, citing twenty-six acres of destroyed grass at $5 per acre, one hundred panels of fence at seventy-five cents each and two acres of wheat and oats for $10 an acre—a total of $225 of damage caused by Jenkins's cavalrymen.[360]

Jenkins and his men enjoyed the respite at Silver Spring Creek, namely because they did not have any plans other than to watch, and perhaps assist, Ewell's infantry attack Harrisburg.[361] Jenkins dispatched many foraging parties that day. Postwar claims for items taken by Jenkins's brigade, mostly stolen horses or crops, spiked rapidly on June 30 in Silver Springs Township, the area west of Silver Springs Creek. This also demonstrates truly how spread out the brigade was on June 30. Jenkins's men were seen north of the Conodoguinet Creek in several places and were reported as far south as the Zacharias Dietz farm, about two miles north of Mechanicsburg. Using the latter information, Jenkins's line—camps, skirmishers and foragers—was about two and a half miles in length.[362] This for a brigade that one Virginian claimed "by reason of detachments and details as scouts and couriers for the infantry…did not number more than five hundred effective men" by June 30, namely due to the fact that the 14th Virginia had been sent back to Carlisle when Jenkins finally learned that Ewell had vacated that city.[363]

Until around noon, Jenkins was in the dark that Ewell had left Carlisle and still expected the attack on Harrisburg that day. Ewell had apparently forgotten to inform his cavalry brigadier. Jenkins could not have been a decoy, considering he went to great lengths to conceal his brigade. The few postwar writings of Jenkins's Virginians stress that they had no idea Ewell was not in Carlisle. But the Yankees did.[364]

The Opening Salvo

Ewen had passed Church Street in White Hall on his return march to Bridgeport when the brigade met a section of Captain Henry Landis's Philadelphia Battery, which had just now arrived to support the brigade. Private Murray of the 22nd noted that they were a "gentlemanly looking and well behaved company." The Philadelphians were informed the reconnaissance was over and told to return to the fort. Scarcely had Ewen resumed his march when he spotted an out-of-breath Lieutenant Stanwood galloping down the pike to overtake the column. Ewen then realized that he had forgotten to notify Stanwood of his return to Bridgeport. The young lieutenant had continued west, where he encountered Southern pickets on the western edge of Sporting Hill. After clearing an abrupt northwest turn in the direction of the pike, Confederate pickets in and about Snavely's Woods on Sporting Hill's western edge opened a sharp fire on the Pennsylvanians, causing them to beat a hasty retreat until they met Ewen at White Hall.[365]

Ewen had a significant decision to make. Smith's orders dictated he return to Bridgeport, but the situation had changed—he now knew where Jenkins was. The New York brigadier called upon a promising twenty-five-year-old artillery lieutenant on Smith's staff, Lieutenant Rufus King Jr., son of the Northern general. Ewen and King spoke for a short time, and King stressed his opinion that, considering it was only around 1:00 p.m., there was plenty of daylight left, enough to organize an attack against Jenkins. "Gen Ewen…

rode along our line talking to the men," recorded Murray, "saying that we ought to return and try to find the enemy and that it was the opinion of the chief of artillery [King] that we should do so."[366]

"Some of the 37th groaned at the Gen'l," continued Murray, "we kept quiet and felt pretty displeased at Gen Ewen because he would not permit us to get back to our quarters, having been away about four hours, hungry[.]" Ewen gave a short speech wanting of inspiration, stating that "the eyes of the country and the state of New York were upon us," and the column about-faced and proceeded west on the Carlisle Pike after Ewen sent a courier informing Smith of his movements. The New Yorkers now looked to defeating Jenkins's cavalry—whose commander at this time was all but composed.[367]

When studying the military career of Albert Jenkins, there are many panicky moments, such as when he retreated from Chambersburg on June 17, fearful for no solid reason of a Yankee advance, and cost the Rebel vanguard precious days in its advance on Harrisburg. On June 30, he was having yet another fright. Somehow the Southern brigadier had got the idea that a force of 10,000-plus men under Couch was coming out of Harrisburg to hunt him down. Jenkins, however, should be commended for the way he interpreted exactly what the Yankees, though only 1,400 in number, were plotting—to cut him off. Because his men were spread out in detachments over the surrounding country, if a determined Union effort broke through his picket lines (which it surely would), his brigade could be picked apart piece by piece. Jenkins determined to send a small force to hold off the Federal attackers as long as possible while he concentrated his brigade. Making matters worse, he had just recently learned Ewell was not in Carlisle. He sent the 14th Virginia galloping to that town to guard his rear.

To fend off the Yankees, he sought Lieutenant Colonel Witcher and his 34th Virginia, who, with Jackson's battery, were detached and personally ordered by Jenkins to "hold the enemy in check at all hazards."[368] Witcher rode forward with his nearly four hundred men to face off against what he thought was a Federal force of numbers he could only imagine.

EWEN MEETS WITCHER AT SPORTING HILL

Shortly after 3:00 p.m., the men of Ewen's brigade marched west up the eastern slope of Sporting Hill on the pike. As they passed by the farm of Samuel Eberly, they could discern puffs of smoke and soon heard bullets whiz over their heads from Moses Eberly's large Dutch barn.[369] Witcher's skirmishers had loopholed the stone-based, wooden barn and would prove themselves a considerable menace to the New Yorkers throughout the coming battle. Witcher, with the majority of his force, remained about five hundred yards farther back in a wood known as Gleim's Grove. The New Yorkers quickly fell to their knees at the command of their officers. The Battle of Sporting Hill had begun.[370]

The baffled Ewen was able to deploy skirmishers, advancing about two hundred yards to within several hundred yards of Eberly's barn.[371] But that was all. Here Ewen made his first of many mistakes in the battle. He left his column in place, with no orders, for about ten minutes, with only skirmishers facing northwest toward the barn. Witcher, meanwhile, was always one to take advantage of such an incredulous opportunity—Ewen, he joyfully realized, had left his left flank open.

Lieutenant King was at the crest of Sporting Hill with Ewen, observing Rebel movements. The group spotted a party of enemy skirmishers cross the pike and deploy in Snavely's Woods, a dense, extensive wood opposite

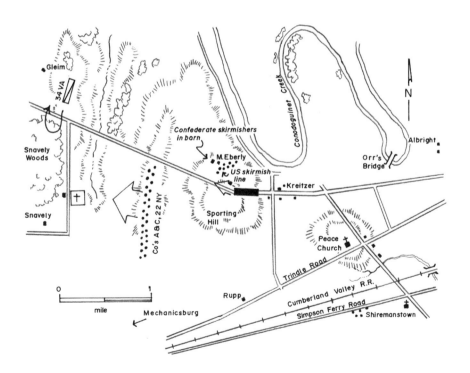

The opening phase of the Battle of Sporting Hill. *Map by John Heiser.*

Gleim's Grove. Ewen either failed to notice it or thought nothing of it. King, however, recognized that the brigade would soon be flanked if the Southerners were allowed to proceed unopposed. On his own responsibility, the young lieutenant detached Companies A and C of the 22nd and ordered them to "seize and hold" Snavely's Woods.[372]

Captain James Otis of Company A led the companies in skirmishing order across Samuel Eberly's wheat field south of the pike by example. "[T]he gallant Capt nerveless and sword in hand led his company in fine style over the fences and Through two wheatfields upon the woods," recalled Private Murray of Company A. Looking back, Otis's men could see that the "eyes of both the 37th and 22nd were upon us." Upon reaching the woods, the Confederates had already cleared out and returned to Gleim's Grove.

As the New Yorkers entered the wood, they spotted a farmer, who turned out to be Henry Snavely. The New Yorkers ordered him to halt. Upon questioning, Snavely told the militiamen in great detail of the picket fight that had occurred between the Rebel pickets in his woods and Stanwood's cavalry and "freely took" the Oath of Allegiance, which was offered him by Captain Otis. He then promised to bring the soldiers bread and milk. After meeting Snavely, Otis set to work deploying his company. In order to be best hidden from the Rebels, Otis ordered his men to lie on their faces and deployed several scouts from his company, whom he placed behind the trees of Snavely's dense wood.[373]

Ewen Waffles to Action

Here ended the first phase of the battle. It was now about 4:00 p.m., and Ewen decided to file his brigade out of column in the pike. South of the pike, he deployed Colonel Lloyd Aspinwall and four companies of his 22nd NYSNG. North of the pike, the other three companies of the 22nd were deployed under command of Major James Cox, along with the 37th.[374]

The first to advance were Aspinwall's four companies. Aspinwall formed his troops on the eastern edge of Samuel Eberly's wheat field, mustering about two hundred men. Either Aspinwall must have forgotten the lessons he learned during his time as an aide with the Army of the Potomac in Virginia or Ewen placed the companies there, as they faced directly west and had their flank about as exposed as possible to the Southern skirmishers in the barn, fewer than four hundred yards distant. Luckily for the New Yorkers, they were in a wheat field, where Aspinwall ordered them to lie down, as the fire coming in on their flank was "becoming warm."[375]

Even while Aspinwall's men took this "warm" fire, Ewen reported that he held the companies in reserve. This would logically mean Ewen considered Aspinwall a reserve for Otis in Snavely's Woods. Ewen had dispatched an officer to a small knoll in Samuel Eberly's wheat field, halfway between Otis and Aspinwall, specifically for communication between the two and reports on the movements of Witcher in Gleim's Grove. Most likely, Ewen was concerned about having a reserve for Otis's two companies so as to guard against a flank attack on that sector of which he seemed to be petrified. Still, the New Yorkers sustained no casualties.[376]

The next advance was a joint movement involving all thirteen companies north of the pike. The terrain in front of them included a small ridge, Eberly's Ridge, on the crest and western slope of which was a wheat field slightly fewer than three hundred yards distant from Moses Eberly's barn. "As the leading files came over the brow of the hill," recalled one New Yorker, "a severe fire was opened upon them[.]" Third Corporal Bowles Colgate, in Company G of the 22nd, was wounded in the neck, as was Second Lieutenant William C. Abbe of Company F, 37th NYSNG, and Thomas L. Wiswall, the drummer

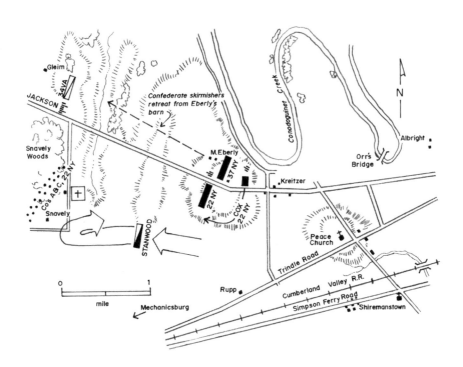

The second and third phases of the Battle of Sporting Hill. *Map by John Heiser.*

A modern overhead view showing the remains of the Moses Eberly barn. *Photo by the author.*

A 1975 photograph of the Moses Eberly barn before the upper structure was destroyed by a minor tornado in 1976. *Courtesy of G. Craig Caba.*

boy of Company H in the 37th, who received a flesh wound in the calf. Cox's three companies scurried to the crest of the ridge, where they lay down and took cover. However, the men of the 37th refused to advance, hugging their chests as close to the ground as possible.[377]

Ewen ordered the 37th to "rise and deploy forward" about thirty yards through the wheat field to the base of Eberly's Ridge, where a post-and-rail fence would provide cover. The 37th refused to budge. A flustered Ewen sent Major J. Henderson Grant of his staff to order Company I of the 22nd to "compel" the 37th using force, bayonets if necessary. Catching wind of this, the 37th hastily obeyed, moving to the bottom of the ridge and taking cover behind the fence.[378]

Thus far, the Yankees had been befuddled by Witcher's numerically inferior force. While Ewen's force did not number anywhere near the 10,000-plus Jenkins supposed, the New York brigadier still mustered a substantial force of 1,400 men, compared to Witcher's 400. However, Ewen had not yet been able to get the 50-some Southern skirmishers out of the Moses Eberly barn, and until he could, the battle would not progress favorably to the Yankee cause.[379]

Jackson's Artillery Takes Center Stage

"This was the position of affairs for about half an hour," reported one witness. Soon a "louder explosion than had yet occurred was heard in the distance, and whirr came a shell directly over our skirmishers, and over the [Cox's] battalion, and exploded just beyond—a beautiful line shot, but a little too high." This sudden artillery fire panicked Cox's New Yorkers, especially when two round shots followed. "Things began to look serious," recalled one, considering Ewen was powerless to respond to Witcher's artillery. Cox's men could take it no longer and began to flee to the south of the pike, where they rallied on Aspinwall's left.[380]

After rallying south of the pike, Cox's men were under orders to advance but made no serious attempt to do so. Apparently Stanwood's cavalry was to advance as well, as it was soon spotted by Otis's men moving along Henry Snavely's farm lane toward Gleim's Grove when Jackson's battery got wind of its move. The Kanawha Artillerymen targeted the Pennsylvania cavalrymen and yanked the lanyard. "Our cavalry wheeled their horses and galloped back from whence they came," observed Private Murray, one of Otis's men. The sight was quite unnerving. Otis's New Yorkers (or at least the enlisted men) had not known that the Rebels were only several hundred yards distant to their right front in Gleim's Grove. "This was a sight for us," penned Murray, "and we laid very quiet."[381] Witcher truly showed his curiosity in Snavely's Woods when he sent a mounted scout to reconnoiter, which was observed by Murray: "We saw one of the Rebels on a fine Horse with his gray uniform on ride boldly out and follow them [Stanwood's cavalry] some distance when he quickly turned back again and disappeared among the trees…this was the first rebel in arms we had seen."[382]

Witcher began concentrating his two artillery pieces on Snavely's Woods. "We could see these men also in gray moving around and smoke rising as if they were cooking," noted Murray. They were cooking up a storm of shells, Murray and his comrades would soon learn. Jackson's artillerymen either could not depress the muzzles of their pieces enough or their aim was off because the damage was limited to tree branches that fell on the men. Some of Otis's men even fell asleep, testifying to the feebleness of the fire. During the period when the Southern focus was concentrated on Snavely's Woods, Captain Otis kept his two companies under strict orders not to fire or in any way give away their position, notwithstanding that the Confederates already knew their position. Witcher also ordered skirmish fire on the two companies, which resulted in no casualties, but one shot came close enough to knock the sight off the rifle of Private William Deere of Company A. Finding his efforts fruitless, Witcher turned his attention elsewhere.[383]

Jackson's fire became sporadic, with no one apparent target in mind. He began aiming at Aspinwall's line—now seven companies strong—in the wheat field. "Our men behaved nobly, not flinching in the least," boasted the *New York Times* correspondent. "A number of shot struck directly in their front, but without causing a panic or doing any great amount of injury." The majority of shells passed over the line, tearing up the ground but completely harmless to the 22nd. Switching his aim to the Yankees north of the pike, Jackson sent one shell into the midst of the 37th, wounding two, one of whom "received a shell scratch from a piece of shell over the eye." In total, the casualties from this sporadic fire totaled one officer and seven enlisted men: two from the 37th and six from Aspinwall's seven companies.[384]

YANKEE ARTILLERY ARRIVES

Baldy Smith could hear the artillery firing from his headquarters at Bridgeport.[385] To assist the embattled Ewen, about 4:00 p.m., Smith dispatched Landis's battery, which had returned to the fort after it was informed that the reconnaissance was over earlier in the day. Shortly after 5:00 p.m., Ewen's men could hear the distant rumbling of artillery wheels. Appearing "around a bend in the road" galloped First Lieutenant Samuel Clarke Perkins's first section, the men getting a free ride on the guns and caissons.[386]

Major Cox of the 22nd tossed his hat in midair with delight. "It was with the utmost difficulty that the men could be kept from cheering," reported one witness. The jubilant New York guardsmen were eventually silenced by their officers after the first round was fired so as not to give away their position to the Confederates.[387] As the Philadelphians galloped to the scene, they passed several slightly wounded New Yorkers limping to the brigade field hospital, the Kreitzer barn—part of the hamlet of several buildings at the intersection of Sporting Hill Road and Carlisle Pike—where brigade surgeons Major Henry W.B. Woodhull and Major Charles Inslee Pardee assured several concerned infantrymen that their wounds were only slight and would not prove mortal.[388]

Lieutenant King ordered Perkins to post his section of two three-inch ordnance rifles in the center of Ewen's line. Perkins posted his guns according to King's direction, the first piece unlimbering on a small knoll in Samuel Eberly's cornfield to the right rear of his barn. The second piece would unlimber several minutes later.[389]

This was the first time the Philadelphians had ever attempted to fire their pieces. As Lieutenant King rode past the first piece, he noted that they were loading the shell fuse first. King quickly dismounted to correct them. King, who had worked with the well-meaning but amateur artillerymen the past several days, explained that loading the shell fuse first, or practically backward, would greatly increase the possibility of premature explosion. The young lieutenant also schooled them on the practice of cutting the fuses, loading the projectile and "such other instructions." King hoped his short artillery lesson would provide results. "[T]he first shell burst in the barn with such effect," recalled an eyewitness, "that instantly its two great doors were swung open and a swarm of Confederate skirmishers came rushing out and made for the woods [Gleim's Grove]."[390] It had taken nearly two hours, but Ewen's 1,400 men had finally managed to force 50 Confederate skirmishers out of Moses Eberly's barn.

The engagement then settled into an artillery duel. Perkins's second piece unlimbered in the center of the Carlisle Pike, almost directly south of the recently abandoned Moses Eberly barn. By most accounts, the artillery duel did not last long. Perkins ably directed his pieces as they continued to "rapidly" exchange fire with Jackson. In Harrisburg, the "reports of the cannon were distinctly heard at several points." At first, the duel was more a

A sketch by Corporal George Wingate of the 22nd NYSNG, showing the first shot fired by Landis's battery at Sporting Hill. *From* History of the Twenty-Second Regiment, *1896.*

contest of who could fire the fastest, but it soon became a contest of aim. One citizen "direct from Mechanicsburg" recalled the fire as "fierce." Another bystander wrote that "the firing was kept up quite briskly for some time." Jackson's weary gunners fell behind, perhaps due to ammunition shortages, and soon enough Perkins's fire blistered Gleim's Grove.[391]

Half an hour into the artillery duel, it was nearing 6:00 p.m. One of Perkins's shells fell among Witcher's soldiers in Gleim's Grove and burst, wounding several. Witcher had seen enough. He hastily ordered his wounded into ambulances, mounted the rest of his men and limbered his two artillery pieces.[392] The Yankees sustained no casualties during this exchange, and only eleven wounded men were counted: eight from artillery fire prior to Perkins's arrival and three from small-arms fire on Eberly's Ridge. These casualties were not troublesome; the most severe wounds from Jackson's artillery were "a slight scratch from a piece of shell over the eye" and, in another case, a wound in the hand. A wide range of numbers is available in relation to the Confederate casualties at Sporting Hill—no definitive number has and likely ever will be disclosed, considering Witcher never filed an official report. The general consensus is around fifteen killed—who were left on the field and buried by a local farmer—and twenty to thirty wounded, four or five of those mortally. Several unmarked graves were found along the roadside on the way to Carlisle several days later. The Confederate dead left on the field were originally buried about one hundred yards west of the Moses Eberly barn until they were reinterred in 1895 at the Washington Confederate Cemetery in Hagerstown, Maryland.[393]

Schuricht's Scrap at Mechanicsburg

Just as Witcher was withdrawing from Sporting Hill, artillery fire was heard to the south. "[T]here were several discharges of artillery on our left," reported Ewen, "demonstrating the existence of a body of the enemy in that direction." Ewen believed he was flanked. "[E]xpecting an immediate attack from that quarter," the New York brigadier refused the flank of Aspinwall's force "to be in readiness to meet and repel it."[394] Further contributing to Ewen's anxiety were reports from Aspinwall's men that the unknown force on the left showed itself by "a few cavalry," notwithstanding these elusive cavalrymen were probably some of Stanwood's cavalry that had skedaddled earlier or all in the minds of the nervous New Yorkers.[395]

This menacing force was German First Lieutenant Hermann Schuricht with Company D, 14th Virginia Cavalry, and one piece of Jackson's battery. Jenkins had ordered Schuricht, with his company, to report to his headquarters. Once there, the Confederate brigadier directed him to "proceed at once with my company and one cannon of Jackson's Battery to Mechanicsburg, to hold this town until ordered otherwise, and to destroy the railroad track as far as possible." This duty flattered Schuricht. "To be entrusted with an expedition, properly belonging to an officer of higher rank," was an honor, he wrote. As Schuricht came within sight of Mechanicsburg, he dispatched patrols to reconnoiter the area.[396]

Frank Murray's Curtin Guards had been operating in the vicinity for the past several days. Shortly after 10:00 a.m., Murray trotted into Mechanicsburg and, finding the town unoccupied, recaptured it but went no farther. Schuricht, his company, Captain Thomas E. Jackson of the Kanawha Artillery and a piece from his battery rode to Mechanicsburg. As Schuricht approached, Murray retreated. Schuricht subsequently passed through Mechanicsburg "without delay," and the town appeared to Schuricht "to be evacuated by the inhabitants; they all kept indoors." The German immigrant advanced to "an elevation east of the town," near where the Trindle Road is crossed by the Cumberland Valley Railroad. After posting pickets nearby, Schuricht ordered his men to demolish the tracks.[397]

Murray had other ideas in mind. He continuously interrupted Schuricht's demolition by advancing frequently from nearby cover and skirmishing with Schuricht. The German immigrant complained that he had to keep up "a lively skirmish all day." Despite Murray's best efforts, Schuricht's men continued to destroy the tracks. However, Schuricht soon "observed many and demonstrative people in the woods some distance to our right [south], and I ordered Lieutenant [Captain Thomas] Jackson to warn them off by some shots." These "demonstrative people" were actually local farmers who had been watching Schuricht and Murray scrapple with each other. Schuricht's fire "chased out" one of the bystanders, who was captured by Schuricht's company and was so frightened that he reportedly died afterward. While this was occurring, Schuricht heard artillery firing from Sporting Hill and, apparently not aware of the battle in progress there, believed he was flanked. The German received orders as Witcher retired to "leave Mechanicsburg after dark and fall back to Carlisle." Schuricht limbered his artillery and raced west on the Trindle Road to join the rest of the brigade, evidently to the citizens of Mechanicsburg "pretty badly alarmed." Schuricht was only able to tear "a few rails" and did not do significant damage.[398]

Both Ewen and Schuricht believed they were flanked. "[T]he discharges of artillery on our left," conjectured Ewen, "had evidently been designed as an intimidation to us, or a signal to the other force of the enemy to retire." The New York brigadier also claimed on the next day as his column proceeded toward Carlisle that "a farmer residing in the vicinity" had informed him "that the force on our left the preceding evening consisted of a body of about 3,500 cavalry, with field pieces." Schuricht did not have more than 70 men if Jackson and his artillery crew were included. Ewen also purported that the menace on his left was Fitz Lee's Confederate brigade that had threatened his left and alleged they pursued his rear as he marched to Carlisle the following day. The engineer-turned-general never learned the flank threat was fewer than 70 men and that they were just as frightened as he was.[399]

JENKINS RETREATS TO CARLISLE

About 2:00 p.m., Colonel James Cochran's 14th Virginia Cavalry entered Carlisle. Jenkins had sent Cochran there to secure his line of communication upon finally learning that Ewell had abandoned Carlisle around noon. "[I]t very soon became evident that they were not under the same discipline which characterized those [of Ewell's corps] which had been here," reported

Cumberland County Deputy Sherriff Simpson K. Donavin. Scarcely had they arrived when they found some liquor that Ewell's soldiers had failed to overturn. It "appeared to madden them," remarked Donavin. "They tore through the streets, cursing and yelling, and playing the demon, as demons only can play it. The feeling of safety which prevailed while Ewel's [*sic*] command was here vanished, and the entire community felt the utmost alarm." The darker it got, the more rowdy the Virginians got. Cochran, who had established his headquarters on the Dickinson College campus, was visited by several citizens pleading with him to stop the rampage of his regiment. He promised that he would carry out Ewell's orders. Although he could not entirely restrain his regiment, he managed to check the progress of the drinking.[400]

It was past midnight when the rest of Jenkins's brigade regrouped in Carlisle; Lieutenant Colonel Witcher placed the time at 1:00 a.m. Jenkins summoned his commanders to a council of war in a house in town. "It was decided," Witcher recalled, "that I should still cover the rear with two pieces of the [Griffin's] Baltimore Light Artillery, and 34th Batt. And 2 Cos. of the 36th, whilst other command threw flankers on both sides of the road." Leaving Carlisle on the Baltimore Pike, Jenkins reached the town of Petersburg, now York Springs, about 2:00 a.m. There the brigade encamped with extreme caution, horses saddled and arms "ready to hand."[401] The following day, Jenkins would proceed to Gettysburg, arriving there in the early evening hours.

REFLECTING ON SPORTING HILL

The Battle of Sporting Hill was the northernmost engagement of the Gettysburg Campaign, but it should also be an account of missed opportunities. Had Ewen constructed a faster and more efficient plan of attack, he could have swept Witcher from the field in minutes and done so with the further effect of reaping havoc on Jenkins's dispersed brigade. Instead, Ewen moved too cautiously, allowing Jenkins time to reorganize his brigade. From a tactical standpoint, Ewen, despite considerably delaying his brigade, did indeed sweep Witcher's lesser force from the field and won. But from a strategic standpoint, Witcher and Jenkins were victorious. Ewen's objective was not to push Jenkins from the Harrisburg area, because Couch already knew Jenkins was or would soon be retiring to follow Ewell's suit, but to inflict considerable damage on Jenkins's brigade. All Ewen did was inflict casualties on Jenkins and scare the living daylight out of his New Yorkers, to no strategic advantage.

Chapter 11

The Shelling of Carlisle

E wen's New Yorkers had retired to Oyster's Point, where they bivouacked in a drenching rain. Wagons had been ordered out from Bridgeport Heights, which enthused the men with the prospect of food, but orders were bumbled and the treasured nourishment was recalled and would not arrive until 2:00 a.m. By then, most of the New Yorkers were fast asleep, although a few arose to devour the provided edibles.[402] News of Ewen's partial triumph had reached Smith, who sent orders for the column to turn around and "follow up the enemy." Ewen deferred to do so, as he reported: "It was then dark. My command had had no food since breakfast, and was destitute of rations and blankets. A considerable portion had also been working in the trenches during the preceding night. I found it, therefore, impracticable to proceed until rations should be procured."[403]

HERMAN HAUPT ARRIVES

Brigadier General Herman Haupt, commander of the U.S. Military Railroad, was charged with facilitating supplies to the field armies. Considering that the Confederates had cut the Baltimore and Ohio Railroad, Haupt "concluded that the most efficient service that I could render would be to go to Harrisburg, ascertain the condition of affairs in Pennsylvania—especially the numbers and position of the forces that had been raised and then make my way across the country on foot, or horseback, and give General Meade all the information I could gather." With this in mind, the engineer-general found he could not use the Northern Central

A wartime photograph of Brigadier General Herman Haupt. *Courtesy of the Library of Congress.*

Railway, as that had been "badly injured," and therefore "was compelled to travel via Philadelphia and Reading." Late on the evening of June 30, Haupt arrived in Harrisburg. He "repaired at once to the capitol, where I found Governor Curtin and his staff. The room was filled with aides and other officers. Much confusion and excitement prevailed. I could get very little information," complained Haupt, so he asked for Colonel Scott.

Curtin's trusty aide, Scott, was "engaged in dispatching troops to protect the bridges on the Pennsylvania Railroad that had been threatened by a cavalry raid." Haupt, who was carrying orders giving him authorization "to do whatever he may deem expedient to facilitate the transportation of troops and supplies," asked Scott to "give me a full and detailed report." Scott informed Haupt that "at an early hour they [Jenkins] had commenced to retreat, and with so much precipitancy that in some cases provisions had been left uncooked; that the artillery had gone through Mechanicsburg at a fast trot." Haupt then inquired what Scott thought these movements meant. Scott's answer was unsatisfactory to Haupt. The colonel conjectured that he and the other officials had successfully deceived the Confederates that they had a force of sixty thousand men. "You are entirely in error," replied Haupt. "These movements do not mean retreat; they mean concentration. Retreat would not be made hastily with no enemy pushing; it would be done deliberately, foraging on the country on the route." Scott consented, with a "I think you are right," and a correct but somewhat arrogant Haupt answered, "I am sure I am."

At 6:00 a.m. the following morning, Haupt sent a report to General in Chief Halleck. "It appears to have been the intention of the enemy to attack Harrisburg yesterday. Our forces, supposed to be [Major General Alfred] Pleasanton's [cavalry], were resisting their movements and...actually succeeded in retarding their advance upon Harrisburg and compelled a retreat." Haupt estimated the Yankee forces in and around Harrisburg at sixteen thousand men. The engineer left Harrisburg that morning and reached Baltimore. He would spend the remainder of the campaign repairing the railroads and assisting the Army of the Potomac.[404]

SMITH MARCHES TO CARLISLE

As Baldy Smith retired on the night of June 30, he had already decided on an advance to Carlisle. As Smith recalled, he and Couch "determined that our duty was to march all the available force[s] to try and get into a position, if possible, to aid Meade in the coming battle." That morning, Smith issued orders for the march to secure the heartland of Cumberland County. Major William Boyd's nearly two-hundred-man contingent of the 1st New York Cavalry was ordered to march to Carlisle by way of Churchtown, where he halted a short while. Boyd's New Yorkers would be the first Federals to reach Carlisle on July 1, entering the county seat early that morning to much merriment before departing to reconnoiter the countryside to the west, where the Confederates were supposed to be. Boyd would not be a factor in the coming engagement.[405]

Smith had already ordered Ewen's brigade, which was now just awakening at Oyster's Point, to march to Carlisle. He turned his attention to Colonel Brisbane, commanding four Pennsylvania militia regiments—the 28th, 30th, 32nd and 33rd. Brisbane's Pennsylvanians drew three days' rations but were delayed due "to a want of transportation" and did not move until 9:00 a.m.[406]

Smith crossed the river into Harrisburg, where he visited General Couch at his headquarters in the capitol. Couch stressed the importance of advancing on Carlisle, while Smith made arrangements for supplies and transportation. Crossing over the river to Fort Washington, Smith found the garrison under General Knipe's command. He gave orders to his experienced brigadier "to march as far as practicable [toward Carlisle] and encamp, and to move at an early hour in the morning."[407] Knipe would only reach Silver Springs Creek, near Jenkins's June 30 location.[408] Smith also ordered Colonel William Barnes's 11th New York Heavy Artillery, acting as infantry, to march to Carlisle. The regiment refused to comply on grounds that it would only fight as artillery. Smith referred the troublesome New Yorkers to Curtin, Couch and Knipe, as he had no time to spare. Couch felt the unit was "of so little use" that he sent it back to New York. Smith left Bridgeport about 3:30 p.m. and hastened to Carlisle.[409]

Meanwhile, within Harrisburg, confidence and spirits rose as news of the affair at Sporting Hill spread. "[T]he Rebels will not be able to carry the entrenchments on the other side of the River[,]" Captain J. Boyd Robinson of the soon-to-be mustered-in 35th PM boasted. "Yesterday their advance was driven back some four miles." Robinson claimed that "[i]f appearances are correct and the people are prompt, two weeks from this" the rebellion would be no more.[410] While unrealistic, Robinson's letter demonstrates the confident mood in the state capital after Sporting Hill.

THE MARCH TO CARLISLE

Several hours ahead of General Smith marched his infantry. That morning, the New Yorkers of Ewen's brigade arose sore and achy. "We are a pretty rough looking lot of troops this morning," penned Private Murray. "The Gen [Ewen] ordered us to march for Carlisle after haranguing the troops like an old sailor on horseback…when the men said that they were suffering…by not being permitted to go back to Bridgeport he said that he suffered as much as they did, we however did not see it in that light as he had a horse to do his marching and plenty of friends to give him victuals."[411] The Yankee soldiers received a ration of three crackers per man. Company B of the 22nd was deployed as skirmishers, followed by Company I of the 22nd as an advance guard. The rest of the New Yorkers were not far behind. The 37th led, followed by the rest of the 22nd, and Perkins's section of Landis's battery brought up the rear. Captain Landis and the other four pieces of the battery, having only recently left Fort Washington, were doing their best to overtake the column.[412]

As the march progressed on the pike, many of the New Yorkers were astonished at how nimble their comrades were when it came to scaling cherry trees. "This country is beautiful in the extreme," raved one New Yorker. The column's pace was slow and cautious until shortly after the men passed the previous day's battlefield at Sporting Hill. After proceeding about a mile beyond, Ewen met a local farmer who informed him that the menace that had harassed his left the previous night had retired. Two miles farther, a short distance beyond Silver Spring Creek, Ewen encountered civilians in wagons on their way from Carlisle to Harrisburg, who notified him of the rapid retreat of Jenkins's brigade the night previous through Carlisle. "This information being soon after confirmed," reported Ewen, "the skirmishers were called in, enabling the column to proceed more rapidly."[413]

"The day was beautiful," wrote George Wingate of the 22nd, "though rapidly becoming too warm for comfort, and by ten o'clock it was scorching hot." He continued:

> The route lay through a most lovely country. Scarcely anywhere can the eye rest on finer scenery, more beautiful fields, more comfortable farm-houses, or more magnificent barns than those of southern Pennsylvania. But the houses were deserted, the farms pillaged, everything of value, everything that could walk, or be eaten or stolen, had been swept away by the invader, and the peaceful population were fugitives…The men of the Twenty-second were stiff, sore and far from amiable when they started, but after a short time, as the fatigue of the previous night wore off, the excitement of the coming fight began to be felt, and the echoes of song and laughter floated down the column and were taken up and re-echoed from the company to company till they died away in the distance, and "all went merry as a marriage bell"—for a time. The roads were good, the air pure, halts had been permitted, there was nothing to find fault with. The people…were as kind and hospitable as could be desired. In Hogestown…and all along the road, wherever there were occupied houses, the women turned out en masse with trays of bread and apple-butter, and buckets of cool spring water for the benefit of the troops, attention which was more appreciated from its contrast with the customs of Harrisburg.[414]

Soon, however, the march in this sultry weather, with raw, unexposed troops, would take its toll. When the soldiers halted at New Kingston about noon for "a few moments," the ladies of the small village brought them pails of water, bread, butter and much more.[415] Contributing to the later fatigue was a race between Ewen's New Yorkers and Brisbane's Pennsylvanians to be the vanguard of the column not long after they left New Kingston. Wingate recalled:

> *A regiment of Pennsylvania reserves, which had started fresh and well fed from Bridgeport that morning, and had gained on the brigade while it had been retarded by the slow progress of the skirmishers…pressed on when the rumor began to spread that Carlisle was evacuated, and, in a manner which was not considered to be consistent with either the rules of war or politeness, undertook to push their way past the* [Ewen's] *brigade "to get in ahead of the Yorkers" and win the honors of the victory from those who thought they had borne the burden and heat of the day. This did not meet with the approval of the commanding officers of the Twenty-second. When, therefore, the new-comers pushed up on the right, the head of the column gently oblique that way close up to the roadside. If they changed to the other side, a simple left oblique rendered passage on that impracticable; and when they attempted, with profound strategy, to come up on both sides, the order, "By company into line," filled the road from fence to fence with a solid front of men and bared their further progress. Then, letting down the fences, the persistent Pennsylvanians took to the field, and attempted to pass in that manner. At the sight of this a wild cry of "double quick" went up from the rear to the front of the column, and, breaking into a "double," the brigade swept on for half a mile, leaving its competitors far in its rear, whence they never emerged to trouble it.[416]*

"Our men felt it not only mean," reported Colonel Aspinwall of the 22nd, "but insulting to be thus treated, and at once struck the 'double quick,' which they would have kept up so long as breath lasted, had I not ordered them to take the route step." Brisbane's Pennsylvanians were not alone in their efforts to take the vanguard. The 22nd also made a run at passing its fellow New Yorkers in the 37th, forcing Roome's guardsmen to move at the double-quick. This brief contest of honor and who could outpace whom soon made painfully evident the effects of marching on such a sultry day. "After the skirmishers were called in [near Silver Spring Creek]," recalled Wingate, "the march had been rapid. It now became forced. That meant, in this instance, a march where speed is such an object that everything must be disregarded, and well, or ill, suffering or not, 'the men must push on.'"[417]

Colonel Lloyd Aspinwall of the 22nd NYSNG. Aspinwall was a staff officer with the Army of the Potomac during the Battle of Fredericksburg. *Courtesy of the MOLLUS-MASS Collection, U.S. Army Military History Institute.*

After clearing New Kingston, the column—totaling six regiments and Landis's battery—did not halt to rest again until they reached Carlisle. The total distance of the march being about fifteen miles, this stretch consisted of nearly seven miles. "It was a very warm and sultry day and we had several thunder storms," reminisced Private Robert Welsh of the 33rd PVM. "Between them the sun came out scorching and there being no breeze we suffered exceedingly. In addition, the red clay soil was ankle deep with mud, which clung like glue."[418]

"The sun now beating down with the sultry heat of an extremely hot July day," detailed Wingate. "[N]o shade, no water, no rest; no complaining now, but men dropping out with frightful rapidity…On every side one would see men flush, breathe hard, stagger to the side of the road and drop almost senseless; but still the column went on, many with feet so blistered that they hobbled rather than marched."[419] As the column crested one of the many hills along the route, the entire left wing of the 37th halted and refused to budge. "It would have been well if the whole brigade had followed their example," later reflected Wingate, but the officers of the 37th soon ushered the men onward.[420] Corporal C. Stuart Patterson of Landis's battery, who was fortunate enough to ride a horse to Carlisle, later wrote:

> *What a ride it must have been for the unfortunates who sat on the limbers and caissons, I can well imagine, for my experience on parade in the city some months before had made me feel forcibly that I could wish my bitterest enemy no worse fate than to ride on a caisson when the horses were trotting. But one of our comrades was the most unfortunate...Charles S. Leland, unable to find room on limber or caisson, had, with admirable fortitude, seated himself astride of a gun in the way that sailors are popularly supposed to ride a horse—with his back turned in the direction the column was moving and his arms clasped round the piece; every jot (and they were not few nor far between) sent him up about three feet, and, most unluckily for him, the law of gravitation did not fail to operate, and consequently he would descend upon his hard steel saddler with a force that would have drawn from most men with some other expression that the German air which he continued to hum with the most unbroken good humor.*[421]

Colonel Roome of the 37th gave out early and followed his command in a wagon. Many other officers followed suit. For the average enlisted men who fell out with exhaustion, wagons followed the column to transport them to Carlisle. But as the wagons became crowded, many were left by the roadside or were taken into the nearby homes.[422] A *New York Tribune* correspondent accompanying the column reported: "In company with a corporal and four privates, I was detailed to act as rear guard, and pick up stragglers; and it was awful to see the boys drop out by the roadside, and lie there, too sick to move. In all cases they were taken into the nearest inhabited houses, the inhabitants of which were very hospitable."[423]

About 4:00 p.m., the column finally neared within a mile of Carlisle. "I was determined that if any honor attached to being the first to occupy an evacuated town," wrote Colonel Aspinwall, "those who have bean [*sic*] in the advance when the enemy were to be attacked should be in front now, and I instructed the advance guard to push forward and enter the town at once[.]" The advance guard, Captain Asa Bird Gardiner and Company I, entered the town and reported it unoccupied. "The first men in Carlisle were of

A wartime photograph of Colonel Charles Roome of the 37th NYSNG. Roome, president of the Manhattan Gas Company and later a brevet brigadier general, remained a well-known citizen of New York City until his death in 1890. *Courtesy of the U.S. Army Military History Institute.*

the Twenty-second regiment," boasted Aspinwall, "and the first Stars and Stripes raised over that place was by a member of my command." General Ewen rode up and ordered the column to halt on the outskirts of town to give the stragglers time to overtake the brigade. "When the colors of the [22nd] regiment arrived," recorded Private Murray, "there were few of the command with them." Wingate claimed that only three hundred men of Ewen's brigade were in the ranks upon arriving at Carlisle. Ewen's officers rode back and forth, cursing the stragglers for their slow pace. Captains and other field officers complained that they had too few in their company. The straggling was less severe among Brisbane's Pennsylvania regiments, who had meanwhile halted in a "nice woods" behind Ewen's New Yorkers. Soon the weary troops marched into Carlisle.[424]

"The reception of the troops at Carlisle was all that could be expected from a patriotic people welcoming those who had been delivered them from a detested enemy," remarked Wingate. "The hurrahs of the men, the smiles and waving handkerchiefs of the ladies, made all forget their privations, and feel that they were engaged in a sacred cause." Tables with foods of all kinds were spread in the town square in front of the courthouse, piled high with bread and butter, "smoking hot" coffee, stacks of sandwiches, ham, apple butter and much more. The men of Carlisle brought hay, oats and water for the horses. It was a merry time, not only for the soldiers—who had to deal no more with gloomy Harrisburg—but also for the citizens of Carlisle, who were finally free of enemy rule.[425]

Around 6:00 p.m., a report came in that the Confederates were returning to Carlisle. Ewen, then senior officer in town, ordered his brigade about a mile and a half south of town on the Baltimore Pike. Carlisle residents gave "uproarious cheers" to the departing militiamen; however, General Ewen hastily stopped the ruckus, asking the cause for "this ridiculous…habit of cheering." Nevertheless, his men felt "refreshed and almost as good as new." Reaching the crest of a hill that "overlooked a broad valley and the main [Baltimore] Road," the first section of Landis's battery, under Lieutenant King, unlimbered with the 22nd and 37th as supports in their rear. Even though most of the exhausted men expected an engagement momentarily, almost three-quarters took this opportunity for slumber.[426]

About 6:30 p.m., Baldy Smith and staff galloped into Carlisle, the general clad in a gray walking suit and "looking more like a country gentleman riding out to inspect his farm." Smith, learning from Brisbane of Ewen's departure, immediately set out to see his untrusted brigadier. Smith was cheered as he left town in his carriage but "paid no attention to the compliment." As he neared Ewen's line, he "was overtaken by an orderly belonging to a company of regular cavalry…who reported that a large force of Confederate cavalry had come in behind them [from the east], capturing some, but had halted on seeing our soldiers in the town." Smith immediately sent orders for Ewen to return to the town and did so himself.[427]

JEB STUART ARRIVES

More Confederates indeed were heading for Carlisle, but they were not from Jenkins's or Ewell's departing columns. Back on June 22, Robert E. Lee had instructed cavalry commander Jeb Stuart to guard the mountain passes with part of his force while the Army of Northern Virginia was still south of the Potomac and then cross river and screen Ewell's right flank. His desired route blocked by the Union Second Corps, Stuart was forced to ride around the Federal army, passing near Washington and, in turn, depriving Lee of

Major General Jeb Stuart commanded the cavalry division of the Army of Northern Virginia. Stuart was legendary for his encircling raids around superior Yankee forces. He would be mortally wounded at the Battle of Yellow Tavern in May 1864. *Courtesy of the MOLLUS-MASS Collection, U.S. Army Military History Institute.*

much of his cavalry. By the end of the month, Stuart, delayed by battles at Westminster and Hanover, was still trying to connect with Ewell. He was now approaching Carlisle from the southeast via York County.

On the morning of July 1, he reached Dover. "The most I could learn was that General Early had marched his division in the direction of Shippensburg," reported Stuart. "After as little rest as was compatible with the exhausted condition of the command, we pushed on for Carlisle, where we hoped to find a portion of the army," as well as replenish his exhausted supply of rations.[428] "On July 1st, our cavalry Corps under Stuart were marching on Carlisle," later wrote Brigadier General Fitzhugh Lee, commanding a brigade in Stuart's division. "[M]y Brigade in advance, the other Brigades were under [Brigadier General Wade] Hampton and [Colonel John R.] Chambliss, the three under Stuart…Our objective point was York, but hearing our army had evacuated that place we turned on Carlisle, hoping to unite with it there."[429]

Stuart sent at least two couriers trying to find the main Southern army—one "on the trail of Early's troops" and another toward Gettysburg—but neither returned before Stuart, Fitz Lee's brigade and James Breathed's 1st Stuart Horse Artillery reached the outskirts of Carlisle on the evening of July 1. Stuart left Wade Hampton at Dillsburg, where later that evening he would be ordered to march toward Gettysburg. Chambliss's brigade halted halfway between Dillsburg and Carlisle and did not participate in the events about to unfold. Staffer Theodore Garnett estimated that, excluding the artillery, about 1,500 seasoned Confederate cavalrymen were present.[430]

THE SHELLING BEGINS

Inside Carlisle it was still relatively calm—for the time being. About 7:00 p.m., several citizens noted a group of unknown cavalrymen at the intersection of the York and Trindle Springs Roads. "It was generally supposed that it was a part of our force," commented Deputy Sherriff Simpson Donavin. "They were within two hundred yards of the town, and sat in their saddles, gazing up the street at the stacked arms of the infantry. It was thought impossible that they could be rebels." One Confederate recalled that Stuart himself rode into the suburbs of Carlisle before he discovered it was Yankees and not Ewell's Confederates occupying the Cumberland County seat. Perhaps partly to blame for Stuart's mishap was that some of the militia regiments wore gray uniforms.[431]

Soon a man "running in from the [south] direction of Mt. Holly gap" cried, "The Rebels are coming!" Most in the plaza either believed he was crying wolf, or they simply could not or did not care to hear it. "I got up and stepped out into the street," recalled Sergeant William L. Nesbit of the 28th PVM, "but could not see anything. I again sat down and almost immediately thereafter another man, carrying a gun, came running in." Rising again, Nesbit could see Southern cavalry as he peered down High Street, the town's main east–west street. But the crowd massed in the square remained unaware of the impending danger. Soon a shell whizzed overhead, giving the appearance, believed Philadelphian C. Stuart Patterson of the four pieces of Landis's battery that rested in the town square, "as if somebody had been popping off a sky-rocket…a tolerably large one, over my head."[432] The battery's Lieutenant Woodruff Jones later reminisced:

> The square was…crowded with ladies, soldiers, and citizens…when the
> sound of a cannon is heard and a shell comes howling over the town. At

This iconic woodcut by artist Thomas Nast depicts the commotion in Carlisle's town square in the early evening hours of July 1. *Author's Collection.*

first not much attention is paid to it, but five or six others arriving in rapid succession, several of which burst overhead, convinced the most confiding that the Rebels had again returned. There followed a scene of indescribable confusion, the soldiers running hither and thither to find their regiments; men, women, and children running about, each trying to find a place of safety. Tables loaded with crockery and food were upset, and piles of baggage were knocked over and strewn about. To add to all this, two or three staff officers, ignorant of the position of the Rebels and their own duties, and feeling anxious that something should be done, ordered troops and guns into fifty different positions at the same time. The guns were drawn up on both sides of the street, the horses were feeding, and the cannoneers without equipment, and drivers were scattered through the crowd.[433]

Yet another rider rode in with the cry, "The Rebels are coming!" and now confusion reigned throughout the square. "Before the soldiers were in line to take their guns from the stack, shells came hurtling through the chimney tops, scattering brick and mortal broad cast," wrote one militiaman. "Such a stampede of women and children you never saw in your life," penned citizen Margaret Murray. "You cannot imagine the confusion that ensued.

A nineteenth-century painting depicting the sheer confusion in the town square. *Courtesy of the U.S. Army Military History Institute.*

It was a disagreeable surprise. Officers calling to their men, who were scattered in all directions, some eating, others worn out with their long march, fast asleep on the Square and pavements; soldiers loading their pieces; the gunners away from their armour [*sic*] and no where to be seen; the excitement was intense."[434]

Brisbane's Pennsylvanians made their way through the dense crowd and grabbed their muskets, which were stacked along the sides of the street. The first few shells, which one Pennsylvania soldier noted "were aimed quite too high," were likely done so purposely to clear the streets of noncombatants. With shells bursting overhead, Lieutenant Colonel John McCleery of the 28th PVM rode around the square ordering the troops to move on the sidewalks to clear the street for the artillery. Still a "good many citizens" occupied the sidewalks, dashing to and fro in a desperate attempt to find their homes. "Please don't fight here," shouted one woman.[435]

While Brisbane and his Pennsylvanians stood aimlessly on the streets, Captain Henry D. Landis—brother-in-law of Major General John F. Reynolds—attempted to organize his battery. Brisbane arrived and ordered Corporal C. Stuart Patterson of Landis's battery to deploy two pieces on the railroad tracks that ran through the center of High Street. Patterson deployed as ordered, pointing his pieces east, while the other section faced south. The battery's limbers and caissons "almost filled up the square."

Meanwhile, Confederate Captain James Breathed placed his four pieces east of town. They commenced lobbing shell and canister at the square. Landis's Philadelphians, however, had trouble responding. "We to clear the houses, had to elevate our guns at such an angle as to throw our shot a mile and a half to their rear," complained one Philadelphian. Only Patterson's gun number two would open fire. Just as Patterson gave the order to fire for the third time, a shell struck him. "Out of the smoke surrounding Patterson's gun I saw a sword blade fly perhaps thirty feet," wrote Charles Leland of the battery, "and then himself [Patterson] borne by two or three men, blood flowing profusely." The shell had taken off two fingers of his right hand and so gashed the other fingers that they required amputation the following day. "My God, I'm shot!" Patterson managed to utter as he was borne from the square. His sword on the other hand had been broken near the hilt.[436]

A wartime photograph of Captain Henry D. Landis, brother-in-law of Union First Corps commander John F. Reynolds, who was killed earlier on July 1 at Gettysburg. Landis had commanded a battery in the militia force commanded by Reynolds the previous fall. *Courtesy of the U.S. Army Military History Institute.*

Patterson, among many others, was removed to the eighteenth-century St. John's Episcopal Church on the square. One surgeon was ready to amputate Patterson's entire arm, but divisional surgeon Dr. John Neill intervened and instead amputated the gashed fingers only. However, Patterson and the surgeons did not remain for long in the church, considering Confederate shells were being lobbed in at a fearfully high rate. Just minutes after Patterson had been removed from the church, a shell tore through the roof and struck at the exact spot where the Philadelphia artilleryman had been lying.[437]

Soon Baldy Smith rode into town. He immediately stopped Landis's fire, which was a good decision considering the only effect it had was attracting Confederate counterbattery fire. Smith ordered Brisbane to take all measures to prevent a cavalry charge into the town.[438] Brisbane formed his four regiments on North Hanover Street and in the square. However, it was soon determined that the Confederates were "firing to kill." Not to overly expose his men, Brisbane ordered them to "enter the private houses, by companies, and rake the rebels as they entered the city." One Confederate of Fitz Lee's 4th Virginia Cavalry recollected that the "houses were filled with Yankees from top to bottom." After about half an hour in the houses, either Smith or Brisbane ascertained that the Rebels would not attempt a charge, and the order was countermanded, "reassembling our regiments and picketing them outside the town, on the main roads where they lay concealed, prone on their faces, awaiting the approach of the enemy till morning." For the most part, the Pennsylvanians remained dispersed throughout and outside the northern section of town.[439] Others wound up in the town square. There they received a heavy pounding of artillery fire, as Captain Nicholas Rice of Company D, 30th PVM, observed:

> *I sat down on the curb and leaned against a shade tree about six inches in diameter. When I rose up…the tree was cut off by a shot, about two feet from the ground, before I was ten feet away. Ten feet is not a close call, but thirty seconds seemed short. Just as we were forming our lines in the street, after coming out of the building, a shell bust over us, and a piece fell in a mud puddle in front of the next company. The mud and water flew over the men. It came so sudden that some of the men lost their heads for a moment, and came rushing through the ranks of my company. It took some forceful language and vigorous commands to bring them to their senses. After order was restored and they realized how like sheep they had acted, they were heartily ashamed of their conduct.*[440]

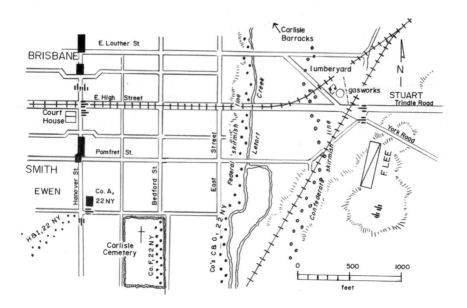

Union and Confederate dispositions at Carlisle, July 1, 1863. *Map by John Heiser.*

Fitz Lee deployed skirmishers at the outskirts of town. They soon met opposition from the five companies of Carlisle home guards, which had disbanded when Ewell occupied the town several days before. Now, with the town in Union hands and Confederates again approaching, these citizens had re-formed with a determination never again to be under enemy control. The companies, each man on his own account, rushed to Letort Creek on the eastern edge of town, there "selecting secure positions" from which they opened fire on the Confederate skirmishers. To their assistance came a contingent of Yankee cavalry, which dashed down Pomfret Street and over a bridge across the creek but was obliged to retire under a hot fire from Confederate skirmishers hidden in bushes in the surrounding area.[441] Brisbane's Pennsylvanians also opened fire from the streets and houses.

All this took place in less than an hour. The shelling ceased, and two Confederates entered the town with a white flag of truce. They were conducted to Smith's headquarters, in the middle of Hanover Street in front of the *American Volunteer* newspaper office. There, "two old ladies who had a little thread and needle store near me, brought to me in the saddle much tea to keep me awake," Smith recalled.[442]

"General Stuart sent an officer and a bugler with a flag of truce demanding the surrender of the town," recalled one of Stuart's staffers.

"It was weird and peculiar to see this officer with a handkerchief tied to his sabre, followed by a bugler, go galloping into town, the latter blowing twice while the former brandished his handkerchief." In a serious and perhaps near-fatal error, these Confederate armistices were not blindfolded. Therefore, they could observe with detail the dispositions in town at their pleasure. "On his return to his commander, he could not have been a more welcome messenger, had he brought an autograph letter from Gen. Smith, minutely detailing the situation, strength and composition of his troops," ranted one Philadelphia artilleryman. Smith was informed by the courier that Fitz Lee had three thousand men (an exaggeration) ready to pounce outside the town. Lee, the bearer explained, demanded the surrender of the town and all military forces within it.

At Smith's headquarters, citizens crowded around. Some begged him to surrender, but many called upon the general to "fight, General fight them; let our property go, only whip the rebels." Judge Graham Bowman decreed that the town should be surrendered, while one woman slapped General Smith in the back and cried, "Don[']t do it, Gen'l, don[']t do it as long as one brick remains on another." Stuart was impatient because the flag "was detained unusually long" by Smith and sent in another courier with a Signal Corps flags. White with a red circle in the center, this banner was custom-fit to be an armistice standard by pinning a white cloth over the red portion. This courier contained a message from Stuart informing Smith if he did not answer in three minutes the town would be shelled and burned. Smith gave a "decided refusal" and, upon being informed that the shelling would proceed, bombastically replied, "Shell away."[443]

The two Southern couriers informed Smith that he would have half an hour to remove all citizens, though comparatively little time was given. Smith sent a Mr. Ward of Harrisburg, his volunteer aide, to inform General Knipe of the situation and for him to inform Couch. Ward also carried orders for Knipe to march at 3:00 a.m. the following morning. "It was, however, at once decided that he [Knipe] was needed for the defence [sic] of Harrisburg and he did not attempt to reinforce me," Smith later wrote. Before deciding the latter, Smith sent another message to Knipe at 11:00 p.m. to move immediately, but the carrier, another volunteer aide named James Dougherty, was captured and his orderly wounded.[444]

Ewen Rejoins Smith

In holding Stuart's armistice bearers for roughly half an hour, Smith had strategic goals in mind. He knew all along he would never surrender the town, but Ewen's brigade of New Yorkers was still south of town on the Baltimore Pike. As the shelling began, General Ewen was busy conversing with a man who claimed to be a local (although most of Ewen's New Yorkers were convinced he was a "Confederate emissary"). The man suggested that Ewen place the section of Landis's battery about a mile to the south, a position that likely "would have insured the capture of the artillery," believed Ewen's New Yorkers. Soon firing was heard to the north, and Ewen remarked, "Verily, gentlemen, it behooves us to look around us." "In this, his command, for once agreed with him," mused Wingate. The New Yorkers could see in their rear only thick columns of smoke and bright flashes of light.[445]

"We supposed that the rebels were only firing at our stragglers," Private Murray recorded, "however we still expected to have some fighting." Ewen's brigade entered town from the south. The 37th deployed opposite the courthouse on Hanover Street, while the 22nd was divided up by companies and sent to several different areas in the southern section of town. The New Yorkers had a dangerous experience as they marched into town, when one of Landis's pieces near the square had its sight trained on them, vigilant that the New Yorkers were a Southern column. Wingate penned that from then on he was "always...thankful that the gentleman who held the lock-string that evening was not a nervous man."[446]

"The condition of affairs which the Twenty-second found on entering Carlisle was not cheering," recalled Wingate. "It was the greatest relief, however, to find that 'Baldy' Smith was there and in command...A well-known and veteran general his presence inspired confidence, and he showed himself fully equal to the emergency." The 22nd halted south of the square and took orders directly from General Ewen, who assumed command of that sector of the town. Company A took position in a small, white two-story house at the corner of Hanover and South Streets, barricading it and filling the windows with its best marksmen. Meanwhile, Companies C and G deployed as skirmishers in a north–south line at Letort Creek, at some places within one hundred yards of their Southern counterparts, exchanging fire regularly.

Company F, under Captain A.N. Francis, together with stragglers from both the 22nd and 37th, a combined two hundred men, were posted behind the thick stone wall of the Carlisle Cemetery, only several hundred yards from the Confederate artillery. Francis was under orders to "hold the

This nineteenth-century painting shows the deployment of the 22nd NYSNG south of town. Lieutenant Perkins's section is visible in the foreground. The white house near the center foreground was occupied by Company A. Beyond the right of the photo is the Carlisle Cemetery. The road shown in the picture is Hanover Street, which leads to the square. Discernible in the left background is the cupola of the county courthouse. *From* History of Company "A" and the Twenty-Second Regiment, *1897.*

position to the last." Lieutenant Perkins's section of Landis's battery was repositioned with one piece pointing south down the Baltimore Pike and another commanding a farm lane that ran east toward the Rebel lines, just south of the home occupied by Company A of the 22nd. These guns were protected by a barricade of wagons and any other wooden implements that could be found. Supporting the section were Companies H and I of the 22nd, under direct command of Colonel Aspinwall. The two companies were lying down in a potato field, "deployed into single rank, with intervals of about six feet between the men." Aspinwall also extended his line to the southwest.[447]

Fitz Lee Shells Carlisle

"[I]t was with much regret I proceeded with hostile intent against Carlisle," later recounted Fitz Lee. "My first military service after graduating at West Point was there. I knew and had received the hospitalities of most of its

Brigadier General Fitzhugh Lee, despite his many and personal connections to Carlisle and its citizens, was the belligerent of the Cumberland County seat on the night of July 1. *Courtesy of the MOLLUS-MASS Collection, U.S. Army Military History Institute.*

citizens. I had warm and earnest and good friends among its inhabitants. Some of the most pleasant days were passed in the hospitable homes of her people—but war—horrid war—was raging then between them and those with me, and my path and their paths had separated."[448]

Not only was it heart-wrenching for Lee to open fire on the town, but it was also physically exhausting for his men. "It is impossible for me to give you a correct idea of the fatigue and exhaustion of our men and beasts at this time," wrote one Confederate cavalryman.[449] Fatigue-filled marches had been combined with little food and little rest for nearly a week. The Southern cavalrymen were fortunate the fight did not escalate into anything larger, considering they were in a deplorable condition to engage even the clumsy Yankee militia.

Captain James Breathed of the 1st Stuart Horse Artillery had placed two of his pieces at the intersection of the York and Trindle Roads and another two on an elevation a short distance to the rear and left of the first two. Early on, the lieutenant of the two pieces in the rear mistook the batteries below as enemy guns and planted his first two shells very near the front pieces. The misled lieutenant was soon ordered to cease firing. Stuart, his staffers and the crews of the first two pieces had to be extremely vigilant; they occupied what they referred to as the angle—the intersection of York and Trindle Roads on the eastern edge of town—taking into mind that the Southerners were only a short distance from the Yankee skirmishers at Letort Creek. Stuart had several close calls near this intersection.[450]

Showing how truly exhausted Lee's command was, "men were falling asleep around the guns, and the present writer slept very soundly within ten feet of a battery hotly firing," remarked staff officer Captain John Esten Cooke. Cooke found one major "leaned against a fence within a few paces of a howitzer in process of rapid discharge, and in that upright position 'forgot his troubles.'" Stuart later told Cooke he "saw a man climb a fence, put one leg over, and in that position drop asleep!" Staffer Theodore Garnett dismounted and fell asleep near the battery, "undisturbed by the music of the guns."[451]

Stuart was present outside town but only until the beginning of the third shelling. Shortly after that had begun, he departed.[452] But for the time being, Stuart was in command. The major general later reported:

> *I disliked to subject the town to the consequences of attack* [but] *at the same time it was essential to us to procure rations. I therefore directed General Lee to send in a flag of truce, demanding unconditional surrender or bombardment. This was refused. I placed artillery in position commanding the town, took possession of the main avenues to the place, and repeated the demand.*[453]

However, contrary to Stuart's report, the second demand for surrender came only after a brutal second shelling. "It was terrific, fiercer, heavier and more devilish than at first," observed Deputy Sherriff Simpson Donavin. Citizens by this time had either fled into the surrounding fields and farms to seek safety or did so trembling in their own cellars. Confederate fire hit a lumberyard near the gasworks on the eastern edge of town. Flames enveloped the stable next to the gasworks. Confederates then applied the torch to the gasworks' purifying house. Southern artillerists targeted the Gasometer, which contained thirty-five thousand feet of gas. The works' superintendent, George Wise, was prohibited by Union troops from going to the works for his own safety, so he instead took the precaution of cutting off the main gas line situated on the outskirts of town to ensure the town would be safe if an explosion occurred.[454]

The Southern artillery fire struck the square with unusual accuracy. Many of the artillery officers knew that the square would be an ideal place to position troops. For one, Lieutenant Richard S. Shreve of Captain William McGregor's 2nd Stuart Horse Artillery (which was not at Carlisle) had likely ridden to Carlisle independently to assist, considering he had graduated from the town in 1860. Shreve "pointed out the various localities, being familiar with them[.]"[455] The men of the 37th NYSNG lay flat on their stomachs in Hanover Street, with portions of Companies B and I of the 12th NYSNG on their left. Detached from duty at Sterrett's Gap, these New Yorkers incidentally fell in with Brisbane's brigade as it marched to Carlisle.

John Gummere of Landis's battery was standing on the steps of the courthouse in the square when a "solid shot struck the…Court House and the pieces fell all around me." The marks of artillery fire (perhaps the shell Gummere speaks of) are still readily visible on the columns of the courthouse. Gummere described the shelling as "3½ hours [of] a perfect hail of shot and shell." Smith maintained his orders for Landis's battery to remain silent as he wisely "deemed the fire too inaccurate, and wished to save my ammunition." The artillerymen lay beside their pieces. Some, including Gummere, managed to fall asleep—a difficult task considering the incoming fire.[456]

Charles Leland of Landis's battery was leaning against a lamppost when a load of grapeshot went through the lamp. "Remembering the story in 'Peter Simple,' and that 'lightning never strikes twice in the same place,'" recalled Leland, "I remained quiet, when there came at once another, smashing what was left of the glass about two feet above my head." A short distance away in the square, an incident of personal bravery occurred. Eighteen-year-old Theodore Fassitt of Landis's battery was detailed to hold four horses in front of a church while the shells came "thick and fast," with one shell decapitating one of the mounts. Fassitt, however, stayed at his post. General Smith rode by and asked him "why the devil he was stopping there." Fassitt replied, "I was ordered to, sir!" Smith told him to go to an alley behind the church, where he spent the remainder of the night.[457]

A deputation of ladies approached General Smith during the middle of the second shelling, asking the general where they would be safest. "I told them I thought the cellars the safest place for them, to which they replied,— 'But they are full of your soldiers.'"[458]

The vicinity of West Louther Street had several particularly terrifying incidents. In one, a shell struck a stone wall that ran along the north side of the street from the corner of North Hanover and Louther Streets. "The shell was deflected by the wall," recalled a witness, "and struck the pavement in front of the Union Engine House, on the same side of Louther Street, richochetted [*sic*], and passed through the weather-boarded house of Mr[.] McPherson, on the southwest corner of Pitt and Louther streets, above the front door on Pitt Street, a little south of the center and lodged between the ceiling and the floor." All this without exploding. Further trepidation came to that neighborhood when two shells struck the home of J. Adam Humerich at 147 West Louther Street. "One of these shells passed through the east gable end, of stone, behind the mantel in the back parlor, and, after passing through the outer wall, exploded in the chimney, and made a hole in the chimney breast at least three feet in diameter. The mantel was split into kindling wood, and at least indentations were made on the walls, ceiling, doors…The piano in the parlor was seriously injured…The other shell, not far apart in time, struck the same side of the building, but above the level of the garret floor, and after passing through the wall and descending, it struck a joist, and richochetted [*sic*] and lodged against the west wall of the building, near the ceiling of the garret room." This shell was later found unexploded.[459]

At the beginning of the second shelling, the 33rd PVM was ordered from the square to form into column and marched double file northeast of town near the barracks in darkness. Less than a mile from the Rebel gunners on the eastern edge of town, the Philadelphians learned they were in prime range when a shell fell just short of them in an orchard along the road. Seconds later, another shell flew over them, and they realized the Southern artillerymen had discovered their movement by the reflection of their bayonets in the moonlight. Another shell sailed over them, and a musket of a nervous Pennsylvanian went off accidentally, wounding Private Robert Wylie of Company D through the knee. Four men of his company carried Wylie on a stretcher to a hospital in town, where his leg was amputated above the knee. The Pennsylvanians remained stationary the rest of the night, deployed as pickets with their bayonets fixed, mostly asleep, all the while "expecting the Cavalry to come down the road and cut us up."[460]

THE BARRACKS BURN

It was now about 10:00 p.m. East of town, in Confederate lines, General Stuart, aloft on his horse near Breathed's artillery, decided he needed to make a statement—namely because he was running short on ammunition.[461] Stuart instructed staff officer Frank Smith Robertson to order Colonel Williams C. Wickham and his 4th Virginia Cavalry to burn the barracks, a longtime symbol of the Federal government's military arm. "Following his point," recollected Robertson, "I rode through sundry dark streets and byways, expecting every minute to have my head blown off from a window or door, and found Colonel Wickham and gave him his orders. In a few moments I saw the grand cavalry barracks begin to glow from many points, and then, with a great burst of flame, light up the scenery for miles around."[462]

"[T]he torch was applied to the barracks, simultaneously to each row of buildings, and by eleven o'clock a great sheet of flame spread over the sky

Colonel Williams Carter Wickham and his 4th Virginia Cavalry were responsible for torching Carlisle Barracks. *Courtesy of the MOLLUS-MASS Collection, U.S. Army Military History Institute.*

in the north east, turning, the terrible scene into sublimity," related Deputy Sherriff Donavin. The 33rd PVM was not far away. "We were within about 50 or 100 yards from the Barracks while the Rebels were burning it down," recorded one Philadelphian. "Just when the scene of fire was grandest the artillery ceased, and a flag of truce bearer entered the town." The bearer passed along the wall of the Carlisle Cemetery, which sheltered Captain Francis's detachment of New Yorkers, who were concealed and crouching in the tall cemetery grass. The Southern armistice bearer stopped at Smith's headquarters but received the same response as his predecessors. Word around Carlisle was that Smith's response "was more decided than courteous, [and Smith] requested the bearer to inform Gen. Lee that he would see him in a hotter climate first."[463]

No sooner had the courier returned to Rebel lines than the shelling resumed. "It did not last as long as either of the others," remarked Deputy Sherriff Donavin. Stuart's horse artillery was running low on ammunition. "The night wore away under a slow fire of artillery which did little or no

This pre-1877 photo shows the Judge Watts town house at left. Watts and his family had fled the area on word of the Rebel advance. Captain Clark and his company of the 28th PVM took position in his house. The home still stands at 20 East High Street. Also note in the bottom foreground the railroad tracks that then ran down the center of High Street. *Courtesy of the Cumberland County Historical Society.*

damage," recalled Smith. The fire soon slackened off, and silence prevailed. "[W]e were kept in a few hundred yards of the town, every man holding his bridle in his hand during the night," reminisced B.J. Haden of the 1st Virginia Cavalry. As this third distinct period of shelling ended, Captain Robert F. Clark of Company C, 28th PVM, managed to gather "most" of his company into Judge Frederick Watts's town house. "Our plan was to await a cavalry charge and fire on them from the house," Clark detailed. "About midnight I superintended the cutting down of Judge Watts' shade trees to give us a fair chance to fire and to make an obstruction in the street."[464]

Around midnight, Stuart sent a third and final request for surrender to Smith, to which he replied that "the message had been twice answered before." By 1:00 a.m., the firing had ceased.[465] About 3:00 a.m., Fitz Lee received orders from Stuart, who had already left, to head southwest for Gettysburg. Before departing, Lee fired three last shots, which he remarked were "merely sent…into the town to let them know that he was still about." Lee then headed south, out of Cumberland County. Never again would Confederate forces occupy the county.[466]

CASUALTIES

Dr. John Neill of Philadelphia, serving as Smith's chief surgeon, secured the West College buildings at Dickinson College for use as a hospital. To assist him were the U.S. Christian and Sanitary Commissions. Neill was a favorite of Smith—he was not only the brother of Brigadier General Thomas Neill of Smith's old division but also "a delightful man," Smith remarked. The shelling had left dozens of men with slight wounds, many of whom are not documented. Seventeen Yankees are documented to have been wounded (see Appendix A), with one man—Private Charles Colliday of the 32nd PM—mortally wounded (see Appendix B).[467] Only one Confederate casualty is documented—artilleryman Private Thomas Yates of Breathed's battery, who reportedly received a wound in the nose (see Appendix A).[468]

Chapter 12
After Carlisle

Baldy Smith's relieved Yankees arose to sultry weather on the morning of July 2. The 33rd PVM, still in position north of the smoldering barracks, "went singly by permission into the city to get our knapsacks" as well as "something to eat," recorded Private Beale. "The house where some of our knapsacks were was shut up, the people had left, so we broke it open and threw the knapsacks out of the windows and shut the house up again."[469]

Company A of the 22nd NYSNG began to leave the small home it had been deployed in, "only to be confronted with a novel adversary," mused New Yorker George Wingate. "The female proprietor appeared and viewed with a housekeeper's consternation the condition of her home. No particular harm had been done, but the furniture was piled in the corners, the beds rolled up and placed at the windows to protect the sharp-shooters, the carpets were covered with mud, and the place looked as if a cyclone had struck it. It must also be confessed," admitted Wingate, "that all the bread and some preserves were missing." Standing in the New Yorkers' exit path, she declared that "not a man should leave that house until she had been all over it and seen just what damage had been done." After a failed attempt to console her, Captain Otis gave the order to "forward march," and "the company shouldered past the irate lady, leaving her still scolding."[470]

John Keagy Stayman, a professor of Latin and French at Dickinson College, opined to a student that Carlisle "looks much altered. But when the merchants get back their goods, and the farmers harvest their crops, and business revives, I think the town will put on its usual appearance." Stayman went on to write that the "barracks have suffered most. They are near a heap of ruins." The professor further pondered, "It will be some years before

CITIZENS

OF THE

CUMBERLAND VALLEY !

The hour has come to arm ! To every man now that can carry a musket, the line of duty is plain. Not satisfied with *revolt, rebellion* and *treason* at home, the misguided men that have sought to tear down our government and destroy our democratic institutions, have turned *ruthless invaders.* They have broken open our stores and our warehouses; they have seized whatever they could use or carry ; they have ravaged private houses and insulted ladies of the highest respectability ; they have plundered peaceable farmers of their horses and cattle, and have wantonly shot such as they could not take away ; they have devastated the valley to the extent of their power.

They have done all this, but they are disappointed. They openly declared that they expected to find a *majority of the people in their favor !* Burn every heart at the indignity of such an imputation ! Flash vengeance every eye on the vile defamers ! *The citizens of this valley are loyal to the heart's core.* Let us show it by deeds. The hour is come. The foe is turned back. He is surrounded.— He is in the net. If he is strong enough, he will break through. If *we* are strong enough we shall crush him. Every right arm that can wield a sword has a duty. Country calls. The deepest interest of humanity demand.

Stay not to discuss the unmeasured degradation of the few in our midst who have been so lost to honor, lost to patriotism, lost to shame, as to " aid and abet the enemy" and find joy in it ! Leave them now. The hour of their reckoning waits. First crush out the invader, then let the *unrelenting justice* due to such miscreants have its course.

Fellow-Citizens ! Rise ! Arm !

Bring your guns. From every neighborhood, gather to the principal towns on the main lines of communication. You will find men to perfect your organization and lead you ; or if not, appoint your own officers. It is the work of an hour. You have men qualified for the duty. Report to the General commanding the army of the valley, and do it promptly. Every hour counts. And now, in the name of country and sacred home, in the name of all that is dear to us and our children, and in the strength of the God of our Fathers march, and " quit you like men."

The printing of the few lines above was intercepted on Wednesday evening by the sudden and unexpected boom of the invaders cannon before Carlisle. The first notice of their presence, to most of the inhabitants, was the swift messenger of death whizzing over their heads. The next came tearing through the tree-tops, by our sides ; the next, crashing into our houses. No moment for women or children to escape, except through the hail storm of shell and grape.

This is the barbarism of civilization ! This the humanity of the modern *chivalry,* self-styled !— Such, the conduct of men whose prating in our midst was incessant of the brutality of *our* officers and of the scrupulous religiousness of *theirs.* Canting hypocrites !

CITIZENS AROUSE ! It is not a war of politics. Former party names have gone to the winds. Patriots and traitors—these are the parties now. There are no others. Men, choose your line; take your stand. If your arms are not needed in the valley now, report to Harrisburg and enlist for the war. No more child's play of three months—FOR THE WAR ! FOR THE WAR !!

CARLISLE, July 3, 1863.   [Circulate through the county.]

On July 3, this provocative banner was printed in Carlisle for circulation throughout the county. It attempted to profit from the shelling two nights previous by calling on men to enlist for the war; "no more child's play of three months[.]" The flier insinuated, "Not satisfied with *revolt, rebellion* and *treason* at home, the misguided men that have sought to tear down our government and destroy our democratic institutions, have turned *ruthless invaders.*" *Courtesy of the Dickinson College Archives.*

the grounds are as beautiful as they were. I think that the Barracks should be rebuilt at once, and in even better style than before. We should have no rebel scar, of that sort left upon the soil of Pennsylvania."[471] In August, a government report found that the officers' quarters, barracks and stable were destroyed by fire, which would cost an estimated $23,200 to rebuild. To restore the entire post would cost an estimated $47,600.[472]

"We came in by way of North Hanover Street," recalled a Carlisle schoolgirl who was reentering her hometown after fleeing the previous evening. At the junction of North Hanover and Louther Streets, she found "a barricade of branches of trees[.]" On the pavement in front of the First Presbyterian Church on the square, she found a dead horse. "Soldiers were in evidence everywhere, many lying wrapped in their blankets on the pavement, men whom the night's vigil had overcome. Reports were made of finding shells embedded in the walls of homes." As she made her way to her home on South Hanover Street, the schoolgirl and her family learned that the southern section of town was closely patrolled by Yankee cavalry, who had issued notices to the residents that the shelling might resume that morning.[473] "Along the central street…the trees and doorsteps are marked by grape, and doors and windows and walls scarred by exploded shell," documented Professor S.D. Hillman of Dickinson College.[474]

At 5:00 a.m., Ewen's brigade—as always, with Landis's battery— marched out of Carlisle, "dispensing with the little formality of breakfast," and proceeded south down the Baltimore Pike. Once they had gone nearly a mile, Ewen deployed his brigade on the crest of a hill—the 22nd in an oat field to the left (east) of the pike, while the 37th was deployed on the right and the artillery unlimbered in the road. There was "nothing to eat with the hot sun pouring down upon us," complained one Yankee. They slept until late afternoon, when food finally came in the form "of a little pork and potatoes," but the tune of irony played its hand when the command "fall in" was issued. The men obeyed, but only after "a universal dash was made at the pans," and each man marched "with a piece of pork in one hand and a potato in the other, eating away for dear life, and forming a *tout ensemble* not often equaled." The brigade bivouacked in an open field near the smoldering barracks, where it spent the night without any cover.[475]

Several of Brisbane's regiments marched to the eastern edge of town, near the Rebel positions of the previous evening. "We were marched to a wheatfield and saw the Rail Road [bridge over Letort Creek] and gas works destroyed last night by the Rebels," penned Private Beale of the 33rd PVM. "The rails were bent and the wooden part burned, the masonry stood[,]

This sketch by artist George Law appeared in the July 18, 1863 issue of *Frank Leslie's Illustrated Newspaper* and depicts the Carlisle Barracks after they were burned by Wickham's 4th Virginia. *From* Frank Leslie's Illustrated Newspaper.

they had tried to knock it down." The Philadelphians were later ordered to another bivouac site, where they happened upon killed beef and dead horses, which were burned "so that we could have pure air to breathe." Without any cover, the 33rd turned in for the night. "The stacks of muskets made a line, then the front rank men laid with their feet toward the stacks and the rear rank with their feet to our heads," described Beale. "The regiment asleep in one grand line looked well by moonlight."[476] By evening, Smith had gathered nearly all the troops in the vicinity of the scorched barracks.

"With the exception of a little picket duty, the next day was devoted, by all hands, to the most energetic resting," Wingate wrote of July 3. One of Smith's concerns was supplying his men with provisions. Due to the recent Rebel presence, the supply trains had not yet appeared, and Smith's attempt to obtain rations from the citizens was "only partially successful." One sutler managed to find his way to the barracks, and in the words of one hungry New Yorker, "his stock disappeared like magic."[477]

REINFORCEMENTS ARRIVE

Smith was also awaiting reinforcements before he would push south. On July 1, General Knipe was ordered to lead his new command, composed of the 8th, 23rd, 56th and 71st NYSNG and E. Spencer Miller's Philadelphia battery—over 2,200 men—to Carlisle. Also accompanying the column was New York National Guard Brigadier Jesse Smith.[478] These New York regiments, many of which had just gotten settled in their camps on Bridgeport Heights, were not pleased to receive marching orders that afternoon. "We were ordered to provide ourselves with two days' cooked rations and to move completely equipped, with packed knapsacks, blankets, and all the paraphernalia of a marching column," recalled John Lockwood of the 23rd. When General Knipe rode through the 71st's camp, he was asked their destination. "Right into the face of the enemy," replied Knipe, to which he received an enthusiastic response.[479]

The sun was setting when the column departed Bridgeport Heights on the pike.[480] "Though the day was warm we kept up a brave spirit for some two or three miles," wrote Lockwood,

> *singing and shouting, stimulated by the exciting expectation of meeting the enemy face to face, and animated by the beauty of the country through which we were passing. But after an hour or so our heavy burdens, the still hot sun, and the roughly macadamised [sic] road began to tell on us. Some becoming exhausted were relieved of a part of their load by their officers, or by comrades who were stronger; field and staff officers in several instances gave up their horses to o'erwearied ones; while other riders piled up knapsacks and blankets…till they were almost sandwiched out of sight.*[481]

Lockwood calculated that the New Yorkers carried roughly forty-four pounds each. "This is about the weight of a healthy boy, eight years," he stated.[482]

Shortly after 10:00 p.m., the column bivouacked in a clover field along Silver Spring Creek. "The night was dark, the sky being overcast," recalled Lockwood. "No sooner had we reached the spot than…far away to the front rose the heavy boom of artillery firing, and a bright light reflected from the clouds indicated that a conflagration was raging…at Carlisle." The New Yorkers began stacking arms and readying sleeping quarters. "We spread out our rubber blankets upon the wet grass, and drawing on our overcoats dropped down to rest, each man behind his musket. Some of the less weary went in search of water to drink, and some had the wisdom to bathe their hot, overworked feet in the neighbouring [sic] brook."[483]

At 3:00 a.m. the following morning, the men were aroused "by a whispered summons" to be in marching order at once—and to do it silently. Rumors were whispered alleging the Confederates were advancing on Harrisburg. As dawn approached, the column was ordered eastward roughly two miles, halting a short distance east of Sporting Hill Road. It did not take long for the eager—not to mention hungry—New Yorkers to spread out and visit local farmhouses. Many took refreshing swims in the Conodoguinet

Creek; some ferried across the creek in a farmer's boat to the opposite bank, where more relatively untouched farmhouses lay. About sunset, the column marched nearly another mile, halting near Orr's Bridge on the southern banks of the Conodoguinet. "It was a pretty place for a bivouac," remarked Lockwood. The southern bank consisted of a rigid, steep slope, which rises rapidly to a relatively flat surface, where the pike rests. From here down to the bridge, Yankees filled every space.[484] Lockwood surveyed the scene:

> *Looking up the stream the centre of the picture was occupied by the bridge, one hundred and fifty yards distant, with woods at either end. In the left foreground lay massed by foreshortening the long lines of stacked arms, with crowds of figures, some moving but most of them at rest. In the distance, under the bridge, this line bent gracefully around to the right of the picture. Half a hundred fires were blazing along the edge of the water, growing brighter every minute as the darkness thickened. Directly over the bridge hung the planet Venus, now moving in that part of her orbit where she shines with the greatest splendor.[485]*

On July 3, the New Yorkers were awakened at 3:30 a.m. and marched for two hours, only "after having braced ourselves for a solid day's work with hot coffee and bread" from the loot they had gathered from local farms the previous day. Around 10:00 a.m., the column halted at New Kingston, where the 8th and 71st visited their "old campaign ground" of a week previous. "By the persuasive force of greenbacks the villagers and outlying farmers were induced to unearth a goodly supply of bread, butter and eggs." After a three-hour rest, the column departed Kingston at 1:00 p.m. and reached Carlisle six hours later, where they camped near the barracks.[486] Also arriving that day was Colonel Joachim Maidhof's 11th NYSNG, which rejoined Ewen's brigade for the first time since June 28.[487]

In addition to Knipe's four regiments, Brigadier General Philip Schuyler Crooke's 980-man brigade of the 13th and 28th NYSNG, two Brooklyn regiments, had been ordered to Smith's assistance. For several days, Crooke had been assisting Brigadier General Charles Yates in defending the approaches to Harrisburg from the west, near the village of Marysville, and had only recently returned to Bridgeport Heights. After dark on July 3, General Hall in Fort Washington received verbal orders from Couch, who ordered him to directly oversee the movements of Crooke's brigade, which was to board the trains for Carlisle that night so as to be there the following morning. At 10:00 p.m., Crooke received orders to leave "everything except blankets, haversacks, and arms." An hour later, Colonel Michael Bennett of the 28th came into camp with a broken ankle. He had been ordered to inspect pickets that dark and rainy evening, and his horse had stumbled and fell on him. "With much sadness he was sent home," reported Crooke. Now, Crooke's two regiments had only one field officer apiece.[488]

Despite such troubles, the brigade boarded the trains "in a hurry" at 2:00 a.m. "As the sun arose," penned Crooke, "we arrived at Carlisle, and saw the ruins of the barracks and the railroad bridge." Under Hall's command, the brigade was marched down High Street and bivouacked in column. Hall received an order from Couch directing him to return to Bridgeport Heights, for which Hall quickly departed. "[T]races of the skirmishing…were fresh," penned L.T. Hyde of the 13th, "the burned barracks, shells exploded and unexploded, trampled wheat fields." General Crooke noted "marks of shell on the buildings." Demonstrating the true rawness and inexperience of the militia, no one had thought to pack rations in the brigade. Crooke telegraphed Couch about this, to which he received a frustrated response from the department commander: "Do troops want me to tell them to breathe? Always have rations in your haversacks."[489]

MARCH TO PINE GROVE

By the time Crooke had arrived in Carlisle, Smith had already left. Reveille was sounded at 3:00 a.m., and in less than three hours, the column began moving south. While experience may have been lacking in this force, it surely had numbers on its side—the column numbered over seven thousand men with a complement of two batteries. Marching through Carlisle, many were shocked to see not "a single fire-cracker or hearing an allusion to the American Eagle, or the flag of our Union" in Carlisle on this Fourth of July.[490]

Smith's purpose in marching south was to lend any assistance possible to Meade's Army of the Potomac, then pitted against Lee's Army of Northern Virginia at Gettysburg. Perhaps Smith's inexperienced but nevertheless numerically strong force coming in on the Confederate rear could cause Lee to divert some of his forces from engaging Meade's army. If the Battle of Gettysburg had lasted several days longer, Smith easily could have become a factor. Smith wanted to reach Pine Grove Furnace, "from which point I hoped to put my command on the road between Chambersburg and Gettysburg," where he expected to interfere with Lee's line of communications.[491]

"The first six miles were well enough," recalled one New Yorker. "We move on slowly, the sun overclouded, the road good…The men talk, laugh, and sing, get water and tobacco from the roadside dwellers, and chaff them with all sorts of absurd questions." At 10:00 a.m., the column reached Mount Holly, just over five miles distant and also known as Papertown because of the Mullen and Kemper Paper Mill (from which Ewell had made his $5,000 "purchase" on June 30). There, the Yankee column was met by enthusiastic cheers from the townspeople.[492] The column's progress was halted upon the arrival of some two thousand paroled Federals from the first day of the Battle of Gettysburg, who were being directed under a flag of truce. "Wishing to prevent the enemy from getting information of our strength," Smith reported, "I was forced to accept the prisoners…and turn the rebel escort back." This matter took two hours to sort out before the march could proceed. The 37th NYSNG remained at Mount Holly as a rear guard.[493]

However, clouds hovered, "and as we rested," recalled Lockwood, "there rose to our ears the distant mutter of thunder, and soon big drops began to fall. Presently a mist was seen to gather around the top of the mountain far above our heads; and soon the top disappeared in the shroud which crept ominously down, down the mountain side. The thunder grew louder, the lightning flashed more and more vividly and the rail fell in torrents." Creeks and streams rose two feet—and then came the order "Forward." "We fell in resignedly and even with good humor," recalled Lockwood, "having by this time been thoroughly soaked…we marched cheerily up the mountain, singing." The men "came to a manufacturing hamlet in a sort of cup of the mountain, the stream on which the mill stood flowing over the edge of the cup at one side as it were." Here the column left the turnpike and turned right onto what was then known simply as Mountain Road, on which they met more Union parolees from Gettysburg.[494]

A short distance farther the column halted because of high water; Hunter's Run and other area streams were overflowing. "The road…was built along the side of the mountain, which was on…[the] right; to the left was a stream…[which] overflowed the road so that the men could not distinguish where the stream and the road parted, and to keep from falling into the former they had to keep as close as possible to the mountains." Often the water was knee- or even waist-deep. Two men of the 23rd nearly drowned when a bridge was carried away and were only rescued "with difficulty[.]" The horse of the 71st NYSNG's adjutant, J.R. Livermore, stepped into a hole and tumbled into the water, the current carrying Livermore. As Lockwood wrote, "A portion of the column succeeded in getting through, though at the imminent peril of being washed away…it was thought prudent to postpone further attempts."

The men of the 23rd countermarched to an abandoned paper mill, which "gave us ample quarters." However, around 5:00 p.m., they were again ordered to proceed to Pine Grove. "On reaching the point of danger we found the water had subsided but little; but orders were imperative, and we plunged in."[495] Lockwood continued:

> *We followed the trail cautiously feeling our way along, and not daring to look to the right or left—our ears filled with the din of the waters, and half carried off our feet by the impetuous flood. Crossing a gully—probably the natural bed of the stream—by a foot bridge, which our engineers had doubtless thrown across, we saw beneath us with a start and shudder of horror the head of a drowned horse and the pole of a wagon sticking up above the torrent…It proved to be a loaded commissary wagon* [belonging to Company D, 32nd PM] *with its team which had been swept away! A number of muskets were lost, and a drum or two; but excepting these casualties we all got across safely.*[496]

The men of the 22nd NYSNG managed to get by the water by felling trees, rolling up their trousers and praying their balance was right. The artillery had the roughest time. After having quite the time ascending the hill, by the time they had crested it, Miller's and Landis's Philadelphians found "neither entreaties nor threats would induce the horses to move."[497] In piecemeal fashion, portions of the column arrived at Pine Grove Furnace. Others, such as Ewen's brigade and the 23rd NYSNG, halted a short distance northeast at Laurel Forge. There Ewen was "to cover the entrance to the narrow valley, and also watch a road leading over the mountain to Bendersville."[498]

Parts of the division arrived at Pine Grove Furnace. The 33rd PVM took shelter at the furnace and surrounding buildings. "We were all wet through, even to the Brigadier Generals," remarked Private Beale. "Our company… got in one of the iron Furnaces and built a large fire in the fire place and a New York Brigadier General and staff dried themselves…with us." Some of the New Yorkers complained that at Pine Grove "the Pennsylvania troops were comfortably provided for in barns and outhouses, while the New Yorkers bivouacked in the rain without any cover." However, on the other hand, this was territory that had not been previously foraged by either side, and "consequently the foraging parties were well rewarded[.]" "Every fence about is converted into fuel," recollected one New Yorker. "The cattle and hogs in the fields are levied upon—shot, dressed, cooked, and eaten."[499]

CROOKE ADVANCES

Meanwhile, Crooke was in Carlisle, clueless about what he was to do. He had absolutely no orders except a hint at instruction left by Couch, who mentioned in correspondence that "you are going into the mountains for a few days." Crooke took a blind guess, which led him to march his brigade south toward Mount Holly, under what L.T. Hyde of the 13th NYSNG called "one of the heaviest rain storms I ever saw." Departing Carlisle about noon, the brigade arrived at Mount Holly "a little before sundown[.]" "The road was lined with the straggler[s] and wounded coming from Gettysburgh [*sic*] and, now and then, a prisoner." Crooke's two regiments—both from Brooklyn—noted with especial interest that "plenty" of these men were of the 14th Brooklyn, a unit in the Army of the Potomac. Clearing Mount Holly, Crooke's soldiers met the same pleasantries experienced by Smith's command—namely waist-deep water. Drummer boys were carried by the men. As darkness came over, Crooke halted his progress at the base of the mountains. The following day he would join Ewen at Laurel Forge.[500]

Epilogue

Crooke's advance from Carlisle essentially ended the period of active operations in Cumberland County and the Harrisburg area. No longer was the Keystone State capital seriously threatened by Confederates. Many more Federal troops would move through the area but mainly via rail and with destinations closer to the Mason-Dixon in mind. As the Battle of Gettysburg raged from July 1 to 3, locals could distinctly hear the roar of cannon. William Sadler of White Hall had a glass of water at his windowsill that "jumped out" due to the tremors caused from the ruckus at Gettysburg.[501] Fort Washington would remain operational late into August. By August 22, only Captain David Mitchell's independent company garrisoned the fort.[502] In 1864, with the Confederacy still appearing able to mount offensives, plans were made "for an elaborate system of fortifications," but as the Southern nation began to crumble, the plans were rendered unnecessary. For the remainder of the war, the earthworks became "a favorite diversion of soldiers from Camp Curtin."[503]

In the early twentieth century, with development threatening, concerned citizens pushed legislation to preserve the earthworks as a state park. Unfortunately, the bill never gained any traction in the state legislature. Fort Couch, however, was preserved as a township park. Unappreciated, the latter fort evolved into a dump until it was restored in the 1950s. In 2005, a monument was erected at the site.[504] The John Rupp House, where Jenkins had his headquarters, is preserved, and in 2005, a monument was dedicated to General Jenkins and his men. Many other historic sites relative to the 1863 Confederate invasion were not as fortunate.

While historic preservation was lacking in the Harrisburg area, the career of one of its chief defendants was not. After the miserable trek

A modern photograph of the monument erected at Fort Couch in 2005 by the Camp Curtin Historical Society. *Photo by the author.*

to Pine Grove, Baldy Smith marched his command to the Mason-Dixon line. However, after ordering New York troops to Frederick, Maryland, so that they could board trains to reach New York City in time to quell the Draft Riots, an order arrived from Secretary of War Stanton directing Couch to arrest Smith. The situation was eventually sorted out, much to Smith's chagrin, and he was "remanded" to commandeer two regiments of volunteers at Hagerstown.

After about a month, Smith was ordered back to New York "to await orders." Soon Smith was sent to the Western Theater, where he was finally appreciated. Assigned to the post of chief engineer of the Army of the Cumberland, he would prove himself a key figure in dislodging Braxton Bragg and his Confederates from Missionary Ridge. He received his long-overdue major general's commission in March 1864 and was brought back to the East by Ulysses S. Grant, who gave him command of the 18th Corps in the Army of the James. Involved at the mishap at Cold Harbor, he later misjudged the formidability of Confederate works at Petersburg in mid-June 1864 and missed an opportunity to shorten the war perhaps by a year. Nonetheless, he served the remainder of the war and did not officially retire from the army until 1867. Smith spent the remainder of his life as president of a cable company, president of the board of police commissioners of New York City and a civilian engineer employed by the government on numerous nonmilitary operations. He died on February 28, 1903, at what had been his home for his last ten years in Philadelphia and is buried in Arlington National Cemetery.[505]

Carlisle embraced Smith as the South did Robert E. Lee. Smith received a beautiful silver pitcher in late September 1863 with a note attached to it from a group of ladies of Carlisle, signed by Mrs. R.C. Woodard, thanking him for his service in defending their city.[506] Smith thanked them but wrote privately:

> *The ladies of Carlisle seemed to think I had protected their homes, while probably if my troops had been in Harrisburg they would not have been disturbed, and the barracks would not have been burned. I was, however, the recipient of a beautiful silver pitcher, on which was engraved a very complimentary legend. A classmate serving with the cavalry in the West wrote to me an amusing letter, saying that his wife in Carlisle had subscribed to the pitcher, and hoped I would recollect him if any one ever proposed to compliment him in that manner. A very old lady who wished to do something in recognition of the siege, painted, from a photograph, a cabinet picture of me and sent it to my family. It was said to be a good likeness in everything but the hair, which was profuse and red!*[507]

Carlisle did forgive and forget—at first. In 1881, the Carlisle GAR Post held a "friendly" reunion at Luray with Confederate veterans from Page County, Virginia. In 1896, Fitz Lee—the man who thirty-three years earlier had shelled the town—was invited to speak at the annual commencement of the Carlisle Indian School, along with former Union 11th Corps commander Oliver Otis Howard. On February 27, Lee addressed the audience: "On these parade grounds I drilled recruits after my return from West Point. Afterwards I was ordered to Texas…and there I became acquainted with the red rovers of the plains, receiving as a memento a scar which I still bear, made by the swift-flying arrow of a Comanche." A brief, unapologetic mention of the shelling served to rile up many citizens. Nevertheless, Fitz added, "But all this is past, and I rejoice with you that there is rust on the sword." Over a span of several days, Carlisle newspapers attacked Lee with unforgiving headlines such as "What He Did."[508]

Darius Couch remained in Pennsylvania for quite some time. Commanding the merger of the Susquehanna and Monongahela Departments—the Department of Pennsylvania—he was at the helm when Chambersburg was burned in July 1864. Later that year, Couch received command of a division of the 23rd Corps in the Western Theater. In December 1864, he was engaged at the Battle of Nashville, where he had a horse killed under him. He was also involved in the 1865 Carolinas Campaign before resigning that May. After the war, Couch's political career never got off the ground due to his strong affiliations with George McClellan and the Democratic Party. He took up residence in Norwalk, Connecticut, where he served as state quartermaster general and adjutant general until his death on February 12, 1897. He is buried in Taunton, Massachusetts.[509]

Unlike Couch and Smith, Albert Gallatin Jenkins would not survive the war. On July 2 at Gettysburg, Jenkins was wounded when a shell burst near him while he was observing Yankee movements from Blocher's Knoll on the first day's battlefield. Jenkins returned to his command that autumn. On May 9, 1864, at the Battle of Cloyd's Mountain near Dublin in southwestern Virginia, he was wounded and captured while attempting to rally troops. A Yankee surgeon amputated his arm at the shoulder, but due to a medical mishap, he died on May 21. Jenkins is buried in Spring Hill Cemetery in Huntington, West Virginia.[510]

Not only did Harrisburg-area Civil War sites disappear physically, but their relevance in history seemed to as well. However, just one day made the difference of an attack by Ewell's corps on Harrisburg. Unfortunately, the actions in the vicinity have oft been relegated to a footnote at best. Writing as an old man in the summer of 1913 during the fiftieth anniversary, Private Robert Vaughan of the 28th PVM—a veteran of Oyster's Point—offered his friend this fitting tribute to the Gettysburg Campaign's northernmost reaches:

> *When a great, big wave rolls in, curves its foam-topped mane and breaks with a roar, we stand back and say, or think—"thus far and no farther," scarce noting the little streamlets or the thin, smooth sheet of water that runs and creeps away up the sands of the sloping beach and so it was at the battle of Gettysburg. The High Water Mark on that field is undoubtedly in its proper place, showing where the crested wave of rebellion dashed in to be broken and hurled back by the solid shore of Loyalty and Patriotism. But the little streams, the thin sheet driven ahead of the big roller, ran away up the beach, until they reached the Susquehanna before they receded. The tremendous events and glorious results at Gettysburg and at Vicksburg drowned all smaller noises and happenings and they were scarcely noted. Yet the sand…[was] wetted… at Oyster's Point, a scant two miles from Harrisburg.[511]*

Casualties during the Shelling of Carlisle

O ne of the most trying aspects of documenting the shelling of Carlisle is accurately reporting the casualties incurred during the encounter. Casualties among Stuart's command number only one: Private Thomas Frank Yates. Born in Leonardtown, Maryland, around 1843, Yates was wounded in the nose at Carlisle. After the war, he went on to become deputy sheriff of Charles County, Maryland, and publish a newspaper titled *St. Mary's Beacon*. In 1894, he entered the Old Soldiers' Home in Pikesville, Maryland, where he died at the age of seventy and is buried in Our Lady's Chapel Cemetery in St. Mary's County.[512]

Federal casualties are a different story. In total, eighteen Yankee casualties resulted from the shelling—at least seventeen wounded and one mortally wounded (see Appendix B). Dozens of men received slight wounds, though only seventeen were serious enough to be documented. Two of the latter number were wounded during the shelling and reportedly died later from their injuries—one man several years later. Additionally, there are other reports that are so lacking in detail as to call into question their accuracy. Following is the most comprehensive list possible of Yankee wounded:

Private Duffield Ashmead, Landis's battery—"Slight" contusion from shell.[513]

Second Lieutenant Henry F. Atherton, Company B, 28th PVM—Unspecified.[514]

Private John Blakison, Company D, 32nd PM—Unspecified.[515]

Captain Asa Bird Gardiner, Company I, 22nd NYSNG—Struck by a shell in the leg in an attempt to deliver a message to General Smith, causing only a slight wound. He was given a horse from General Ewen, which he was forced to ride for several days. For this and his actions at the Battle of Sporting Hill, Gardiner was awarded a Congressional Medal of Honor, which he was later asked to return. Gardiner termed this "a scandalous act."[516]

PRIVATE J.P. HUBBARD, Company K, 37th NYSNG—Scalp wound from shell.[517]

CORPORAL MARCUS HUNTER, Company B, 28th PVM—Contusion from shell on right leg, early in the shelling.[518]

PRIVATE FRANK KROFF, Company F, 30th PVM—Injured "slightly" from a fall.[519]

PRIVATE HENRY B. LELAND, Landis's battery—Brother Charles Leland recalled, "As we were not firing, I and the rest of the men of the gun were lying on the ground to escape the shells, but my brother…stood upright in his place just beside me. There came a shell which burst immediately, and very closely over our heads, and a piece of it struck my brother exactly on the brass buckle in his belt on the spine. The blow was so severe that the buckle was bent in two. It cut through his coat and shirt, and inflicted a slight wound two inches in length. But the blow on the spine had produced a concussion or disorganisation [sic] of the brain, which proved, after years of suffering, the cause of his death. At first he was quite senseless, but as he came to, and I asked him anxiously if he was hurt, he replied sternly, 'Go back immediately to your place by the gun!'" Henry still partook in the battery's march to Pine Grove, where, wrote Charles, "the wound on my brother's brain manifested itself in a terrible hallucination…Taking me aside he informed me that as he had a few days before entered a country-house, contrary to an order issued, to buy food, he was sure that Captain Landis meant as soon as possible to have him shot, but that he intended, the instant he saw any sign of this, at once to attack and kill the captain!" Charles was able to quell his brother's insanity, "but he was never the same person afterwards[.]"[520]

PRIVATE GEORGE MCNUT, Company C, 33rd PVM—Shell wound, right leg.[521]

CORPORAL HENRY C. MECKLEIN, Company C, 37th NYSNG—Shell wound, right knee.[522]

PRIVATE J.W. MORTON, Company B, 22nd NYSNG—"Foot cut by a piece of shell…he was the only one [in the 22nd] who was injured enough to go to the hospital."[523]

CORPORAL C. STUART PATTERSON, Landis's battery—Shell wound, right hand, removing two fingers and necessitating amputation of others.[524]

PRIVATE JOHN J. SCALLY, Company C, 37th NYSNG—Contusion from shell.[525]

PRIVATE WALTER SCOTT, Landis's battery—Shell wound in head, which reportedly caused his death.[526]

FIRST LIEUTENANT WILLIAM PROVOST TREADWELL, Company K, 37th NYSNG—Wound in right hand.[527]

CORPORAL BAXTER W. WALTER, Company H, 32nd PM—Shell wound on face and right ear.[528]

PRIVATE ROBERT WYLIE, Company D, 33rd PVM—Friendly-fire gunshot wound through knee, limb amputated above the knee.[529]

The Death of Private Charles Colliday at Carlisle

A lifelong resident of Philadelphia, Charles W. Colliday had seen prior service in the 32nd PM—or, as it was better known, the Gray Reserves—during the 1862 Maryland Campaign, when the regiment was designated the 7th Pennsylvania Militia. In 1863, after arriving in Harrisburg on June 18, the Philadelphians were mustered in on June 26 and remained in Camp Curtin until nearly sundown on June 28, when Couch dispatched the Grays to Smith's aid. By July 1, the regiment, commanded by Colonel Charles S. Smith and numbering 894 officers and men, had joined in company with three other Pennsylvania regiments under Colonel Brisbane.[530]

As Stuart's artillery opened upon Carlisle, the Grays were formed in line just off the square on North Hanover Street. Private Theodore Justice of Company D was next to Colliday in line of battle. It was during the second shelling, after Smith had refused Stuart's first armistice bearers, Justice recalled, that Colliday was struck by a shell and badly wounded "as he stood in line." Private Frank L. Neall, on the other side of the wounded Colliday, cried out in a sentence that betrayed his and Justice's Quaker faith, "Theodore, is thee hurt?" For the remainder of the campaign, recalled Justice, he was greeted oft with that same query as "the use of the phraseology of the non-combatant Quakers amidst the carnage of war appealed to the soldiers' sense of humor[.]"[531] By Justice's account, Colliday was wounded while standing in line. Noncombatant Isaac Harris of the U.S. Sanitary Commission recorded he was informed that Colliday "attempted to run across the road, but a shell winged him in the right leg."[532] Justice's account is more trustworthy considering that he was at Colliday's side when his comrade received the wound, while Harris heard it

Private Charles W. Colliday of Company D, 32nd Pennsylvania Militia, was mortally wounded at Carlisle. He is presumably the northernmost Union fatality of the Gettysburg Campaign. *Courtesy of the U.S. Army Military History Institute.*

secondhand. Therefore, it is safe to say Colliday received the wound while standing in line of battle.

In its comprehensive reporting on the shelling's casualties, the *Philadelphia Daily Evening Bulletin* listed Colliday's wound as a compound shell fracture of his right thigh.[533] Colliday was taken to the home of Jacob Rheem in Carlisle, where the amputation of his leg "was successfully performed by Drs. Darrow and [S.B.] Kieffer [Keefer]." "For two weeks he got along finely, the stump healing rapidly," reported A.K. Rheem, editor of the *Carlisle Herald*, "but his weak constitution finally gave way, and though he received the most careful attention and kindly nursing, he gradually succumbed" at 1:00 a.m. on July 27.[534]

Abbreviations

ALPL	Abraham Lincoln Presidential Library, Springfield, IL
BC	Border Damage Claims, RG 2, Pennsylvania State Archives, Harrisburg, PA
CBC	Carlisle Barracks Collection, U.S. Army Military History Institute, Carlisle, PA
CCHS	Hamilton Library, Cumberland County Historical Society, Carlisle, PA
CDP	Casper Dull Papers, Dauphin County Historical Society, Harrisburg, PA
CWD	Civil War Document Collection, U.S. Army Military History Institute, Carlisle, PA
CWM	Civil War Miscellaneous Collection, U.S. Army Military History Institute, Carlisle, PA
CWTI	*Civil War Times Illustrated* Collection, U.S. Army Military History Institute, Carlisle, PA
DC	Waidner-Spahr Library, Dickinson College, Carlisle, PA
DP	John W. Daniel Papers, Alderman Library, University of Virginia, Charlottesville, VA
GNMP	Gettysburg National Military Park Library, Gettysburg, PA
HCWRT	Harrisburg Civil War Round Table Collection, U.S. Army Military History Institute, Carlisle, PA
HRL	Stewart Bell Jr. Archives, Handley Regional Library, Winchester, VA
HSDC	Alexander Family Library, Historical Society of Dauphin County, Harrisburg, PA
HSP	Historical Society of Pennsylvania, Philadelphia, PA

KRK	Keith R. Keller Collection, U.S. Army Military History Institute, Carlisle, PA
LC	Library of Congress, Washington, D.C.
MDHS	H. Furlong Baldwin Library, Maryland Historical Society, Baltimore, MD
MMA	Mechanicsburg Museum Association, Mechanicsburg, PA
MWP	Micajah Woods Papers, University of Virginia, Charlottesville, VA
NARA	National Archives and Records Administration, Washington, D.C.
NT	*National Tribune*, Washington, D.C.
NYHS	New-York Historical Society, New York, NY
NYSA	New York State Archives, Albany, NY
OR	U.S. War Department, *The War of the Rebellion: A Compilation of the Official Records of the Union and Confederate Armies* (Washington, D.C.: Government Printing Office, 1889), Series I
PASA	Pennsylvania State Archives, Pennsylvania Historic and Museum Commission, Harrisburg, PA
PDEB	*Philadelphia Daily Evening Bulletin*
PGS	Philip German Scrapbook, Historical Society of Dauphin County, Harrisburg, PA
PPM	Pennypacker Mills Historic Site, Schwenksville, PA
RG-19	Record Group 19, Records of the Department of Military and Veterans Affairs, Civil War Muster Rolls & Related Records, PASA
RLB	Robert L. Brake Collection, U.S. Army Military History Institute, Carlisle, PA
SHC	Southern Historical Collection, Louis Round Wilson Library, University of North Carolina, Chapel Hill, NC
SOR	Janet Hewett, ed., *Supplement to the Official Records of the Union and Confederate Armies* (Wilmington, NC: Broadfoot, 1996)
SPL	Simpson Public Library, Mechanicsburg, PA
"Thirty Days"	Anonymous, "Thirty Days with the Seventy-first Regiment," *Continental Monthly* 4, no. 4 (October 1863)
UNC	University of North Carolina, Chapel Hill, NC
USAMHI	U.S. Army Military History Institute, Carlisle, PA
UVA	Alderman Library, University of Virginia, Charlottesville, VA
VTHS	Leahy Library, Vermont Historical Society, Barre, VT
WRHS	Western Reserve Historical Society, Cleveland, OH

Notes

Chapter 1

1. Couch, "Chancellorsville Campaign," in *Battles and Leaders*, 171.
2. Glazier, *Peculiarities of American Cities*, 199–202; Penn, "John Penn's Journal," 290–91.
3. Cazenove, *Cazenove Journal*, 51–54.
4. Washington, *President Washington's Diaries*, 56.
5. Henry Wirt Shriver to Frederick Augustus Shriver, June 17, 1863, Shriver Family Papers, MS 2085, Box 9, MDHS.
6. Theodore Burr to John Downey, May 21, June 12, 1812, Burr Papers, MG 57, PASA.
7. Ibid., May 28, 1814.
8. Harrisburg Bridge Company Minutes, September 17, 1847, MG 112, HSDC.
9. Ibid., November 6, 1850.
10. *OR* 27:3, 914.
11. Warner, *Generals in Blue*, 95–96; William F. Smith Typescript Memoir, Smith Papers, VTHS. In his memoir, Smith, who records this account (which he likely heard secondhand via Couch), opined that Lincoln's offer was likely more to "see if self interest was behind Couch's action."
12. *OR* 27:3, 54–55. Brooks received a promotion to major general in June 1863, but the War Department later revoked this rank.
13. Ibid., 2, 211.
14. Ibid., 3, 68–69.
15. Ibid., 79–80.

16. Kamm, "Civil War Career of Thomas A. Scott," 151–52.
17. A.F. Mathis to Curtin, June 13, 1863, Benjamin Reinhold to Curtin, June 16, 1863, Commissions File, RG 19, PASA.
18. Garrett Ramsey to Curtin, June 14, 1863, ibid.
19. B.H. Hyde to Curtin, June 15, 1863, ibid.
20. Samuel Comfort Jr. to A.L. Russell, June 22, 1863, ibid.
21. A.N. Brice to Eli Slifer, June 26, 1863, Slifer Papers MC 2003.4, DC.
22. A. Beil to Curtin, June 29, 1863, Commissions File, RG 19, PASA.
23. George Osborn to A.L. Russell, June 18, 1863, ibid.
24. Jones to Curtin, June 15, 1863, ibid.
25. Arthur Wolff to Curtin, June 15, 1863, ibid.
26. *OR* 27:2, 211–12.
27. Ibid., 3, 76–77.
28. Ibid.
29. Ibid., 95.
30. Andrew Carnegie to George Lauder Jr., June 21, 1863, Carnegie Papers, LC.
31. McClure, *Lincoln and Men of War Times*, 244–45.
32. *OR* 27:3, 97.
33. Ibid., 111.
34. Pleasonton, *Third Annual Report*, 11.
35. *OR* 27:3, 134–35.
36. Ibid., 2, 212.
37. *PDEB*, June 13, 1863.
38. Pennypacker, "Six Weeks in Uniform," 307–9.
39. *OR* 27:3, 138.
40. Ibid., 2, 227.
41. Wingate, *Twenty-Second Regiment*, 150.
42. Isaac Harris Diary, June 25, 1863, CWD, USAMHI.
43. E. Burd Grubb, "How the 23rd of N.J. Came Here in 1863," PGS, HSDC; Foster, *New Jersey and the Rebellion*, 512–13; Toombs, *New Jersey Troops in the Gettysburg Campaign*, 86–87.
44. *OR* 27:2, 212.
45. Ibid., 3:264.
46. *Philadelphia Press*, June 26, 1863.
47. Harris Diary, June 29, 1863, CWD, USAMHI.
48. *OR* 27:3, 496.
49. Smith Typescript Memoir, VTHS.
50. Warner, *Generals in Blue*, 95–96, 159–60, 462–63; Smith, *Autobiography*, 66–67.

51. William B. Franklin to William F. Smith, June 23, 1863, Smith Papers, VTHS.

52. Wingate, *Twenty-Second Regiment*, 206; Warner, *Generals in Blue*, 462–63.

53. *OR* 27:3, 330.

CHAPTER 2

54. J.B. Wheeler Report to Chief of Engineers, August 31, 1863, RG 77, NARA.

55. John Wilson Diary, June 14 1863, HSP.

56. Ibid., June 15, 1863; Gottschalk, *Notes of a Pianist*, 210; *PDEB*, June 17, 1863.

57. Lockwood, *Our Campaign Around Gettysburg*, 24–25.

58. *PDEB*, June 16, 1863.

59. Wilson Diary, June 15–16, 1863, HSP; *New York Tribune*, June 17, 1863; Wheeler Report, NARA; Gottschalk, *Notes of a Pianist*, 212.

60. Wilson Diary, June 16–23, 1863, HSP.

61. R. Went Diary, June 15–17, 1863, MG-6, PASA.

62. Gottschalk, *Notes of a Pianist*, 208–12.

63. *PDEB*, June 17, 1863.

64. Wingate, *Twenty-Second Regiment*, 179.

65. William Robinson Diary, June 18, 1863, CWM, USAMHI.

66. Went Diary, June 16–17,1863, PASA.

67. Wingate, *Twenty-Second Regiment*, 169–70; Harris Diary, June 24, 1863, CWD, USAMHI.

68. Minutes of the Harrisburg Bridge Company, January 4, 1864, HSDC; E.J. Moore to Wife, June 19, 1863, E.J. Moore Collection, LC.

69. Lockwood, *Our Campaign Around Gettysburg*, 23.

70. *OR* 27:2, 256–57.

71. L.T. Hyde, "Campaign of Brooklyn City Guard June and July 1863," KRK, USAMHI.

72. Lockwood, *Our Campaign Around Gettysburg*, 23.

73. Jacob Spangler to Dear Mother, June 18, 1863, Box 7, Strokes L. Roberts Papers, MG 198, PASA

74. *OR* 27:3, 203; Gambone, *Enigmatic Valor*, 280 n. 43; Moore to Wife, June 17, 1863, LC.

75. Pennypacker, "Six Weeks in Uniform," 311–13.

76. Editorial Correspondence with Co. B, 28th PVM, *Montrose Democrat*, July 2, 1863.

77. Charles Sayles to Dear Caroline, June 18, 1863, GNMP.
78. Shriver to Frederick Augustus Shriver, June 17, 1863, Shriver Family Papers, MDHS.
79. Moore to Wife, June 19, 1863.
80. Parson, "History of 'Co. A,'" 92.
81. "History of the 27th Pennsylvania Emergency Men," CWD, USAMHI.
82. Shriver to Frederick Augustus Shriver, June 17, 1863, Shriver to Uncle, June 20, 1863, Shriver Family Papers, MDHS.
83. Moore to Wife, June 16, 17, 19, 1863, LC.
84. *PDEB*, June 20, 1863.
85. Shriver to Frederick Augustus Shriver, June 17, 1863, Shriver Family Papers, MDHS.
86. Moore to Wife, June 17, 1863, LC.
87. Curtin to Kate Curtin, June 25, 1863, Military Dispatches, Transportation and Telegraph Department, RG 19, PASA.
88. *OR* 27:3, 347–48.
89. Burr, *James Addams Beaver*, 62–64.
90. Went Diary, June 17, 1863, PASA.
91. *OR* 27:3, 223.
92. *Philadelphia Press*, June 26, 1863.
93. Pleasonton, *Third Annual Report*, 87; Jones, *1st Philadelphia Light Artillery*, 7.
94. Wheeler Report, NARA.
95. *OR* 27:2, 232; "Forts Washington and Henry Clay," Kelker Family Collection, MG 405, HSDC; Pleasonton, *Third Annual Report*, 87.
96. Lockwood, *Our Campaign Around Gettysburg*, 31.
97. "History of the 27th Pennsylvania Emergency Men," CWD, USAMHI.
98. *OR* 27:3, 391, 448; Jones, *1st Philadelphia Light Artillery*, 7; John Gummere Diary, June 27, 1863, HSP; *Harrisburg Evening Telegraph*, June 29, 1863; Hyde, "Campaign," KRK, USAMHI.
99. H.H. Snavely War Sketch, "Personal War Sketches," Col. H.I. Zinn Post 415, SPL.
100. Editorial Correspondence with Co. B, 28th PVM, *Montrose Democrat*, July 2, 1863; Smith, "Marches and Exposures of the 28th Regiment," Palmer Collection, WRHS; Zeamer, *Cumberland Blue Book*, 93.
101. Wheeler Report, NARA.
102. Pleasonton, *Third Annual Report*, 87.
103. Lockwood, *Our Campaign Around Gettysburg*, 48–49.
104. Wheeler Report, NARA.
105. *Harrisburg Daily Patriot and Union*, June 24, 1863.

106. Shriver to Frederick Augustus Shriver, July 8, 1863, Shriver Family Papers, MDHS; Newspaper Scrapbook, PPM.

107. Welsh, "Some Personal Experience," Nye Papers, GNMP.

108. Lockwood, *Our Campaign Around Gettysburg*, 33.

109. Hyde, "Campaign," KRK, USAMHI.

110. Shriver to Frederick Augustus Shriver, July 8, 1863, Shriver Family Papers, MDHS.

111. Lockwood, *Our Campaign Around Gettysburg*, 33–34.

112. Ibid., 34–35.

113. Hyde, "Campaign," KRK, USAMHI.

114. Henry Wirt Shriver Diary, June 29, 1863, Shriver Family Papers, MDHS.

115. Pennypacker, "Six Weeks in Uniform," 363.

116. Ibid., 363–65; Shriver to Frederick Augustus Shriver, July 4, 1863, Shriver Family Papers, MDHS.

117. Pennypacker, "Fort Washington," 242–43; *Harrisburg Evening Telegraph*, June 29, 1863.

118. Pleasonton, *Third Annual Report*, 86.

119. Pennypacker, "Six Weeks in Uniform," 365; John Irvin Murray Diary, June 22, 1863, NYHS; PGS, DCHS.

120. Shriver to Mary Winebrenner and Frederick Augustus Shriver, June 29, 1863, Shriver Family Papers, MDHS.

121. Klinefelter, "Historical Sketch," GNMP.

122. PGS, HSDC.

123. *OR* 27:2, 229–30.

124. Ibid., 234; Murray Diary, June 20–22, 1863, NYHS; Wingate, *Twenty-Second Regiment*, 168–69.

125. Murray Diary, June 22, 1863, NYHS.

126. Ibid., June 25, 1863.

127. *OR* 27:2, 234–35.

128. Murray Diary, June 27, 1863, NYHS; Wingate, *Twenty-Second Regiment*, 175.

CHAPTER 3

129. Warner, *Generals in Gray*, 154.

130. Dickinson, *16ᵗʰ Virginia Cavalry*, 16.

131. Armstrong, *19ᵗʰ and 20ᵗʰ Virginia Cavalry*, 10.

132. Thomas L. Feamster to J.F. Watts, May 31, 1863, Feamster Family Papers, LC.

133. Scott, *36th and 37th Battalions Virginia Cavalry*, 2–3.

134. Driver, *14th Virginia Cavalry*, 176.

135. Moore, *Graham's Petersburg*, 36–55.

136. Baltimore Battery Monument, Antietam National Battlefield.

137. Pfanz, *Richard S. Ewell*, 20–21, 28.

138. Ibid., 263–90.

139. Turner, *Ted Barclay*, 84.

140. Samuel Dunbar Letter, May 20, 1863, CWTI, USAMHI.

141. Ibid.

142. Busey and Martin, *Regimental Strengths and Losses*, 278.

143. David Zable Speech, December 12, 1903, RLB, USAMHI.

144. Daniel Sheetz to Brother, June 18, 1863, GNMP.

145. George Daugherty to Dear Friends, June 20, 1863, Daugherty Papers, USAMHI.

Chapter 4

146. Washington, *President Washington's Diaries*, 56–62.

147. Harris Diary, June 19–22, 1863, CWD, USAMHI.

148. Francis, *History of the 71st Regiment*, 260-62.

149. Williams, *From the Cannon's Mouth*, 252.

150. Sullivan, *Boyhood Memories*, 14–15.

151. Charles Himes to Dear Rood, October 2, 1863, Himes Papers MC 2000.1, DC.

152. Francis, *History of the 71st Regiment*, 262–63; *Philadelphia Press*, July 1, 1863; *Carlisle American*, "Rebel Occupancy of Carlisle," July 15, 1863; Pleasonton, *Third Annual Report*, 70; "Thirty Days"; Robinson Diary, June 24–25, 1863, CWM, USAMHI.

153. Knipe to Couch, June 25, 1863, CDP.

154. *OR* 27:3, 344, 814.

155. *Philadelphia Press*, July 1, 1863; Francis, *History of the 71st Regiment*, 263; Pleasonton, *Third Annual Report*, 70; Robinson Diary, June 25, 1863, CWM, USAMHI; "Thirty Days."

156. *Philadelphia Press*, June 29, 1863; *Harrisburg Evening Telegraph*, June 27, 1863.

157. Schaumann, *Taverns of Cumberland County*, 168–70. The tavern is known by three different names: Stone Tavern, Moore's Tavern and Cumberland Hall.

158. *Philadelphia Press*, June 29, 1863; *Harrisburg Evening Telegraph*, June 27, 1863; *Harrisburg Daily Patriot and Union*, June 29, 1863. The ten men captured were Joseph Weaver, Jacob Stiner, Richard Bucher, John Dobert, Jacob Feig, James Irvin, John Stormfeltz, D. Slack, Rudy and Bates.

159. Charles Leeds, "Invasion of Carlisle," Miscellaneous Newspaper Clippings, CBC, USAMHI.

160. Isaac V. Reynolds to Dear Wife, August 9, 1863, ALPL.

161. Eunice Stewart to Dear Parents, June 24 [25], 1863, HCWRT, USAMHI; Goldsborough, *Maryland Line*, 284; Stevenson, *"Boots and Saddles,"* 211.

162. *OR*, 27:2, 565–66.

163. Reynolds to Dear Wife, July 20, 1863, ALPL.

164. Harris, *Autobiography*, 91–92.

165. Goldsborough, *Maryland Line*, 285; *Carlisle American*, "Rebel Occupancy of Carlisle," July 15, 1863.

166. Dickinson and Dickinson, *Gentleman Soldier of Greenbottom*, 95.

167. *Carlisle American*, "Rebel Occupancy of Carlisle," July 15, 1863.

168. May, *Journal and Letters*, 105.

169. Harris Diary, June 20, 1863, CWD, USAMHI.

170. Cazenove, *Cazenove Journal*, 58.

171. Washington, *President Washington's Diaries*, 62–63.

172. Stewart to Dear Parents, June 24, 1863, HCWRT, USAMHI.

173. Samuel Pickens Diary, June 26, 1863, GNMP.

174. Ibid.

175. J.C. Attick Diary, June 26, 1863, CWTI, USAMHI.

176. Douglas, *I Rode With Stonewall*, 237.

177. John William Ford Hatton Memoir, June 23, 27, 1863, LC.

178. *Carlisle American*, "Rebel Occupancy of Carlisle," July 15, 1863.

179. Ibid., "A Few Days of Rebel Rule," August 5, 1863.

180. Sullivan, *Boyhood Memories*, 17–18.

181. Thomas, *History of the Doles-Cook Brigade*, 8; John Harris Diary, June 28, 1863, GNMP; Pryor, *Post of Honor*, 369.

182. Goodyear, *Lee's Invasion of Carlisle*, 2–4; James E. Green Diary, June 27, 1863, RLB, USAMHI.

183. Pickens Diary, June 27–28, 1863, GNMP; Park, "Sketch of the Twelfth Alabama Infantry," 243.

184. R.K. Hitner to Mrs. David Hastings, July 6, 1863, CBC, USAMHI; Jones, *Campbell Brown's Civil War*, 200–1; *Carlisle American*, "Rebel Occupancy of Carlisle," July 15, 1863.

185. Jones, *Campbell Brown's Civil War*, 201.

186. Pfanz, *Richard S. Ewell*, 28–30, 60–63, 299–300.

187. *OR*, 27:2, 443.

188. Eugene Blackford to Dear Father, June 28, 1863, GNMP; John F. Coghill to Dear Pappy Ma and Mil, July 10, 1863, Coghill Papers, SHC, UNC; William Marston Diary, June 28 1863, Confederate Miscellany Collection, Robert Woodruff Library, Emory University.

189. Blackford to Dear Father, June 28, 1863, GNMP.

190. Purifoy, "With Ewell and Rodes," 464.

191. Park, "Sketch of the Twelfth Alabama Infantry," 243.

192. *Carlisle American*, "Rebel Occupancy of Carlisle," July 15, 1863; Mingus, "Grandest Affair."

193. Pfanz, *Richard S. Ewell*, 299; See, Douglas, *I Rode With Stonewall*, 237–38, which also mentions this encounter.

194. *Carlisle American*, "Rebel Occupancy of Carlisle," July 15, 1863.

195. Requisition Order, CBC, USAMHI.

196. *Carlisle American*, "Rebel Occupancy of Carlisle," July 15, 1863; Goodyear, *Lee's Invasion of Carlisle*, 3–4.

197. Pfanz, *Richard S. Ewell*, 299; Jedediah Hotchkiss to Darling Sara, June 28, 1863, Hotchkiss Papers, LC.

198. Clemmer, *Old Alleghany*, 458.

199. McKim, "Steuart's Brigade," 292.

200. Schaumann, *Taverns of Cumberland County*, 194–95.

201. Hatton Memoir, June 27, 1863, LC.

202. *Newville Valley Times-Star*, "The Big Spring and the Big Spring Turnpike," March 4, 1956.

203. Samuel Firebaugh Diary, June 27, 1863, Wayland Collection, HRL.

204. Peffer, "History of Springfield," CCHS; Wing, *History of Cumberland County*, 25.

205. Thomas Tolson Diary, June 27, 1863, 1ˢᵗ Maryland Battalion Newspaper Clippings, GNMP; McKim, *A Soldier's Recollections*, 165–66.

206. Tolson Diary, June 27, 1863, GNMP; Wallcut, *Journal of Thomas Wallcut*, 35; Cazenove, *Cazenove Journal*, 62. The mill later became renowned for shipping flour to Queen Victoria.

207. "Rebels Invade Springfield at Head of Big Spring During Civil War," Newspaper Clipping, Newville Historical Society.

208. Firebaugh Diary, June 28, 1863, HRL; Tolson Diary, June 28, 1863, GNMP; Goldsborough, *Maryland Line*, 125; McKim, "Steuart's Brigade," 292.

209. Goldsborough, *Maryland Line*, 125–26.

210. Ibid., 127.

211. Sharpe, "A Boy's Experience," *Pennsylvania History*, 166.

212. Nettie Jane Blair Reminisce, 1934, Numbered Box Collection 120-13, CCHS.

213. *Altoona Tribune*, June 16, 1863.

214. L. Brown to John Lingle, July 9, 1863, HCWRT, USAMHI.

215. Bond, "Company A, First Maryland Cavalry," 78; Gill, *Courier for Lee and Jackson*, 41–42.

216. William McCandlish Diary, June 27–29, 1863, Newville Historical Society; Zenas J. Gray Account, Newville Historical Society; John Lefever Diary, June 29, 1863, Newville Historical Society; Martha B. Munn to Martha Jane, March 1929, CCHS.

217. C.B. Niesley to Dear Parents, July 1, 1863, HCWRT, USAMHI.

218. *Carlisle Sentinel*, "Tablet Unveiled at Spot Where Rebels Turned," October 26, 1929; McCandlish Diary, June 27, 1863, Newville Historical Society.

219. Hufham, "Gettysburg," 451–56; Clark, *Histories of the Several Regiments*, 2:233.

220. George Wills to Dear Sister, June 28, 1863, Wills Papers, SHC, UNC; Jones, *Campbell Brown's Civil War*, 200–1; Clark, *Histories of the Several Regiments*, 2:525–26.

221. Jones, *Campbell Brown's Civil War*, 201–3; Hotchkiss Diary, June 28, 1863, Hotchkiss Papers, LC.

222. Trimble, "Battle and Campaign of Gettysburg," 116–28.

223. Thomas, *History of the Doles-Cook Brigade*, 8.

224. Sheffey, *Soldier of Southwestern Virginia*, 154–55.

225. *OR* 27:2, 552.

CHAPTER 5

226. Zeamer, *Cumberland Blue Book*, 76–77; Schaumann, *Taverns of Cumberland County*, 139.

227. Murray Diary, June 30, 1863, NYHS.

228. Bowman, "Map of Historical Points," CCHS.

229. *New York Times*, "Obituary: Gen. William Hall," May 4, 1874.

230. *OR* 27:2, 232; Pennypacker, "Six Weeks in Uniform," 359.

231. Gorgas Narrative, CDP.

232. Smith Typescript Memoir, VTHS.

233. *SOR*, 59:2, 338, 341–42; Joseph Boggs Beale Diary, June 24–27, 1863, HSP; Correspondence of the 33rd PVM, *Philadelphia Public Ledger*, July 3, 1863.

234. *New York Times*, "Col. William Everdell," November 6, 1912.

235. Lockwood, *Our Campaign Around Gettysburg*, 39–42; Vaughan to German, 1913, PGS, HSDC; Brinton, Sawyer and Shopp Narratives, CDP.

236. Beale Diary, June 27–28, 1863, HSP.

237. Ibid.; John Mater and Rupp Narratives, CDP.

238. Whittemore, *Seventy-First Regiment*, 76; Lithograph of 11th NYSNG, PGS, HSDC; Sadler Narrative, CDP; Pleasonton, *Third Annual Report*, 70–71; Robinson Diary, June 27, 1863, CWM, USAMHI.

239. Bowman Narrative, CDP.

240. Gorgas Narrative, CDP.

241. Charles Macdonald to Samuel Pennypacker, July 11, 1892, PPM.

242. Brinton and Sawyer Narratives, CDP.

243. John Mater and George Mater Narratives, CDP.

244. Brinton and Bowman Narratives, CDP.

245. Shriver to Frederick Augustus Shriver, July 4, 1863, Shriver Family Papers, MDHS.

246. Gorgas Narrative, CDP.

CHAPTER 6

247. Schuricht, "Jenkins' Brigade," 339–50; Reynolds to Dear Wife, August 9, 1863, ALPL.

248. *Cumberland Valley Journal*, "The Rebel Invasion," July 23, 1863.

249. Schuricht, "Jenkins' Brigade."

250. Goldsborough, *Maryland Line*, 285.

251. *New York Daily Tribune*, June 30, 1863.

252. Schuricht, "Jenkins' Brigade"; *Cumberland Valley Journal*, "The Rebel Invasion," July 23, 1863; Hauck's Centennial Directory of Mechanicsburg, 1876, MMA; *Philadelphia Press*, July 1, 1863; Goldsborough, *Maryland Line*, 285; Moore, *Rebellion Record*, 7:18; Hoke, *Great Invasion*, 182–83.

253. This interpretation of the Confederate deployment on both the pike and the Trindle Springs Road varies drastically from earlier versions. However, the interpretation for this book was done with several new pieces of crucial historical evidence, which, when carefully interpreted, render

past theories implausible. See, Stewart, *History of the Cumberland Valley*, 101; Vincent A. Witcher to John W. Daniel, March 15, 1900, January 26, 1906, March 1, 1906, March 22, 1906, DP, UVA; *Richmond Enquirer* account, reprinted in Schuricht, "Jenkins' Brigade."

254. *Richmond Enquirer* account, Schuricht, "Jenkins' Brigade"; Micajah Woods to Dear Mother, June 30, 1863, MWP, UVA; *Cumberland Valley Journal*, "The Rebel Invasion," July 23, 1863; Niesley to Dear Parents, July 1, 1863, HCWRT, USAMHI.

255. Hauck's Directory, 1876, MMA.

256. *Cumberland Valley Journal*, "The Rebel Invasion," July 23, 1863.

257. Ibid.; Hauck's Directory, 1876, MMA; *Richmond Enquirer* account, Schuricht, "Jenkins' Brigade"; Niesley to Dear Parents, July 1, 1863, HCWRT, USAMHI; Schuricht, "Jenkins' Brigade"; information courtesy of Andrew Sheely, Mechanicsburg, Pennsylvania.

258. *Cumberland Valley Journal*, "The Rebel Invasion," July 23, 1863; Hauck's Directory, 1876, MMA; Niesley to Dear Parents, July 1, 1863, HCWRT, USAMHI; "Paging Through Our Past," 11–12, SPL; Schuricht, "Jenkins' Brigade."

259. Woods to Dear Mother, June 30, 1863, MWP, UVA.

260. *Cumberland Valley Journal*, "The Rebel Invasion," July 23, 1863.

261. Hauck's Directory, 1876, MMA; Brown to Lingle, July 9, 1863, HCWRT, USAMHI.

262. *Cumberland Valley Journal*, "The Rebel Invasion," July 23, 1863; Hauck's Directory, 1876, MMA.

CHAPTER 7

263. Jacob Otstot Claim, BC. Otstot later filed a damage claim for $3.20 per gallon, a total of $146.25, but was only approved for $121.25 and, like many, never refunded.

264. Crist, "Highwater 1863," 181.

265. Pleasonton, *Third Annual Report*, 71; J.P.S. Lower, "The Tablet at Oyster's Point," *NT*, November 13, 1913; "Thirty Days"; Robinson Diary, June 28, 1863, CWM, USAMHI; Whittemore, *Seventy-First Regiment*, 76; Beale Diary, June 28, 1863, HSP. The reference to the Rebels advancing likely refers to Confederate skirmishers.

266. Woods to Dear Mother, June 30, 1863, MWP, UVA. Some have questioned whether Woods's account actually applies to the June 28

affair or, rather, the Skirmish of Oyster's Point on June 29. After careful analysis, the author finds that several factors demonstrate his account refers to June 28; first, on June 29, Jenkins could not have been present during the majority of the engagement as Woods states he was; second, Woods writes the encounter lasted roughly thirty minutes, while the June 29 bombardment lasted two hours. Also, if Woods and Jackson's battery weren't there, who was? Griffin certainly was not. Additionally, it is likely Jackson's entire battery was present, two guns deployed, as Woods would have likely mentioned if the battery had split.

267. Pleasonton, *Third Annual Report*, 71.
268. "Thirty Days"; Woods to Dear Mother, June 30, 1863, MWP, UVA.
269. Whittemore, *Seventy-First Regiment*, 76; *Carlisle Evening Sentinel*, "Fort Washington and the Home Guard," October 16, 1897; Beale Diary, June 28, 1863.
270. Woods to Dear Mother, June 30, 1863, MWP, UVA.
271. Lockwood, *Our Campaign Around Gettysburg*, 40–42; PGS, HSDC; 11th NYSNG Lithograph, PGS, HSDC.
272. Statement of Mrs. Lawrence Landis, Nye Papers, MS, GNMP.
273. J.B. Reeser Claim, BC.
274. Brinton, Bowman, Sawyer, Sadler and Smith Narratives, CDP.
275. Schuricht, "Jenkins' Brigade."
276. *Harrisburg Patriot*, "'Peace Church' on Trindle Road," November 18, 1927.
277. Woods to Dear Mother, June 30, 1863, MWP, UVA.
278. Bowman Narrative, CDP.
279. *Harrisburg Patriot*, "'Peace Church' on Trindle Road," November 18, 1927.
280. Reynolds to Dear Wife, August 9, 1863, ALPL; Witcher to Daniel, March 15, 1900, DP, UVA.
281. Beale Diary, June 28, 1863, HSP; Nicholas Rice, "Memoir," 79, Rice Papers, USAMHI; *Philadelphia Inquirer*, June 29, 1863.
282. Rice, "Memoir," 79, Rice Papers, USAMHI.
283. Beale Diary, June 28, 1863, HSP; Whittemore, *Seventy-First Regiment*, 76; Smith Typescript Memoir, VTHS.
284. Rice, "Memoir," 80, Rice Papers, USAMHI; *Philadelphia Press*, July 1, 1863.
285. Vaughan to German, 1913, PGS, HSDC; Welsh, "Some Personal Experience," GNMP; Editorial Correspondence with Co. B, 28th PVM, *Montrose Democrat*, July 9, 1863; Smith, "Marches and Exposures," WRHS.

286. Vaughan to German, 1913, PGS, HSDC.

287. Shopp Narrative, CDP.

288. Editorial Correspondence with Co. B, 28th PVM, *Montrose Democrat*, July 9, 1863.

289. Bowman Narrative, CDP; Welsh, "Some Personal Experience," GNMP.

290. Welsh, "Some Personal Experience," GNMP.

291. Ibid.

292. Editorial Correspondence with Co. B, 28th PVM, *Montrose Democrat*, July 9, 1863; Beale Diary, June 28, 1863, HSP.

293. Murray Diary, June 28, 1863, NYHS.

294. Lockwood, *Our Campaign Around Gettysburg*, 42–51.

295. Ibid., 42–43.

296. Murray Diary, June 28, 1863, NYHS; Wingate, *Twenty-Second Regiment*, 177–80.

297. *OR* 27:2, 234–35; Murray Diary, June 28, 1863, NYHS; Wingate, *Twenty-Second Regiment*, 180.

298. *New York Tribune*, June 30, 1863.

299. *OR* 27:2, 439, 551–52.

300. Bigler, Hemminger, Boyer, Rogers Claims, BC.

301. Boyer Claim, BC.

302. *OR* 27:2, 259–61.

303. Shopp Narrative, CDP.

304. Hoke, *Great Invasion*, 110.

305. *Harrisburg Daily Patriot and Union*, June 29, 1863.

306. Brinton Narrative, CDP.

307. Vaughan to German, 1913, PGS, HSDC; *Richmond Enquirer* account, Schuricht, "Jenkins' Brigade"; Beale Diary, June 28, 1863, HSP.

308. Vaughan to German, 1913, PGS, HSDC; Beale Diary, June 28, 1863; Smith, "Marches and Exposures," WRHS; Whittemore, *Seventy-First Regiment*, 76–77; "Thirty Days"; *New York Tribune*, June 30, 1863; *Philadelphia Inquirer*, June 30, 1863.

309. *OR* 27:3, 385.

310. Ibid., 387.

311. Murray Diary, June 28, 1863, NYHS; Wingate, *Twenty-Second Regiment*, 181.

312. Wingate, *Twenty-Second Regiment*, 181–82.

313. Ibid.; Murray Diary, June 28, 1863, NYHS.

314. Beale Diary, June 28, 1863, HSP.

315. Zeamer, *Cumberland Blue Book*, 99.

316. Witcher to Daniel, March 15, 1900, January 26, 1906, March 1, 1906, March 22, 1906, DP, UVA.
317. Witcher to Daniel, March 22, 1906, DP, UVA.

Chapter 8

318. *Harrisburg Evening Telegraph*, June 29, 1863; Brown to Lingle, July 9, 1863, HCWRT, USAMHI.
319. Henry C. Demming to Casper Dull, October 15, 1900, CDP, HSDC.
320. Ibid.
321. Ibid.
322. *New York Tribune*, "The Reports from Harrisburg," June 22, 1863.
323. John Mater Narrative, CDP; Hoke, *Great Invasion*, 123.
324. John and George Mater Narratives, CDP.

Chapter 9

325. Beale Diary, June 29, 1863, HSP.
326. "Thirty Days."
327. Ibid.
328. *Philadelphia Inquirer*, June 30, 1863.
329. *OR* 27:2, 220.
330. *Richmond Enquirer* account, Schuricht, "Jenkins' Brigade"; Smith Narrative, CDP.
331. Woods to Dear Father, July 10, 1863, MWP, UVA.
332. *OR* 27:3, 407; Whittemore, *Seventy-First Regiment*, 77; Beale Diary, June 29, 1863, HSP; Robinson Diary, June 29, 1863, CWM, USAMHI.
333. Beale Diary, June 29, 1863, HSP; Newspaper Correspondence of the 28th PVM, *Philadelphia Inquirer*, July 3, 1863; Smith and Bowman Narratives, CDP; Lower, "The Tablet at Oyster's Point," *NT*, November 13, 1913.
334. Lockwood, *Our Campaign*, 56–58. In his report, Elwell states that the 8th was deployed north of the pike and the 23rd south. However, his reference to the 8th being deployed "beyond the railroad" could only refer to the Cumberland Valley Railroad, south of the pike.
335. Witcher to Daniel, March 22, 1906, DP, UVA; Whittemore, *Seventy-First Regiment*, 76–77.

336. Rupp, Smith, Sadler and Wolf Narratives, CDP; *Carlisle Evening Sentinel*, "Fort Washington and the Home Guard," October 16, 1897.

337. Bowman, Sawyer, Rupp, Sadler, Wolf and Smith Narratives, CDP.

338. Beale Diary, June 29, 1863, HSP. Not only was Company F engaged, but so were ten men of Captain Stephen T. Souder's Company B, 33rd PVM, who fought with the 71st NYSNG. See, *SOR*, 59:2, 342.

339. Bowman, Smith, John Mater and Sawyer Narratives, CDP.

340. Sadler Narrative, CDP.

341. Ibid., Sawyer and Wolf Narratives; Whittemore, *Seventy-First Regiment*, 77; "Thirty Days." While some historians have written that the Confederates forgot the lone artillery piece in their haste to retire and had to return to retrieve it, local Benjamin F. Sawyer recorded that when the cannon fell back it did so with the Confederate cavalrymen.

342. *Richmond Enquirer* account, Schuricht's Diary entry, Schuricht, "Jenkins' Brigade"; Hotchkiss Diary, June, 29, 1863, Hotchkiss Papers, LC.

343. Gorgas Narrative, CDP.

344. Freeman, *Lee's Lieutenants*, 3:34.

345. Hotchkiss Diary, June 29, 1863, LC; James E. Green Diary, June 29, 1863, RLB, USAMHI; Pickens Diary, June 29, 1863, GNMP.

346. *OR* 27:2, 443, 552. The expectation of a Rebel advance was present among citizens as well. "There was quite an excitement about the rebels," penned a Millersburg schoolteacher in his diary. "It was reported that they are about crossing the river to invade our valley." The teacher fully expected a battle at Harrisburg and added that "before long" the Rebels would be stealing his property. See Josiah Weaver Diary, June 29 and July 1, 1863, PASA.

347. Green Diary, June 30, 1863, Brake Collection, USAMHI; Pickens Diary, June 30, 1863, GNMP; *Daily Evening Express*, July 2, 1863.

348. Bond, "Company A," 78.

CHAPTER 10

349. Welsh, "Some Personal Experience," GNMP.

350. *OR* 27:3, 434.

351. Ibid., 2, 220.

352. Scharf, *History of Westchester County*, 1:2, 767.

353. Wingate, *Twenty-Second Regiment*, 153.

354. Ibid., 192–93; *OR* 27:2, 220, 235; Murray Diary, June 30, 1863, NYHS; Wilson Diary, June 30, 1863, HSP.

355. Henry M.M. Richards to Samuel Pennypacker, July 5, 1892, PPM.

356. Haupt, *Reminiscences*, 211.

357. Murray Diary, June 30, 1863, NYHS; Leland, *Memoirs*, 253, 307; *Philadelphia Inquirer*, July 1, 1863.

358. Witcher to Daniel, March 6, 1906, DP, UVA.

359. Leland, *Memoirs*, 253, 307.

360. Coble Claim, filed by John Sample, guardian of heirs, BC.

361. *Richmond Enquirer* account, Schuricht, "Jenkins' Brigade."

362. Baker, Bristline, Clepper, Coble, Dietz, Fought, Hemminger, Herman, Simmons, Snyder and Spahr Claims, BC.

363. *Richmond Enquirer*, "Gen. Jenkins' Brigade," July 17, 1863.

364. Witcher to Daniel, March 6, 1906, March 22, 1906, DP, UVA; Wingate, *Twenty-Second Regiment*, 197; Schuricht, "Jenkins' Brigade."

365. *OR* 27:2, 235; Murray Diary, June 30, 1863, NYHS.

366. Murray Diary, June 30, 1863, NYHS.

367. Ibid.; *OR* 27:2, 235.

368. Wingate, *Twenty-Second Regiment*, 197; Witcher to Daniel, March 1, 1906, DP, UVA.

369. Though many sources call it the McCormick barn, it was not sold to James McCormick until the spring of 1864. See, Wingert, *Battle of Sporting Hill*, 18.

370. *OR* 27:2, 235; Wingate, *Twenty-Second Regiment*, 194–95.

371. Wingate, *Twenty-Second Regiment*, 194–95.

372. Ibid.

373. Ibid.; Murray Diary, June 30, 1863, NYHS.

374. Wingate, *Twenty-Second Regiment*, 194–95; *OR* 27:2, 220, 235; Moore, *Rebellion Record*, 7:20; Wingate, *History of Company A*, 29; Lloyd Aspinwall Letter, *New York Times*, July 26, 1863.

375. Wingate, *Twenty-Second Regiment*, 194.

376. *OR* 27:2, 235; Murray Diary, June 30, 1863, NYHS; Moore, *Rebellion Record*, 7:20; Aspinwall Letter, *New York Times*, July 26, 1863; Wingate, *Twenty-Second Regiment*, 194.

377. *OR* 27:2, 235; Wingate, *Twenty-Second Regiment*, 194–95; *New York Herald*, "Skirmish at Sporting Hill," July 1, 1863; *New York Times*, "Harrisburgh," July 3, 1863; Wingert, *Battle of Sporting Hill*, 27–29.

378. *OR* 27:2, 235; Wingate, *Twenty-Second Regiment*, 194–95.

379. *OR* 27:2, 219.

380. Wingate, *Twenty-Second Regiment*, 195–96.

381. Ibid., 194–95; Murray Diary, June 30, 1863, NYHS.

382. Murray Diary, June 30, 1863, NYHS.

383. Ibid.; Wingate, *Twenty-Second Regiment*, 194–95.

384. Wingate, *Twenty-Second Regiment*, 194–95; *OR* 27:2, 235; Wingert, *Battle of Sporting Hill*, 34; *New York Herald*, "Skirmish at Sporting Hill," July 1, 1863.

385. *Harrisburg Evening Telegraph*, "A Skirmish-Rebels Retreat," July 1, 1863.

386. *OR* 27:2, 220; Pleasonton, *Third Annual Report*, 88; *New York Times*, "Famous Twenty-Second," June 28, 1896; Wingate, *Twenty-Second Regiment*, 195.

387. Wingate, *Twenty-Second Regiment*, 196.

388. Jones, *1st Philadelphia Light Artillery*, 10.

389. Ibid.; *OR* 27:2, 235; Wingate, *Twenty-Second Regiment*, 196; Pleasonton, *Third Annual Report*, 82, 88.

390. Wingate, *Twenty-Second Regiment*, 196.

391. *OR* 27:2, 235; Jones, *1st Philadelphia Light Artillery*, 10–11; *New York Times*, "Famous Twenty-Second," June 28, 1896; Wingate, *Last Campaign*, 11; Wingate, *Twenty-Second Regiment*, 196; Pleasonton, *Third Annual Report*, 82, 88; *Harrisburg Evening Telegraph*, "A Skirmish-Rebels Retreat," July 1, 1863; *Harrisburg Daily Patriot and Union*, "The Situation," July 1, 1863; *Philadelphia Press*, "Cavalry Skirmish Near Mechanicsburg—The Rebels Forced to Retire," July 1, 1863.

392. Jones, *1st Philadelphia Light Artillery*, 11; *Harrisburg Daily Patriot and Union*, "The Situation," July 1, 1863.

393. Wingert, *Battle of Sporting Hill*, 51–52; *New York Herald*, "Skirmish at Sporting Hill," July 1, 1863; *Cumberland Valley Journal*, "The Rebel Invasion," July 23, 1863.

394. *OR* 27:2, 235.

395. Wingate, *Twenty-Second Regiment*, 196.

396. Schuricht, "Jenkins' Brigade."

397. Ibid.; *Cumberland Valley Journal*, "The Rebel Invasion," July 23, 1863.

398. Schuricht, "Jenkins' Brigade"; *Cumberland Valley Journal*, "The Rebel Invasion," July 23, 1863; Brinton Narrative, CDP.

399. *OR* 27:2, 235–37.

400. *Carlisle American*, "Rebel Occupancy of Carlisle," July 15, 1863.

401. Witcher to Daniel, March 15, 1900, January 26, 1906, March 1, 1906, March 22, 1906, DP, UVA; Schuricht, "Jenkins' Brigade."

Chapter 11

402. Wingate, *Twenty-Second Regiment*, 197–200.

403. *OR* 27:2, 236.

404. Haupt, *Reminiscences*, 208–13.

405. *OR* 27:2, 220; *Carlisle American*, "Rebel Occupancy of Carlisle," July 15, 1863; Smith Typescript Memoir, VTHS.

406. *OR* 27:2, 220; Smith, "Marches and Exposures," WRHS.

407. *OR* 27:2, 220.

408. *Harrisburg Evening Telegraph*, "The Impending Battle," July 2, 1863.

409. *OR* 27:2, 220, 27:3, 613; Smith, *Autobiography*, 67.

410. J. Boyd Robinson Letter, July 1, 1863, Pardee-Robinson Collection, USAMHI.

411. Murray Diary, June 30–July 1, 1863, NYHS.

412. Ibid., July 1, 1863; Wingate, *Twenty-Second Regiment*, 201; Pleasonton, *Third Annual Report*, 88. As Brisbane's brigade left Oyster's Point, the barricade near the tollgate was still in place, and the men had to march around it, through an orchard and a wheat field, "so as to go around it and allow all to look at it." See Beale Diary, July 1, 1863, HSP.

413. *OR* 27:2, 236; Murray Diary, July 1, 1863. Note that Company I remained in front as the advance guard; only Company B, the skirmishers, was recalled.

414. Wingate, *Twenty-Second Regiment*, 202–3.

415. Ibid., 204–5, 208; Murray Diary, July 1, 1863, NYHS.

416. Wingate, *Twenty-Second Regiment*, 202–4.

417. Ibid., 204; Aspinwall Letter, *New York Times*, July 26, 1863; Murray Diary, July 1, 1863, NYHS.

418. Welsh, "Some Personal Experience," GNMP.

419. Wingate, *Twenty-Second Regiment*, 214–15.

420. Wingate, *Last Campaign*, 17.

421. Wingate, *Twenty-Second Regiment*, 214–15.

422. Ibid., 206–8, 228.

423. Ibid., 208.

424. Ibid., 208–9; *OR* 27:2, 236; Murray Diary, July 1, 1863, NYHS; Beale Diary, July 1, 1863, HSP.

425. Wingate, *Twenty-Second Regiment*, 209–10; Jones, *1ˢᵗ Philadelphia Light Artillery*, 12; Welsh, "Some Personal Experience," GNMP; Rice, "Memoir," 80, Rice Papers, USAMHI. As they marched into Carlisle, the Yankees were some of the last to ever lay eyes on the old Carlisle Barracks and Gas Works. Murray Diary, July 1, 1863, NYHS.

426. *OR* 27:2, 220, 236; Wingate, *Twenty-Second Regiment*, 210–14.
427. Wingate, *Twenty-Second Regiment*, 215; *OR* 27:2, 220–21; Smith, *Autobiography*, 67; *Carlisle American*, "Rebel Occupancy of Carlisle," July 15, 1863; Smith Typescript Memoir, VTHS.
428. *OR* 27:2, 696.
429. Fitzhugh Lee to J.T. Zug, August 25, 1882, Civil War Correspondence 24-101-015, CCHS.
430. Theodore Garnett to George Wingate, May 31, 1892, published in Wingate, *Twenty-Second Regiment*, 221–25.
431. *Carlisle American*, "Rebel Occupancy of Carlisle," July 15, 1863; Margaret Murray to Harmar Murray, July 3, 1863, Numbered Box Collection 18-15, CCHS; Trout, *In the Saddle with Stuart*, 77; Beale Diary, July 1, 1863, HSP.
432. Nesbit's reminiscences appear in *Carlisle Evening Sentinel*, May 9, 11 and 26, 1923; Rice, "Memoir," 80, Rice Papers, USAMHI; Jones, *1s Philadelphia Light Artillery*, 12; Editorial Correspondence of Co. B, 28th PVM, *Montrose Democrat*, July 9, 1863; Beale Diary, July 1, 1863, HSP; Leland, *Memoirs*, 253; Pleasonton, *Third Annual Report*, 89–90.
433. Jones, *1st Philadelphia Light Artillery*, 12–13.
434. Rice, "Memoir," 80, Rice Papers, USAMHI; Murray to Harmar Murray, July 3, 1863, CCHS; *Carlisle Evening Sentinel*, May 9, 1923.
435. *Carlisle Evening Sentinel*, May 26, 1923.
436. Jones, *1st Philadelphia Light Artillery*, 13, 16; Pleasonton, *Third Annual Report*, 89–90; Beale Diary, July 1, 1863, HSP; Wingate, *Twenty-Second Regiment*, 216; Leland, *Memoirs*, 256, 267.
437. *Carlisle Evening Sentinel*, "Shelling of Carlisle Is Recalled," May 2, 1923.
438. Smith, *Autobiography*, 67; Pleasonton, *Third Annual Report*, 83.
439. Wingate, *Twenty-Second Regiment*, 216–19; Jones, *1st Philadelphia Light Artillery*, 14; Rice, "Memoir," 81, Rice Papers, USAMHI; Beale Diary, July 1, 1863; *Carlisle Evening Sentinel*, May 26, 1923; Correspondence of the 33rd PVM, *Philadelphia Public Ledger*, July 17, 1863; Editorial Correspondence with Co. B, 28th PVM, *Montrose Democrat*, July 9, 1863; Robert Vaughan, "The Pennsylvania Militia: They Rendered Important Service During the Gettysburg Campaign," *NT*, April 1, 1915; John Armstrong Memoir, CWTI, USAMHI.
440. Rice, "Memoir," 81, Rice Papers, USAMHI.
441. *Carlisle American*, "Rebel Occupancy of Carlisle," July 15, 1863.
442. Smith Typescript Memoir, VTHS.
443. *Carlisle American*, "Rebel Occupancy of Carlisle," July 15, 1863; *Carlisle American*, "A Few Days of Rebel Rule," August 5, 1863; Jones, *1st*

Philadelphia Light Artillery, 13–14; Hitner to Mrs. Hastings, July 6, 1863, CBC, USAMHI; Trout, *In the Saddle with Stuart*, 77–78; Smith Typescript Memoir, VTHS; Pleasonton, *Third Annual Report*, 91; Conway Hillman to Dear Morgan, September 9, 1930, Conway Hillman Letters, DC; Garnett to Wingate, May 31, 1892, in Wingate, *Twenty-Second Regiment*, 221–25; Gummere Diary, July 1, 1863, HSP.

444. *OR* 27:2, 221; Smith, *Autobiography*, 67–68; Garnett to Wingate, May 31, 1892, in Wingate, *Twenty-Second Regiment*, 221–25; Conway Hillman to Dear Morgan, September 9, 1930, DC; *Carlisle American*, "Rebel Occupancy of Carlisle," July 15, 1863.

445. *OR* 27:2, 236; Wingate, *Twenty-Second Regiment*, 213, 219–20, 222.

446. *OR* 27:2, 236–37; Wingate, *Twenty-Second Regiment*, 213, 219–20, 222; Murray Diary, July 1, 1863, NYHS.

447. Wingate, *Twenty-Second Regiment*, 229–31.

448. Fitzhugh Lee to J.T. Zug, August 25, 1882, Civil War Correspondence 24-101-015, CCHS.

449. Beale, *Lieutenant of Cavalry*, 114.

450. Garnett to Wingate, May 31, 1892, in Wingate, *Twenty-Second Regiment*, 221–25.

451. Ibid.; Cooke, *Wearing of the Gray*, 244–45.

452. Lee to Zug, August 25, 1882, CCHS.

453. *OR* 27:2, 696–97.

454. *Carlisle American*, "Rebel Occupancy of Carlisle," July 15, 1863; *Carlisle Herald*, July 31, 1863.

455. George Shreve, "Reminiscences in the History of the Stuart Horse Artillery, C.S.A.," 10, R.P. Chew Papers, Jefferson County Museum, Charlestown, WV.

456. *OR* 27:2, 221; Wingate, *Twenty-Second Regiment*, 233–34; Gummere Diary, July 1, 1863, HSP; Jones, *1ˢᵗ Philadelphia Light Artillery*, 16.

457. Leland, *Memoirs*, 254–55.

458. Smith Typescript Memoir, VTHS.

459. Christian P. Humerich Narrative, Himes, "Shelling of Carlisle," CCHS.

460. *SOR*, 59:2, 338; Beale Diary, July 1, 1863, HSP.

461. *OR* 27:2, 697.

462. Trout, *In the Saddle with Stuart*, 77–78.

463. *Carlisle American*, "Rebel Occupancy of Carlisle," July 15, 1863; Beale Diary, July 1, 1863, HSP; Wingate, *Twenty-Second Regiment*, 233; Smith, "Marches and Exposures," WRHS. After the war, Smith stated that the barracks were "too far for me to protect." See, Smith Typescript Memoir, VTHS.

464. *Carlisle American*, "Rebel Occupancy of Carlisle," July 15, 1863; Smith Typescript Memoir, VTHS; Haden, *Reminiscences*, 24. Clark's letter appears in *Columbia Democrat and Bloomsburg General Adviser*, July 18, 1863.

465. *OR* 27:2, 221.

466. *Carlisle American*, "Rebel Occupancy of Carlisle," July 15, 1863.

467. *Carlisle Evening Sentinel*, June 2, 1923; *Philadelphia Public Ledger*, July 4, 1863; Murray to Harmar Murray, July 3, 1863, CCHS; *New York Times*, "Harrisburgh, Thursday, July 2," July 3, 1863; Smith Typescript Memoir, VTHS.

468. Moore, *1ˢᵗ and 2ⁿᵈ Stuart*, 181.

CHAPTER 12

469. Beale Diary, July 2, 1863, HSP.

470. Wingate, *Twenty-Second Regiment*, 244–45.

471. John Stayman to Dear Edgar, July 1863, File I-MachemerA-1975-I, DC.

472. Edward Clark to M.C. Meigs, August 7, 1863, CBC, USAMHI.

473. *Carlisle Evening Sentinel*, "Another Reader Who Recalls the Days of the Rebel Invasion," May 11, 1923.

474. *Carlisle American*, "A Few Days of Rebel Rule," August 5, 1863.

475. Wingate, *Twenty-Second Regiment*, 249; Murray Diary, July 2, 1863, NYHS.

476. Beale Diary, July 2, 1863, HSP.

477. *OR* 27:2, 224–25; Wingate, *Twenty-Second Regiment*, 250.

478. *OR* 27:2, 219, 224, 245; Pleasonton, *Third Annual Report*, 71.

479. Lockwood, *Our Campaign Around Gettysburg*, 59; "Thirty Days."

480. Robinson Diary, July 1, 1863, CWM, USAMHI.

481. Lockwood, *Our Campaign Around Gettysburg*, 59–60.

482. Ibid., 61.

483. Ibid., 61–63; Whittemore, *Seventy-First Regiment*, 77.

484. Lockwood, *Our Campaign Around Gettysburg*, 65–77.

485. Ibid.

486. Ibid., 83–84; Francis, *History of the 71ˢᵗ Regiment*, 265–66; Robinson Diary, July 3, 1863, CWM, USAMHI.

487. *OR* 27:2, 237.

488. Ibid., 2:232, 241.

489. Ibid., 241–42; Hyde, "Campaign," KRK, USAMHI.

490. *OR* 27:2, 215–16, 219; Lockwood, *Our Campaign Around Gettysburg*, 86; Wingate, *Twenty-Second Regiment*, 252.

491. Smith Typescript Memoir, VTHS.

492. Lockwood, *Our Campaign Around Gettysburg*, 87; "Thirty Days"; Francis, *History of the 71ˢᵗ Regiment*, 266.

493. *OR* 27:2, 221, 225.

494. Lockwood, *Our Campaign Around Gettysburg*, 88–91.

495. Ibid., 90–93; Wingate, *Twenty-Second Regiment*, 261; Francis, *History of the 71ˢᵗ Regiment*, 266; *OR* 27:2, 246.

496. Lockwood, *Our Campaign Around Gettysburg*, 93–97. See Wingate, *Twenty-Second Regiment*, 261.

497. Wingate, *Twenty-Second Regiment*, 261–69.

498. Ibid.; *OR* 27:2, 221

499. Beale Diary, July 4, 1863, HSP; Francis, *History of the 71ˢᵗ Regiment*, 266; "Thirty Days."

500. *OR* 27:2, 242–43; Hyde, "Campaign," KRK, USAMHI.

Epilogue

501. Sadler Narrative, CDP.

502. *Harrisburg Evening Telegraph*, August 22, 1863.

503. PGS, DCHS.

504. Ibid.

505. Warner, *Generals in Blue*, 463–64; Smith Typescript Memoir, VTHS.

506. *Carlisle American Volunteer*, November 5, 1863.

507. Smith Typescript Memoir, VTHS.

508. Thompson, "Fitzhugh Lee Returns," CCHS.

509. Warner, *Generals in Blue*, 96.

510. Warner, *Generals in Gray*, 154–55.

511. PGS, DCHS.

Appendix A

512. Moore, *1ˢᵗ and 2ⁿᵈ Stuart*, 181.

513. *Philadelphia Public Ledger*, July 4, 1863.

514. Smith, "Marches and Exposures," WRHS.

515. *New York Times*, "Harrisburgh, Thursday, July 2," July 3, 1863.

516. Wingate, *Twenty-Second Regiment*, 243; Wingert, *Battle of Sporting Hill*, 27–28.
517. *Philadelphia Public Ledger*, July 4, 1863.
518. Ibid.; Smith, "Marches and Exposures," WRHS.
519. *Philadelphia Public Ledger*, July 4, 1863.
520. Leland, *Memoirs*, 257–58.
521. *Philadelphia Public Ledger*, July 4, 1863
522. Ibid.
523. Wingate, *Twenty-Second Regiment*, 243.
524. Leland, *Memoirs*, 256.
525. *Philadelphia Public Ledger*, July 4, 1863.
526. Ibid.; Wingate, *Twenty-Second Regiment*, 243; Scrapbook F644s, CCHS.
527. *Philadelphia Public Ledger*, July 4, 1863.
528. Ibid.
529. Beale Diary, July 1, 1863, HSP.

Appendix B

530. *OR* 27:2, 216, 3:387.
531. *Carlisle Evening Sentinel*, "Shelling of Carlisle Is Recalled," May 2, 1923.
532. Harris Diary, July 1, 1863, CWD, USAMHI.
533. *Philadelphia Daily Evening Bulletin*, July 4, 1863.
534. *Carlisle Evening Sentinel*, "Carlisle Shelled by Rebels 60 Years Ago," June 2, 1923; *Carlisle Herald*, "Death of a Union Soldier," July 31, 1863.

Bibliography

BOOKS

Armstrong, Richard L. *19th and 20th Virginia Cavalry.* Lynchburg, VA: H.E. Howard, 1994.

Bates, Samuel P. *History of Pennsylvania Volunteers, 1861–5.* Harrisburg, PA: B. Singerly State Printer, 1869–1871.

Beale, George W. *A Lieutenant of Cavalry in Lee's Army.* Boston: Gorham Press, 1918.

Burr, Frank. *Life and Achievements of James Addams Beaver.* Philadelphia: Ferguson Brothers, 1882.

Busey, John W., and David G. Martin. *Regimental Strengths and Losses at Gettysburg.* Highstown, NJ: Longstreet House, 1982.

Casler, John O. *Four Years in the Stonewall Brigade.* Repr., Dayton, OH: Morningside, 1982.

Cazenove, Theophile. *Cazenove Journal 1794.* Edited by Rayner Kelsey. Haverford: Pennsylvania History Press, 1922.

Clark, Walter. *Histories of the Several Regiments and Battalions from North Carolina, in the Great War 1861–'65.* Raleigh, NC: E.M. Uzzell, 1901.

Clemmer, Gregg. *Old Alleghany: The Life and Wars of General Ed Johnson.* Staunton, VA: Hearthside Publishing, 2004.

Cole, Scott C. *34th Battalion Virginia Cavalry.* Lynchburg, VA: H.E. Howard, 1993.

Cooke, John Esten. *Wearing of the Gray.* New York: E.B. Treat; Baltimore: J.S. Morrow, 1867.

Dickinson, Jack L. *16th Virginia Cavalry.* Lynchburg, VA: H.E. Howard, 1989.

Dickinson, Jack L., and Kay Dickinson. *Gentleman Soldier of Greenbottom: The Life of Brig. Gen. Albert Gallatin Jenkins, CSA*. Huntington, WV: Dickinson, 2011.

Douglas, Henry Kyd. *I Rode With Stonewall: Being Chiefly the War Experiences of the Youngest Member of Jackson's Staff...* Chapel Hill: University of North Carolina Press, 1940.

Driver, Robert J., Jr. *14ᵗʰ Virginia Cavalry*. Lynchburg, VA: H.E. Howard, 1988.

Foster, John Y. *New Jersey and the Rebellion*. Newark, NJ: M.R. Dennis, 1868.

Francis, Augustus T. *History of the 71ˢᵗ Regiment, N.G.N.Y.* New York: Eastman Publishing Co., 1919.

Freeman, Douglas Southall. *Lee's Lieutenants: A Study in Command*. New York: Chas. Scribner's Sons, 1951.

Gambone, A.M. *Enigmatic Valor: Major-General Darius Nash Couch*. Baltimore, MD: Butternut and Blue, 2000.

Gill, John. *Courier for Lee and Jackson*. Shippensburg, PA: Burd Street Press, 1993.

Glazier, William. *Peculiarities of American Cities*. Philadelphia: Hubbard Bros., 1883.

Goldsborough, William. *The Maryland Line in the Confederate States Army*. Baltimore, MD: Kelly, Piet, 1869.

Goodyear, Samuel. *General Robert E. Lee's Invasion of Carlisle, 1863*. Carlisle, PA: Hamilton Library, 1942.

Gottschalk, Louis Moreau. *Notes of a Pianist: During His Professional Tours in the United States, Canada, the Antilles, and South America*. London: J.B. Lippincott, 1881.

Haden, B.J. *Reminiscences of J.E.B. Stuart's Cavalry*. Charlottesville, VA: Progress Publishing Co., n.d.

Harris, Nathaniel. *Autobiography: The Story of an Old Man's Life with Reminiscences of Seventy-Five Years*. Macon, GA: J.W. Burke, 1925.

Haupt, Herman. *Reminiscences of General Herman Haupt*. Milwaukee, WI: Wright & Joys Co., 1901.

Hoke, Jacob. *The Great Invasion of 1863 or General Lee in Pennsylvania*. Dayton, OH: W.J. Schuey, 1887.

Jones, Terry L. *Campbell Brown's Civil War with Ewell and the Army of Northern Virginia*. Baton Rouge: LSU Press, 2001.

Jones, Woodruff. *1ˢᵗ Philadelphia Light Artillery in the Army of the Susquehanna, 1863*. Edited by Cooper Wingert. Camp Hill, PA: Wingert, 2011.

Kamm, Samuel Richey. "The Civil War Career of Thomas A. Scott." Dissertation, University of Pennsylvania, 1940.

Leland, Charles. *Memoirs*. New York: Appleton, 1893.

Leslie, Frank. *Frank Leslie's Illustrated History of the Civil War*. New York: Mrs. F. Leslie, 1895.

Lockwood, John. *Our Campaign Around Gettysburg*. Brooklyn: A.H. Rome and Brothers, 1864.

May, John. *Journal and Letters of Col. John May*. Cincinnati, OH: Robert Clarke & Co., 1873.

McClure, A.K. *Lincoln and Men of War Times*. Philadelphia: Times Publishing Co., 1892.

McKim, Randolph. *A Soldier's Recollections: Leaves from the Diary of a Young Confederate*. New York: Longmans, Green, 1910.

Miller, William J. *The Training of an Army: Camp Curtin and the North's Civil War*. Shippensburg, PA: White Maine, 1990.

Moore, Frank. *The Rebellion Record: A Diary of American Events, with Documents, Narratives, Illustrative Incidents Poetry, Etc.* New York: D. Van Nostrand, 1864.

Moore, Robert H., II. *The 1st and 2nd Stuart Horse Artillery*. Lynchburg, VA: H.E. Howard, 1998.

———. *Graham's Petersburg, Jackson's Kanawha, and Lurty's Roanoke Horse Artillery*. Lynchburg, VA: H.E. Howard, 1996.

Pfanz, Donald. *Richard S. Ewell: A Soldier's Life*. Chapel Hill: University of North Carolina, 1998.

Pleasonton, A.J. *Third Annual Report of Brigadier General A.J. Pleasonton, Commanding the Home Guard of the City of Philadelphia, to the Hon. Alexander Henry, Mayor for 1863*. Philadelphia: King & Baird, 1864.

Pryor, S.G. *A Post of Honor: The Pryor Letters, 1861–1863*. Edited by Charles Adams Jr. Fort Valley, GA: Garret Publications, 1989.

Robertson, Frank Smith. *In the Saddle with Stuart: The Story of Frank Smith Robertson of Jeb Stuart's Staff*. Edited by Robert Trout. Gettysburg, PA: Thomas Publications, 1998.

Scharf, J. Thomas. *History of Westchester County, New York…* 2 vols. Philadelphia: L.E. Preston & Co., 1886.

Schaumann, Merri Lou Scribner. *Taverns of Cumberland County, Pennsylvania, 1750–1840*. Carlisle, PA: Cumberland County Historical Society, 1994.

Scott, J.L. *36th and 37th Battalions Virginia Cavalry*. Lynchburg, VA: H.E. Howard, 1986.

Sheffey, John Preston. *Soldier of Southwestern Virginia: The Civil War Letters of Captain John Preston Sheffey*. Edited by James Robertson. Baton Rouge: Louisiana State University, 2004.

Smith, William F. *Autobiography of Major General William F. Smith, 1861–1864*. Edited by Herbert Schiller. Dayton, OH: Morningside, 1990.

Stevenson, James. *"Boots and Saddles": A History of the First Volunteer Cavalry of the War*. Harrisburg, PA: Patriot Publishing Co., 1879.

Stewart, Harriet W. *History of the Cumberland Valley, Pennsylvania*. N.d., n.p.

Sullivan, John W. *Boyhood Memories of the Civil War, 1861–'65*. Carlisle, PA: Hamilton Library Assoc., 1933.

Thomas, Henry. *The History of the Doles-Cook Brigade Army of Northern Va.* Atlanta: Franklin Publishing, 1903.

Toombs, Samuel. *New Jersey Troops in the Gettysburg Campaign*. Orange, NJ: Evening Mail Publishing House, 1888.

Trout, Robert. *In the Saddle with Stuart: The Story of Frank Smith Robertson of Jeb Stuart's Staff*. Gettysburg, PA: Thomas, 1998.

Turner, Charles, ed. *Ted Barclay, Liberty Hall Volunteers: Letters from the Stonewall Brigade (1861–1864)*. Natural Bridge Station, VA: Rockbridge Publishing, 1992.

Wallcut, Thomas. *Journal of Thomas Wallcut in 1790*. Cambridge, MA: University Press, 1879.

Warner, Ezra. *Generals in Blue: Lives of the Union Commanders*. Baton Rouge: Louisiana State University, 1964.

———. *Generals in Gray: Lives of the Confederate Commanders*. Baton Rouge: Louisiana State University, 1959.

Washington, George. *President Washington's Diaries: 1791 to 1799*. Compiled by Joseph Hoskins. Summerfield, NC, 1921.

Whittemore, Henry. *History of the Seventy-First Regiment, N.G.S.N.Y.* New York: McDonald & Co., 1886.

Williams, Alpheus. *From the Cannon's Mouth: The Civil War Letters of General Alpheus S. Williams*. Detroit: Wayne State University Press, 1959.

Wing, Conway. *History of Cumberland County, Pennsylvania, With Illustrations*. Philadelphia: J.D. Scott, 1879.

Wingate, George. *History of Company A and the Twenty-Second Regiment, N.G.N.Y., 1861–1901*. New York: Styles & Clash, 1901.

———. *History of the Twenty-Second Regiment of the National Guard of the State of New York: From Its Organization to 1895*. New York: E.W. Dayton, 1896.

———. *The Last Campaign of the Twenty-Second Regiment, N.G.S.N.Y. June and July, 1863*. New York: C.S. Westcott & Co., 1864.

Wingert, Cooper. *The Battle of Sporting Hill: A History & Guide*. Camp Hill, PA: Wingert, 2011.

Zeamer, Jeremiah. *The Cumberland Blue Book*. Camp Hill, PA: J.R. Schwarz, 1908.

OFFICIAL DOCUMENTS

Hewett, Janet B., ed. *Supplement to the Official Records of the Union and Confederate Armies*. Wilmington, NC: Broadfoot Publishing Co., 1996–1997.

U.S. War Department. *The War of the Rebellion: A Compilation of the Official Records of the Union and Confederate Armies*. Washington, D.C.: Government Printing Office, 1889.

ARTICLES AND PERIODICALS

Anonymous. "Thirty Days with the Seventy-first Regiment." *Continental Monthly* 4, no. 4 (October 1863).

Bond, Frank. "Company A, First Maryland Cavalry." *Confederate Veteran* 6 (1898).

Couch, Darius. "The Chancellorsville Campaign." In *Battles and Leaders of the Civil War* vol. 3 by Robert U. Johnson and Clarence C. Buel. Repr., New York: Castle Books, 1991.

Crist, Robert G. "Highwater 1863: The Confederate Approach to Harrisburg." *Pennsylvania History* 30, no. 2 (April 1963).

Hufham, J.D., Jr. "Gettysburg." *The Wake Forest Student*, April 1897.

McKim, Randolph. "Steuart's Brigade at the Battle of Gettysburg." *Southern Historical Society Papers* 5 (1878).

Park, Robert E. "Sketch of the Twelfth Alabama Infantry." *Southern Historical Society Papers* 33 (1905).

Parson, William. "History of 'Co. A,' 26th Regiment, P.V.M." *Pennsylvania College Monthly* 3, no. 3 (April 1879).

Penn, John. "John Penn's Journal of a Visit to Reading, Harrisburg, Carlisle, and Lancaster in 1788." *Pennsylvania Magazine of History and Biography* 3.

Pennypacker, Samuel. "Fort Washington in 1863." *Transactions of the Historical Society of Dauphin County, Pennsylvania* 1, no. 1 (1903).

———. "Six Weeks in Uniform." in *Historical and Biographical Sketches* by Samuel Pennypacker, Philadelphia: Robert Tripple, 1883.

Purifoy, John. "With Ewell and Rodes in Pennsylvania." *Confederate Veteran* 30 (1922).

Schuricht, Hermann. "Jenkins' Brigade in the Gettysburg Campaign." *Southern Historical Society Papers* 24 (1896).

Sharpe, John. "A Boy's Experience During the Civil War." *Pennsylvania History* 6, no. 3.

Trimble, Isaac. "The Battle and Campaign of Gettysburg." *Southern Historical Society Papers* 26 (1898).

NEWSPAPERS

Altoona Tribune, Altoona, PA, 1856–19??

Carlisle American, Carlisle, PA, 1855–1864

Carlisle American Volunteer, Carlisle, PA, 1814–1909

Carlisle Evening Sentinel, Carlisle, PA, 1889–1984

Carlisle Herald, Carlisle, PA, 1845–1881

Columbia Democrat and Bloomsburg General Adviser, Columbia, PA, 1850–1866

Cumberland Valley Journal, Mechanicsburg, PA, 1863

Daily Evening Express, Lancaster, PA, 1856–1876

Daily Patriot and Union, Harrisburg, PA, 1858–1868

Evening Telegraph, Harrisburg, PA, 1863–1864

Montrose Democrat, Montrose, PA, 1849–1876

National Tribune, Washington, D.C., 1877–1917

Newville Valley Times-Star, Newville, PA, 191?–present

New York Herald, New York, NY, 1840–1920

New York Times, New York, NY, 1851–present

Philadelphia Daily Evening Bulletin, Philadelphia, PA, 1856–1870

Philadelphia Inquirer, Philadelphia, PA, 1860–1934

Philadelphia Press, Philadelphia, PA, 1857–1880

Philadelphia Public Ledger, Philadelphia, PA, 1836–1925

Richmond Enquirer, Richmond, VA, 1815–1867

MANUSCRIPTS

ABRAHAM LINCOLN PRESIDENTIAL LIBRARY, SPRINGFIELD, IL:
Isaac V. Reynolds Letters.

CUMBERLAND COUNTY HISTORICAL SOCIETY, HAMILTON LIBRARY, CARLISLE, PA:
Nettie Jane Blair Reminisce, 1934.

Bowman, Addison. "Map of Historical Points of Interest in Camp Hill, Cumberland County, Pennsylvania, Regarding the Northern Raid of the Confederates During the War of the Rebellion."

Himes, C.F. "The Shelling of Carlisle Cumberland Co. Penn'a by the Confederates, July 1863. Personal Observations,—Narratives and Notes."

Fitzhugh Lee to J.T. Zug, August 25, 1882.

Martha B. Munn to Martha Jane, March 1929.

Margaret Murray to Harmar Murray, July 3, 1863.

Peffer, Georgia. "History of Springfield."

Scrapbook F644s.

Springfield Drop File.

Thompson, D.W. "Fitzhugh Lee Returns, and Returns."

DICKINSON COLLEGE, WAIDNER-SPAHR LIBRARY, CARLISLE, PA:
Conway Hillman Letters
    Conway Hillman to Dear Morgan, September 9, 1930.
Charles Himes Papers
    Charles Himes to Dear Rood, October 2, 1863.
Eli Slifer Papers
    A.N. Brice to Slifer, June 26, 1863.
    John Stayman to Dear Edgar, July 1863.

EMORY UNIVERSITY, ROBERT W. WOODRUFF LIBRARY, ATLANTA, GA:
William Marston Diary.

GETTYSBURG NATIONAL MILITARY PARK LIBRARY, GETTYSBURG, PA:
Eugene Blackford to Dear Father, June 28, 1863.
John Harris Diary.
Klinefelter, Frederick. "An Historical Sketch of 'Company A,' 26th Penna. Volunteer Militia."
Samuel Pickens Diary.
Charles R. Sayles to Dear Caroline, June 18, 1863.
Daniel Sheetz to Brother, June 18, 1863.
Thomas Tolson Diary, 1st Maryland Battalion Newspaper Clippings.
Welsh, Robert A. "Some Personal Experience." Wilbur S. Nye Papers.

HANDLEY REGIONAL LIBRARY, STEWART BELL JR. ARCHIVES, WINCHESTER, VA:
Wayland Collection
    Samuel Firebaugh Diary.

BIBLIOGRAPHY

HISTORICAL SOCIETY OF DAUPHIN COUNTY, ALEXANDER FAMILY LIBRARY, HARRISBURG, PA:
Casper Dull Papers.
Philip German Scrapbook.
Kelker Family Collection
    "Forts Washington and Henry Clay."
Minutes of the Harrisburg Bridge Company.

HISTORICAL SOCIETY OF PENNSYLVANIA, PHILADELPHIA, PA:
Joseph Boggs Beale Papers.
John Gummere Diary.
John A. Wilson Diary.

JEFFERSON COUNTY MUSEUM, CHARLES TOWN, WV:
Roger Chew Papers
    Shreve, George W. "Reminiscences in the History of the Stuart Horse Artillery, C.S.A."

LIBRARY OF CONGRESS, WASHINGTON, D.C.:
Andrew Carnegie Papers
    Carnegie to George Lauder Jr., June 21, 1863.
Feamster Family Papers
    Thomas Feamster Letters.
John William Ford Hatton Memoir.
Jedediah Hotchkiss Papers
    Jedediah Hotchkiss to Darling Sara, June 28, 1863.
    Jedediah Hotchkiss Diary.
E.J. Moore Letters.

MARYLAND HISTORICAL SOCIETY, H. FURLONG BALDWIN LIBRARY, BALTIMORE, MD:
Shriver Family Papers
    Henry Wirt Shriver Diary.
    Henry Wirt Shriver Letters.

MECHANICSBURG MUSEUM ASSOCIATION, MECHANICSBURG, PA:
Hauck's Centennial Directory of Mechanicsburg, 1876.

SCOTT L. MINGUS SR., YORK, PA:
Mingus, Scott, Sr. "A Grandest Affair Ever Set on Foot: The Gettysburg Campaign Begins, June 10–July 1, 1863." Unpublished manuscript.

NATIONAL ARCHIVES AND RECORDS ADMINISTRATION, WASHINGTON, D.C.:
Record Group 77
  J.B. Wheeler Report to Chief Engineer, August 31, 1863.
  J.B. Wheeler, "Sketch of Defensive Works and Approaches of Harrisburg, Pa."

NEWVILLE HISTORICAL SOCIETY, NEWVILLE, PA:
Zenas J. Gray Account.
John Lefever Diary.
William McCandlish Diary.
Newspaper Clippings Related to Confederate Invasion.

NEW-YORK HISTORICAL SOCIETY, NEW YORK, NY:
John Irvin Murray Diary.

PENNSYLVANIA STATE ARCHIVES, PENNSYLVANIA HISTORIC AND MUSEUM COMMISSION, HARRISBURG, PA:
Manuscript Group 6, Diaries and Journals Collection
  Josiah Weaver Diary.
  R. Went Diary.
Manuscript Group 57, Theodore Burr Papers
  Theodore Burr Letters.
Manuscript Group 198, Strokes L. Roberts Papers
  Jacob Spangler to Dear Mother, June 18, 1863.
Record Group 2, Records of the Department of the Auditor General
  Border Damage Claims.
Record Group 19, Records of the Department of Military and Veterans Affairs
  Commissions File.
  Commission Requests, June–July 1863.
  Military Dispatches.
  Transportation and Telegraph Department.

PENNYPACKER MILLS HISTORIC SITE, SCHWENKSVILLE, PA:
Charles Macdonald to Samuel W. Pennypacker, July 11, 1892.
Newspaper Scrapbook.

SIMPSON PUBLIC LIBRARY, MECHANICSBURG, PA:
Pamphlet. "Paging Through Our Past: The History of the Joseph T. Simpson
    Public Library."
Personal War Sketches." Col. H.I. Zinn Post 415.

UNIVERSITY OF NORTH CAROLINA, LOUIS ROUND WILSON LIBRARY, CHAPEL
    HILL, NC:
Southern Historical Collection
    John Coghill Papers.
    George Wills Papers.

UNIVERSITY OF VIRGINIA, ALDERMAN LIBRARY, CHARLOTTESVILLE, VA:
John W. Daniel Papers
    Vincent Witcher Letters.
Micajah Woods Papers
    Micajah Woods Letters.

U.S. ARMY MILITARY HISTORY INSTITUTE, CARLISLE BARRACKS, CARLISLE, PA:
Robert L. Brake Collection
    James E. Green Diary.
    Col. David Zable Speech, 1903.
Carlisle Barracks Collection
    Edward Clark to M.C. Meigs, August 7, 1863.
    Confederate Requisition Order.
    R.K. Hitner to Mrs. David Hastings, July 6, 1863.
    Leeds, Charles H. "Invasion of Carlisle." Miscellaneous Newspaper
    Clippings.
Civil War Document Collection
    Isaac Harris Diary.
    "History of the 27th Pennsylvania Emergency Men."
Civil War Miscellaneous Collection
    William Robinson Diary.
Civil War Times Illustrated Collection
    John E. Armstrong Memoir.
    J.C. Attick Diary.
    Samuel Dunbar Letter, May 20, 1863.
George Daugherty Papers
    George Daugherty to Dear Friends, June 20, 1863.

Harrisburg Civil War Roundtable Collection
  L. Brown to John B. Lingle, July 9, 1863.
  C.B. Niesley to Dear Parents, July 1, 1863.
  Eunice Stewart to Dear Parents, June 24 [25], 1863.
Keith R. Keller Collection
  L.T. Hyde, "Campaign of Brooklyn City Guard June and July 1863."
Pardee-Robinson Collection
  J. Boyd Robinson Letter, July 1, 1863.
Nicholas Rice Papers
  Nicholas Rice, "Memoir."

VERMONT HISTORICAL SOCIETY, LEAHY LIBRARY, BARRE, VT:
William F. Smith Papers
  William Franklin to William F. Smith, June 23, 1863.
  William Smith Typescript Memoir.

WESTERN RESERVE HISTORICAL SOCIETY, CLEVELAND, OH:
William Palmer Collection
  Smith, Charles H. "Marches and Exposures of the 28th Regiment, P.V.M.
  Col. James Chamberlin, Commanding, During the Emergency."

Index

About the Author

Cooper Wingert is a South Central Pennsylvania student who has authored and edited four books on the Gettysburg Campaign, as well as several articles in periodicals such as *Gettysburg Magazine*. He regularly speaks to area Civil War Round Tables, historical societies and other groups.

Visit us at
www.historypress.net